The Psychology of Fear in Organizations

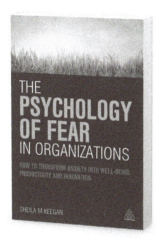

The Psychology of Fear in Organizations

How to transform anxiety into well-being, productivity and innovation

Sheila M Keegan

KoganPage

LONDON PHILADELPHIA NEW DELHI

Publisher's note

Every possible effort has been made to ensure that the information contained in this book is accurate at the time of going to press, and the publishers and author cannot accept responsibility for any errors or omissions, however caused. No responsibility for loss or damage occasioned to any person acting, or refraining from action, as a result of the material in this publication can be accepted by the editor, the publisher or the author.

First published in Great Britain and the United States in 2015 by Kogan Page Limited

2nd Floor, 45 Gee Street
London EC1V 3RS
United Kingdom
www.koganpage.com

1518 Walnut Street, Suite 1100
Philadelphia PA 19102
USA

4737/23 Ansari Road
Daryaganj
New Delhi 110002
India

ISBN   978 0 7494 7254 2
E-ISBN 978 0 7494 7255 9

British Library Cataloguing-in-Publication Data

A CIP record for this book is available from the British Library.

Library of Congress Cataloging-in-Publication Data

Keegan, Sheila.
  The psychology of fear in organizations : how to transform anxiety into well-being, productivity and innovation / Sheila Keegan.
     pages cm
  ISBN 978-0-7494-7254-2 (paperback) – ISBN 978-0-7494-7255-9 (ebk)   1. Organizational behavior.
2. Fear.   3. Management — Psychological aspects.   4. Organizational effectiveness.   I. Title.
  HD58.7.K4195 2015
  658.3′14—dc23
                                                                                            2014043314

Typeset by Amnet Systems
Print production managed by Jellyfish
Printed and bound by CPI Group (UK) Ltd, Croydon CR0 4YY

CONTENTS

PREFACE

Some decades ago, as a psychology student just starting university, I opted for a module on industrial psychology, as it then was. It is now called organizational psychology. I had no idea what it was about, but it sounded as if it might be fun, whereas cognitive psychology sounded like hard work. I don't remember much about the module, except for one research project that just leapt out at me. It intrigued me then and it still intrigues me today. It was the famous Hawthorne experiments, which were some of the first industrial psychology experiments, carried out in the United States in the 1920s. The experiments were simple – deceptively so. They involved changing the lighting conditions in a huge electrical factory in Chicago that housed thousands of female production line workers.

The research question was, 'Would an increase in lighting affect productivity?' The answer, it turned out, was an unsurprising Yes. Productivity *did* increase with brighter light. So, obviously, the next research question had to be, 'Would a reduction in light decrease productivity?' Of course the answer was obvious: it *would* reduce productivity. To my surprise it turned out that, contrary to expectations, the answer was No. Reducing light actually *improved* productivity. This didn't make any sense to me. It was irrational and counter-intuitive. In fact, instinctively, it still seems wrong to me. Surely better lighting would enable employees to work more efficiently? If you are familiar with the Hawthorne experiments you will already know the answer to this conundrum. We will discuss it further in Chapter 6. However, at that time, this was all a bit of a puzzle. How could my undergraduate brain make sense of this? Having shown some aptitude for the sciences when I was young, I was shepherded off to be indoctrinated in 'the scientific method', as it was then called. It was a regime designed to foster a rational, scientific brain and preserve us from the fanciful ideas of the flighty 'art tarts' who studied the poets.

So when I later discovered psychology it was quite an eye-opener. To accept that people could not be understood solely in terms of rational behaviour was exciting, particularly in those more literal days. It was not that I was unaware of the non-rational; I had simply assumed that if I was studying science, then only rational thought counted. At that time, within mainstream academic psychology, the non-rational was still rather suspect. Rats and mazes were all the rage.

However, my younger self was intrigued to discover that psychology encapsulated a great many conundrums like the Hawthorne experiments. In fact it incorporated the whole gamut of human behaviour, both rational and non-rational: the sensible, the bizarre, the physical and the emotional, the unbelievable, our intuitions and feelings, both individual and crowd behaviour and much more. Many years on, I try to keep hold of that first sense of excitement about how we human beings 'work'. It still intrigues and excites me. There are so many different perspectives from which we can view the world.

In some ways, organizational life has changed out of all recognition since the Hawthorne experiments of the 1920s. More recently, we have seen fashions in management theory and practice come and go. For instance we had the Balanced Score Card and Total Quality Management (TQM) to mention just two. These initiatives generally involved greater control and monitoring of staff, in my view overdoing the science and downplaying the human. However, what I do find surprising and depressing is that organizational life in recent decades has not changed in ways that favour employees. Arguably, it has made their lives more difficult, as fear within organizations rises.[1,2] In many large organizations there appear to be crises at senior levels, with weak and short-term leadership. Meanwhile job security at lower levels has been sacrificed. As the writer and management guru Margaret Wheatley puts it:

> I'm sad to report that in the past few years, ever since uncertainty became our insistent 21st-century companion, leadership has taken a great leap backwards to the familiar territory of command and control.

The focus on measurement and control predominates in many large organizations and, in my experience, there is often scant attention given to understanding human behaviour and values – and how these can be employed effectively in the workplace. We are all creatures of habit. It is sometimes hard to avoid becoming over-mechanized in our thinking and working practices. In workplaces that are increasingly and unthinkingly adopting technological models as a template for life, the challenge, for both individuals and groups, is to find ways of staying alert, ways of experiencing the world through different lenses and trying, as best we can, to stay human.

There is a considerable body of research that points to the rise of fear within organizations and indeed a *climate of fear* that is widespread and contagious.[3] Employees feel fearful of job loss, of being demoted, bullied, shamed or humiliated. This level of fear can become self-sustaining so that it is difficult to separate the causes of fear; fear at work becomes normalized.

In this book we will examine the nature of fear in the workplace and how it affects us physiologically, psychologically and emotionally. Fear can be a force for change – positive or negative – and it can be a barrier to change. We are all familiar with the phrase 'feel the fear and do it anyway'. Not all of our fears are proportionate to the degree of risk. Perhaps more frightening are the risks that we cannot know or that we cannot evaluate.

Throughout this book we explore how some work environments have become psychologically dangerous places. We have moved on from the physical dangers that were inherent in the workplaces of the Industrial Revolution, but in some cases we have substituted them with psychological ones. As we will discuss in Chapters 3 and 4, the proportions of people who say they feel frightened at work, who are afraid to speak out, who feel bullied or humiliated by their managers, who are afraid of losing their jobs, who feel helpless and unable to change their situation, is quite shocking, as evidenced by the number of studies that show similar findings.[4]

However, describing fear at work without offering any solution is of little help. While the first part of this book addresses the experience and effects of fear in the workplace, the second part explores the ways in which we might reduce fear and, in doing so, become more productive and also get more enjoyment and a sense of achievement from our work.

Board members and senior managers are often pivotal in both inducing and reducing fear. However, they may not be obvious confidants and they are not the only place to start when seeking change. Building resilience by changing our own beliefs, attitudes and behaviours; being more conscious of our use of language; developing stronger, more collaborative working groups, possibly across diverse organizational sectors and traditional work demarcations; initiating innovation – these are just some of the ways in which productivity and engagement may be strengthened.

Of course, not all workplaces are unhappy and we need to acknowledge those people within very many large organizations who work very hard at developing an engaged and happy staff. This is important, not least because most of the studies in this area indicate that engaged and happy employees are more productive. We all know that when we are happy and productive we work more effectively. When we feel miserable and downtrodden we may work harder in the short term, because we feel under threat, but it is unsustainable. In addition, the more stressed we feel, the more we treat our work in a mechanical fashion. Creativity, innovation and initiative go out the window – and these are some of the qualities most needed in modern organizations.

This book is not predominately about these healthy organizations, although they can act as exemplars of good practice – and of course none of us can be good all the time. It is predominately about those organizations towards the opposite end of the spectrum, who are struggling to develop an engaged and productive workforce. At the same time, however, we need to be careful not to polarize organizations into good and bad. The best organizations contain pockets of fear just as the most fear-ridden often have areas or departments where cooperation and productivity thrive. Similarly, the climate within individual departments can shift over time, depending on the internal dynamics, the manager in charge, gaining or losing staff and so on.

And then, we bring our own human programming along with us into the workplace, shaped as it is by our upbringing, beliefs and values. How could we not? We tend to underestimate the value of our intuitive knowledge and are reluctant to either trust it or make it visible. In a work context particularly, we tend to overemphasize our rational responses and underestimate and suppress emotional, intuitive and instinctive reactions. This is a shame – and a great loss. If we can learn to utilize our often underdeveloped skills of human perception, such as our intuition, our creativity and our ability to connect and develop ideas, it will stand us in very good stead, on a personal level as well as within an organizational context. Sadly, when we are fearful, we tend to freeze rather than open up and this restricts our ability to think more creatively. We achieve the opposite state to the one we hope to achieve.

Fear is one of the most powerful of emotions. It evolved for a reason: to warn us, to protect us and to give us the power of self-preservation. In a sense we have voluntarily welcomed fear into our organizations. We have allowed it to grow and thrive in situations that are not life-threatening and in which fear is counterproductive. Fear thrives in organizations in which the more powerful can terrorize the less powerful, where people are silenced because they do not toe the company line, where there are unnecessary rules and regulations designed to reduce and intimidate employees rather than foster new thinking and fresh ideas. If we want to develop workforces that are motivated, that go the extra mile, that are proud of what they have achieved, then we need to first *understand*, and second *work with* the human drives, motivations, needs and ambitions that staff inherently possess. In essence, we need to treat staff (including ourselves) with respect as valuable human beings, acknowledging their worth and helping them to achieve.

As I write this, I feel a sinking in my stomach. All this talk of respecting employees sounds so clichéd. It is easy to say and so difficult to achieve. And yet, at the same time, I believe it. I know from my training and from 30 years of experience working within a wide range of organizations that it is true.

It is tempting for managers to describe *what we need to do to employees to make them work better.* Maybe it is time to change the broken record. The starting point is to understand what it is to be human and what we human beings need in order to be engaged, motivated and productive, and to enjoy going to work.

Notes

1 Ashkanasy, M and Nicholson, G J (2003) Climate of fear in organisational settings: Construct definition, measurement and a test of theory, *Australian Journal of Psychology*, 55 (1) pp 24–9

2 Tran, V (1989) The role of the emotional climate in learning organizations, *The Learning Organization* 5 (2) pp 99–103

3 Work intensification, fear at work and job-related well-being in Britain: First findings from the Skills and Employment Survey 2-12 [online] www.cardiff.ac.uk/socsi/newsandevents/events/work-intensification-fear-at-work-and-jobrelated-well-being-in-britain.html

4 Harter, J K, Schmidt, F L and Hayes, T L (2002) Business-unit-level relationship between employee satisfaction, employee engagement, and business outcomes: a meta-analysis, *Journal of Applied Psychology* [online] http://psycnet.apa.org/index.cfm?fa=buy.optionToBuy&id=2002-12397-006

PART ONE
The nature of fear and how it shapes organizations

The paradox of fear

Fear doesn't shut you down; it wakes you up. **VERONICA ROTH**

In this book we will explore the emotion of fear within large organizations: how it arises, how it can be recognized and how we can deal with it. The book is in two parts. Part One explores the paradoxical nature of fear itself and its various manifestations in the workplace. We examine how a widespread culture of fear has emerged, fuelled largely by the recent economic downturn, and how it has spread its tentacles throughout many organizations and indeed through society as a whole. In particular, we will examine how fear can infiltrate workplaces and the impact it can have on employees, at all levels of the organization.

Part Two explores the ways in which we can both combat the effects of fear and tap into its energy. By examining different approaches to utilizing fear we can harness it for our own benefit, particularly in relation to creativity, productivity, innovation and risk-taking within organizations. Most importantly, we can attempt to create healthy organizations in which people want to work.

The scope of this book

We will examine some of these issues within the context of working life in a range of organizations. The book is based in part on commissioned research and organizational change projects carried out by Campbell Keegan Ltd, a business consultancy that I have jointly run, along with my co-director Rosie Campbell, for the last 30 years. I also include academic input from books, papers, conferences and innumerable conversations with colleagues working in the areas of research and organizational change over the years.

My aim in writing this book is to encourage thoughts, comments and discussion among those who work with and within organizations so that we can share experiences and further develop ideas on the growth and nature of organizations. We are moving out of the time of austerity, yet many of us still carry the baggage of anxiety and, all too often, fear, instilled by the recession. My initial aim was to direct this book towards psychologists, research practitioners and those who work in organizational change. However, as I wrote, I came increasingly to the view that, as almost all of us work in, or interact with, organizations, it may have broader relevance.

The book draws on both the academic and the practical. It includes some theory and a scattering of case studies. It is also coloured by my ongoing interest in the complexity sciences, in particular the work of Professor Ralph Stacey[1] who explores complexity theory within the workplace. The complexity sciences challenge our traditional thinking and practice; arguably, they can change the way in which we view the world. Put crudely, the Western perspective tends to see the world as a collection of static things (a door, a person, a viewpoint etc) whereas a complexity perspective emphasizes interconnectivity, relationships and unpredictability (change, flow, emergence etc).[2] Of course, both perspectives are important and this is a question of perspective. How we work with these different perspectives is something we will return to throughout this book.

Much of Campbell Keegan's work over the years has involved qualitative research. This is a form of research seeking useful directions to explore and pursue in order to help solve problems or create new concepts. Qualitative research is a form of *emergent inquiry*[3] that allows the researcher to explore, hypothesize and experiment. It is therefore concerned less with measurement and statistics (as is quantitative research).

However, 'qualitative' and 'quantitative' perspectives are two sides of the same coin. Overemphasis on measurement and statistical significances skews understanding, just as exclusive attention to qualitative findings potentially distorts understanding in a different way. Both elements need to be in balance. As we will see, this is particularly relevant in the context of organizational development as well as the development of new ideas, products or services in a range of sectors.

The recession has eased, but its psychological effects may well be with us for some years to come. Both employers and employees are still wary. In many organizations tough decisions had to be made to ensure the company's survival and it will take time for the scars to heal. It is perhaps not a gross overstatement to say that, just as the Second World War shaped the attitudes of a generation, so too the recent recession will shape the attitudes, behaviours and fears within organizational life for some decades to come.

What instils fear in organizations?

We will start by briefly introducing the topic of fear within organizations. Although we will examine fear in many different contexts throughout this book and probe into its manifestations and effect on different aspects of our lives, fear in organizations is our prime concern. This is not a new subject – you could argue that there is not an organization in the world that does not have at least some employees who are fearful on some occasions – but research from around the world provides strong evidence that fear is a more invasive and disabling influence than ever before. Fear is part of our human lot, for better and worse, and we cannot avoid it. However, when we get to the point where significant numbers of employees express the view that 'work is a source of fear and anxiety', we have to ask ourselves: What is going on here? How have we created this situation? How is it possible that working environments that should provide us at the very least with an income, job satisfaction and a sense of community become places to avoid or even to dread? It must be that fear improves employees' performance, their thinking, their speed, their creativity. Well, on the whole, *no*, it doesn't. Fear is much more likely to inhibit productivity than to foster it. So, why has a culture of fear developed? This is one of the key issues we will explore in this book.

You may ask, 'Is fear that big a deal in contemporary life In developed countries we are unlikely to be savaged by wild animals, die of starvation on be unable to access medical care.' This is a big question and one that is not easily answered. Fear is a very powerful force and it is one that is difficult to define. Or at least it is difficult to find a way of describing it that everyone would agree with. What one person experiences as fear might be brushed away by another as a minor irritant.

Fear as a cultural norm

The sociologist Barry Glassner describes America as 'engrossed with fear'.[4]

He claims that three out of four Americans say they feel more fearful today than they did 20 years ago but, he believes, it is our perception of danger that has increased, not our actual level of risk. He points out that the huge amount of attention given to airline safety is disproportionate to the risk. 'Hazards that kill and injure many more people receive much less attention.' In the mid 1990s, while the press obsessed over airline accidents – which resulted in fewer than a dozen deaths in the best years and a few hundred in the worst – more than 5,000 Americans died in work-related injuries each year. It seems that some risks are simply more sexy than others. If the issue is that we overestimate fear, that we see fear where there is none, perhaps we simply need to address our *perceptions* of fear rather than trying to avoid *situations* that induce it.

The climate of fear

Fear and uncertainty are the backdrop against which this book is set, and fear is the emotion that many of us try hardest to avoid; although paradoxically we may also court it. Fear reaches back into the origins of mankind and, at the same time, it lurks in the dark alleyways of our 21st-century minds, biding its time, waiting to pounce in our moments of weakness. It can be a figment of our imagination – or it can be all too real. Sometimes it is unclear which it is – or maybe it is both at the same time. Fear is an emotion that is widely viewed as a pariah. Many of us feel afraid of fear itself, but fear can be our friend as well as our foe. It can sharpen our senses. It can steer us through danger. Whatever you may currently think about fear, my aim is to convince you that fear is not all bad news. Fear is a chameleon. It surprises us. It shocks. But, paradoxically, it can help us to perform to the best of our abilities, sometimes to a level way beyond our wildest dreams. In certain circumstances it can even make us superhuman. We will examine the conundrum of fear; how it can be so ubiquitous, so adaptable and so scary, all at the same time.

We will explore fear in order to better understand our complex and quixotic relationship with it, particularly within the context of our working lives. Humans try, with varying degrees of success, to manage our relationship with fear. Much of the time we may feel that we have the upper hand. Fear is a distant rumble, barely discernible. We forget about it. But at other times fear can loom large in our lives, oppressing us and undermining our confidence and our ability to function well in our working lives. Occasionally we feel that it has defeated us and, however much we try, we cannot overcome it. In these situations, fear hangs onto our coat-tails and we can never seem get rid of it.

Fear gets a bad press

In general, fear gets a very bad press in contemporary life. We easily forget that fear is a double-edged sword, both friend and foe. We tend to focus on the negative aspects of fear; how we struggle to suppress it when we are delivering a presentation or convening a workshop, or when we have to make a public speech, or in a variety of work contexts that make us feel anxious, uncomfortable and out of our comfort zone. In some circumstances feeling frightened is an appropriate response to the situation in which we find ourselves. More than this, the complex pattern of fear responses that cut in when we are – or feel that we may be – in danger can be literally life-saving. Fear is both our brother in arms and our nemesis. It is all around us but, like the air we breathe, it is invisible. It is not until it rears up, wrapping us in panic and anxiety, that we remember its power and feel cowed by it.

The shame and embarrassment of fear

Fear is also the emotion that we most deny; the emotion that we hide from others and even, sometimes, from ourselves. Fear makes us feel childlike. Why are we so embarrassed to display fear, especially in a work context? Is it a help or a hindrance? How can we overcome our fears? Should we even try to conquer fear? But then, what about the positive side of fear? Fear gives us the strength to run and the wit to hide. If we can understand and befriend fear, perhaps we can harness its strengths to help us achieve our goals or to protect us from danger. When we are able to harness fear, we can absorb its energy and focus. We can feel invincible.

Emotional contagion

Although we will talk about fear in organizations, this is something of a misnomer. As we have already touched upon, fear does not recognize categories and never stays neatly where we put it. Work-related fears and worries seep into our work lives and our home lives. Fear has a tendency to spread, joining with diverse worries to create a mass of anxiety. We have a niggling worry and, like Chinese whispers, off it goes. It cannot be recaptured, but it can grow and morph into some other fear. This is particularly true in fear-ridden organizations. The hierarchical nature of large organizations means that it is more difficult for managers to refute rumours. They expand to fill the void.

Fear in different organizations

We will move on to explore how fear impacts on our lives in a work environment; how it subtly – and not so subtly – influences our decision-making; how it encourages or prevents us from taking certain paths. Many of us work in environments which, at least some of the time, are scary; we are afraid to speak out, we feel anxious about job security, about our role or our relationship with our manager. We keep our heads down and are fearful of the future. We will explore the roots of these fears and how the structures and practices within many contemporary organizations often contribute to a culture of fear at work.

Organizations come in all shapes and sizes. Some are small, informal groups. Others are formal and heavily structured. We will concentrate on large organizations in this book. This does not mean that fear does not exist in small organizations. However, we need to impose some boundaries or this book will be never-ending. Large organizations have some degree of similarity in their structures, even if they differ in style, priorities, culture and so on. Smaller organizations tend to be more diverse and idiosyncratic and therefore it is more difficult to categorize them.

Organizations old and new

Organizations are not a new phenomenon. Human beings are, first and foremost, social animals and organizations have been with us since cavemen roamed the plains, organizing themselves into groups for protection, hunting for food and huddling fearfully together in caves to hide from predators. Over subsequent millennia, groups and organizations of all shapes and sizes, with different functions, structures and ambitions, have come and gone. Human beings have been initiated into warrior tribes, they have become conscripts and formed into armies. Secret societies have formed to carry out dastardly deeds; centres of learning have been created; religious groups have thrived and diminished. And still we manage to construct new configurations of organizations.

Large organizations under pressure

It is interesting that the hierarchical model of top-down power, which is still prevalent within most large organizations, is struggling under the pressures of contemporary business life. It is more difficult than it has ever been for senior managers to monitor staff, control and steer their organization in the face of a deluge of data, fast turnarounds, fragmented work groups, diverse sites, international connections, cultural specialization, technological advances and the many other aspects of business life that have changed in recent decades.

And yet, some things don't change

Notions of fear and safety within groups and organizations are hard-wired into the human psyche. We find comfort in groups, yet at the same time they can present a threat. We spend much of our lives managing the tension between on the one hand *being an individual* and doing what we want to do, and on the other hand *being part of the group*, which is necessary for our physical and emotional well-being. From the moment we are born, we are part of a group – the family – and as babies we cannot survive without care from our family group. Human beings are social animals through and through. Even if we became hermits, took ourselves off to a cave high up in the Himalayas and never met another human being for the rest of our lives, we would bring our social baggage along with us. That is the way in which our brains are configured; our emotions and our drives are what make us human. Human beings need social contact and affirmation if we are to survive and thrive, even if it is the memory of socializing that the hermit retains from his childhood. We need to be acknowledged for who we are and recognized for what we have achieved.

We see this need in its simplest form in young children who rush up to their parent waving a scribbled drawing, seeking praise and attention. As adults, we too have a need for affirmation from our family and friends. It's a primal need; it does not diminish. And although we may deny it, we need affirmation or validation from our work colleagues too. Equally, our colleagues and friends need affirmation from us. It therefore makes good *human* sense, as well as good *business* sense to try to make our shared journey in life, both inside and outside work, a more pleasurable experience and, in the process, a more productive one.

Throughout this book we will examine what it is to be human; how we have evolved, what we are today and what this means in terms of our thinking, behaviours, emotions, drives and aspirations in the workplace. These human characteristics have developed over millions of years and they will not change overnight. The challenge for all organizations, whether they are large or small, traditional or leading edge, whether they make widgets or solar panels, whether they have 10 employees or 20,000, boils down to human relationships. Without constantly nurturing, monitoring, training and listening to staff, building resilience, trust and engagement – and encouraging lines of communication, formal or otherwise – organizations will flounder. This is an obvious thing to say, a self-evident observation on human nature, but one which has all too apparently been forgotten within many organizational cultures. All may seem well in the short term, but it will not last. The basic hierarchy of needs and aspirations that Abraham Maslow defined in 1943 and in which he prioritized human needs and aspirations has not basically changed.[5]

The impact of the recession

We will concentrate on fear within large contemporary organizations and focus primarily on the period from the beginning of the recent recession, around 2007, to the present day – and beyond. We will investigate the ways in which the recession has changed the psychology of the workforce in the UK and elsewhere, and assess the effects of the recession on employees' confidence, their willingness to take risks and to experiment, as well as their sense of involvement, well-being, satisfaction and productivity at work. Has the recession encouraged greater mutual support among employees across diverse workforces? Has it helped some and not others? Has it promoted a keener sense of purpose in employees and a resolve to support the industry, company and department in which they work?

Alternatively, has it depressed the workforce, undermined confidence, left people feeling unsupported, scared that they might lose their jobs and yearning for security? Of course there can be no neat answers, but exploring these areas helps us to differentiate those factors that encourage 'healthier' organizational behaviours from those that foster fear and mistrust.

Practices in different countries, regions, companies, industries and among individuals will differ. However, by employing reputable academic studies, using established published data and extensive interviewing with a wide variety of employees at all levels and within a range of organizations, we can identify the priorities, practices and attitudes that are likely to foster productive, healthy and innovative working environments; environments that instil a strong work ethic and practices that support a positive outcome for both employees and companies. Equally, we can identify those practices, attitudes and environments that are likely to result in 'negative' workplaces; where cooperation is undermined, where there is a weak work ethic and where productivity within the organization is low due to a demoralized and fearful workforce, with poor productivity and limited innovation.

Organizational diversity

You may find some descriptions of workplaces in this book familiar, in that they resemble places you have worked. Others will seem alien. Organizations differ and the rules, norms, expectations, loyalties and protocols inevitably vary. In spite of this, there are some common cultural themes that spread across organizations, their tentacles touching companies that may be very different in style but have a common philosophy, ethos or shared ambition. For instance, there are now many 'green' companies with common values, although they may work in very different industries. Equally, there are companies that position themselves at the cutting edge of technology; they feel an affinity with other tech-focused companies, regardless of their product portfolio. Other companies may represent the face of cultural heritage and be involved in preserving historical buildings, yet feel an affinity with companies that focus on contemporary design. Incorporating the vast diversity of organizational styles and aspirations that exist within the huge spectrum of organizations worldwide is clearly impossible within one book.

Organizational styles

Large organizations need strong management teams and clear structure; without sufficient structure the organization risks descending into chaos. Paradoxically too much structure can lead to stagnation, as employees feel that there is no scope for personal initiative. Bigger organizations also tend to be at particular risk of losing their agility and they may become less able to adapt to changing market conditions; they can become set in their ways. Within all organizations, regardless of size, there is an ongoing tension between *the established* and *the new* because we humans, on the whole, tend to resist change. To be most effective, employees need to be able to play the tension between the established 'how we do it round here' and new ways of thinking and doing. This requires well-designed staff training, permission to experiment and greater knowledge sharing across different parts of the organization. It is a critical issue and one that is too often neglected. Knowledge and best practices are often lost in the drive for innovation. Conversely, we also need to be wary of 'best practice'. It can become enshrined in corporate behaviour. We need to remember that best practice is simply 'what we have always done'. It is not written in stone.

Psychological health at work

In talking about organizations in general, I do not want us to get too pinned down with definitions of different types of organization or talking specifically in terms of the number of employees, turnover, sites or industry type. I am more interested in the ways in which people behave in organizations; what influences this behaviour and the cumulative effect of the ongoing interaction between all employees, from the most junior to the most senior, regardless of job function. How do these behaviours impact on the organization as a whole? There is clear evidence that enthusiastic, collaborative, engaged and experimental workforces are much more likely to lead to healthier workplaces and organizations that are good for employees from top to bottom; that is, they deliver a happy, productive, resilient and engaged workforce.

Managing and using fear

But let us focus, for a moment, on fear as our friend, not just something to suppress or avoid. In particular, fear can be a stimulus for innovation, enabling us to work creatively, to encourage a mindset of curiosity, experimentation and innovation. If we can learn to harness the energy of fear, it can help us to think and work more effectively. These are qualities that we desperately need if we are to develop strong, productive and profitable organizations, in both the private and public sectors; organizations that people feel proud to be part of, where they are happy to work and feel both supported and challenged.

If we can learn to manage fear, if we can use the energy that can be released by channelling it into useful directions, if we can 'feel the fear and do it anyway', if we can support one another to minimize the fear, if we can become so enthusiastic and caught up in what we are doing that we no longer even feel the fear . . . then there is a possibility to change ourselves, to change our working environment and to change the fortunes of the organization in which we are working.

Of course, there is nothing new about this. For many decades management theorists have been talking about the relationship between a happy workforce and a productive one and there is ample research to support this link. For instance in his book, *Happiness: Lessons from a new science*,[6] the economist Richard Layard places work as ranking third in the 'Big Seven factors affecting happiness' (after family relationships and financial situation). Sheer common sense tells us that if we are happy in our work, we are likely to do a better job because we are more motivated and enjoy what we do.

Re-humanizing the workplace

So, are happy, productive and innovative workforces what we want? If yes, then the million-dollar question is, 'Why haven't we got them?' We are swamped with hundreds of business books, articles and papers on organizations and how to make them bigger, better, more productive, more efficient, more visible; merging them, growing them, diversifying them. And here am I offering yet another book on this subject. With so much information, why are we in a situation where people feel more miserable at work than they have ever been? Fear of job loss, ritual humiliation at work, being excluded and being shamed are regular occurrences in some organizations. Why do we allow this? These are some of the issues that we will explore in the following chapters.

We already have more information than we know what to do with and 'Big Data' will ensure that we will be never be at a loss for it in the future. However, it seems that information is not enough. At least it is not enough to instigate change within organizations. Our rational brain is insufficient on its own. For organizational culture to begin to shift from one of fear and withholding to one of openness and engagement, we need to embrace all of our *human* abilities – and in particular our senses – right across and up and down the workplace.

Brene Brown, in her very interesting book *Daring Greatly*,[7] describes a woman in her thirties that she interviewed. The woman – we will call her Jill – had made a mistake at work: the first mistake after two years of what her employer called 'outstanding, winner's work'. Her mistake resulted in the agency losing a client. As a consequence, her boss put her on the 'losers list'. She went from the top of the winners list to the top of the losers list. Jill was traumatized. Her confidence sank. She felt ashamed, fearful and unable to function. After a couple of weeks, she resigned from her job.

How is it possible in this day and age that staff who are trying their best to do a good job are treated in his humiliating and degrading way? Significantly Jill was handled in a manner that tapped into and recreated her childhood feelings of being shamed, insignificant and powerless. As an adult, this is one of the most undermining of experiences. This story is not a one-off occurrence. In the course of interviewing people for this book, such stories were depressingly common. I only had to mention the topic of my book before friends, relatives and even complete strangers offered to tell me of their experiences. Significantly, after individuals had spoken about their experience, they added, anxiously, 'But you won't say my name, will you?' Public humiliation is still one of our greatest fears.

As I write Jill's story, I find myself asking: How have we as a society lost the plot? Where is the appreciation for the simple, human purpose of work, an activity that gives us satisfaction and the means to live comfortably and provide for our families? We criticize bankers for their greed, for their hungry grasping at power and wealth. Are we just jealously trying to emulate them by putting up with abuse at work in order to maintain excessive lifestyles? Or are we just ground down by the fear of losing our job, of being humiliated at work, by an ongoing sense of weariness and anxiety about the future?

And why, I wonder, does this climate of fear appear to be stronger in larger organizations? I say 'appear' because it is difficult to establish whether or not smaller organizations have more or less fear. Smaller organizations are more diverse. They cannot easily be compared. So I am not saying that fear cannot exist in smaller organizations, but from my experience it is different and idiosyncratic. Also, smaller organizations are more likely to operate, to varying degrees, on a family model, where people know one another and there are strong pressures to get along together.

Many large organizations have become obsessed with control within the workplace: measurement, monitoring, compliance, performance targets, regulatory controls, procurement, protocols, directives for individuals and groups. At best these targets can provide useful steers. At worst, they can pervert productivity and undermine morale. There are many examples of poorly thought-out targets that undermine staff morale and employees' sense of self-worth. Attempting to monitor and control the workforce has reached near-epidemic proportions, sometimes to the point where the humanity of the employee is forgotten. When did mutual trust just evaporate? Trust between employees, regardless of level, is the bedrock of a healthy organization. The obsession with measurement, in its various forms, is indicative of a lack of trust.

Of course, all employees at all levels of the organization deserve respect, honesty and acceptable working conditions. In return, it is reasonable to expect that they will fulfil their work requirements to the best of their ability. Is it naive to talk in these terms nowadays? Is human dignity a quaint anachronism? For me, there is one word that sums up the disposability and inhumanity that have become part and parcel of normal conversation within some workplaces. The word is 'culling'. Google Search defines 'to cull' as 'to reduce the population of (a wild animal) by selective slaughter'. Culling is part of the normal vocabulary in some contemporary organizations. It is no longer used with irony or maverick self-mockery. As one interviewee, Mary, explained:

> The management consultants are coming and they instil a lot of fear. A third of us are culled every year – there's a lot of fear there. She [the management consultant] is going to decide if we will axe this whole department so we can streamline and save money.

There are parallels with the later stages of the Industrial Revolution in the late 19th and early 20th centuries. New materials, the use of new energy sources, the steam engine and so on enabled increased production with smaller expenditure of human energy. In particular, a new organization of work known as the 'factory system', which entailed an increased division of labour and specialization of function, became common. In essence, this involved breaking a job down into its component parts so that the workers could do their job in a mechanistic and supposedly more efficient fashion. It was an effective method of controlling and monitoring the workforce.

Now we are comfortably ensconced in the 21st century. We believe that we are much more sophisticated nowadays, huddled in in our digitalized workplaces, tweeting and emailing, Skyping and blogging. Perhaps it's true. However, the drive to mechanize and monitor employees is still alive and well. As we will see, the desire to control the workforce is atleast as powerful today as it was in the time of the Industrial Revolution. In particular, performance targets, in one shape or another, define many workplaces and can result in a wide range of unintended consequences that perversely undermine productivity in the long term.

If we genuinely want to foster healthy organizations, in the sense of encouraging well-being among the workforce and enabling a productive, financially viable organization, it may mean rethinking the way in which we organize work. Perhaps we need to reassess how the organization is structured and the hours staff work. It may mean more collaborative working, less target-driven tasks, or flexible targets that act as a steer rather than a rod for the employee's back. It may mean more autonomy for the workforce. Perhaps this sounds idealistic, but there is considerable evidence, for example from Daniel Goleman,[8] that happy employees who feel both stretched and supported in their work are more likely to contribute and help build successful and profitable organizations. Most importantly we need to change the way we think about the work. This is hardly rocket science.

We all know from our own experience that when we enjoy what we do we tend to do a better job. So, at the end of the day, it is in the interests of all staff in an organization, at all levels, to contribute in the best way they can. Within many workplaces, over the years of the recession, cutbacks and downsizing, employees at all levels of organizations have become nervous, anxious and fearful. We have become habitually cautious. As the green shoots of recovery grow stronger and the recession gives way to greater optimism, we have to relearn what it means to be bold and adventurous. It is time to embrace a new era of optimism and productivity. It is up to all of us, from the CEO to juniors, to put the necessary effort into changing our organizations, moving them towards places in which we enjoy working, which are productive, innovative and explorative. This will obviously be easier in some organizations or departments than others. It will require collaborative effort and it will not always be Straightforward – but think of the sense of achievement, even if we only manage 50 per cent improvement within our own department.

Notes

1   Stacey, R (2003), *Complexity and Group Processes: A radically social understanding of individuals*, Brunner-Routledge

2   For an excellent introduction to complexity sciences, I recommend Margaret J Wheatley's 1999 book *Leadership and the New Science: Discovering order in a chaotic world,* Berrett-Koehler

3   Keegan, S,(2011) *Qualitative Research as Emergent Inquiry: Reframing qualitative practice in terms of complex responsive processes*, Emergent Publications

4   Glassner, B (2009) *The Culture of Fear: Why Americans are afraid of the wrong things*, Basic Books

5   Maslow, A (1943) *A Theory of Human Motivation*

6   Layard, R (2005) *Happiness: Lessons from a new science*, Penguin Press

7   Brown, B (2012) *Daring Greatly: How the courage to be vulnerable transforms the way we live, love, parent and lead,* Portfolio Penguin

8   Goleman, D (1996) Chapter 10, *Managing with Heart* in *Emotional Intelligence: Why it can matter more than IQ*, Bloomsbury Publishing

The cultural backdrop of fear

02

The tragedy of our day is the climate of fear in which we live, and fear breeds repression. **ADLAI STEVENSON, 1952**

The backdrop of fear and uncertainty within the workplace

No organization exists in isolation. It is always influenced by the broader context in which it nestles: its history, its competition, the wide variety of factors that influence its progress and so on. In this chapter we will discuss some of the effects of the recent worldwide recession, which have had a significant impact on most workplaces over the past decade and which continue to shape the way in which our working cultures have developed and are still developing. The backdrop of fear and uncertainty, a residue of the protracted slowdown, acts as a restraint, in the face of which even successful companies show caution.

It is more than 60 years since Adlai Stevenson, then governor of Illinois and a US presidential candidate, made the comment above. The focus of our fear may have changed since then, but we are still very familiar with fear itself. For many of us, the unknown is right up there in our top ten fears. This is hardly surprising. We spend a great deal of our time trying to make the unknown known. We save for our retirement so we will not be penniless in our old age. We service our car so we can be sure that it will start on a cold frosty morning. We put our boots by the door so we know where they are when we rush out to work. We take a job in a reputable organization in the hope of being guaranteed a regular salary and maybe a decent pension. But, try as we might, we can never quite achieve the certainty we seek.

Of course, people vary in the extent to which they crave certainty and this changes as we pass through life, but all of us, in some way or another, seek a degree of structure and certainty – although life doesn't necessarily oblige. We could die tomorrow. The company we work for may go bust.

We navigate as best we can through the vagaries of life, and are pleasantly surprised when our boots are still by the door. However, at other times we are horrified to find that our expectations have been cruelly and disastrously confounded.

2007/8 and the cold winds of recession blew in

The recession started towards the end of August 2007 and escalated throughout 2008. The year had started calmly enough. It was a leap year. Cyprus and Malta accepted the euro as their currency. The Indian cricket team drew with Australia and the price of petroleum hit US$100 a barrel for the first time. All seemed well, at least as far as the general public was concerned. Then, seemingly out of the blue, life changed unexpectedly. Markets around the world plunged amid growing fears of a US recession, fuelled by the subprime mortgage crisis. It was the start of the worldwide recession and central banks eventually had to step in, lending to the banking market. This was just the beginning. Who could have predicted that by the end of the year a number of international banks would have crashed, triggering a collapse in national economies, and that we would be plunged into the worst recession since the 1930s, a recession that would force us to re-evaluate structures, systems, lifestyles and assumptions that had once seemed invincible? As Gordon Brown, then prime minister, put it, 'What we did not see, nobody saw, was the possibility of markets failure.'[1]

Certainly the general publics across much of the developed world did not expect the crash. The UK, for example, had enjoyed 16 years of unprecedented growth, fuelled by steady interest rates and easy access to credit. Yet, with hindsight, the indicators were visible. The most telling was the exponential growth in consumer credit in the UK and elsewhere. Perhaps it was the case that nobody wanted the good times to end and we were in a state of collective denial.[2] But, at the time, the general public was not privy to the knowledge that the major banks and the government possessed and we felt angry, frightened and deceived. The boots were no longer by the door. How had this happened?

In fact, the boots were nowhere to be seen. With the financial crash, our certainties were shaken in a way that had not happened before, at least within our lifetimes. Research among the general public reinforced the mood of gloom, fear and uncertainty.[3] As Maggie, a 45-year-old woman with two teenage children, summed it up: 'I am almost frozen about what to do. I'm so worried I might lose my job, I have to re-mortgage but I don't know what's right . . . I wish I could see into the future.'

Maggie was not alone in wanting to see what was coming next. Leaders across the globe were probably wishing the same thing. The economic crisis dented our collective confidence in the future and now, as we see the green shoots of recovery, it is still difficult for many people to plan ahead. We cannot easily judge what will happen to our jobs, our families, levels of employment, how our societies will pan out. According to the neuroscientist Jonah Lehrer, we are much more comfortable with risk than we are with uncertainty.[4] And we have not been short of uncertainty in recent years. Many of us, to varying degrees, are afraid for our own futures and those of our children.

It got worse. In the UK, public sector finance was slashed as the recession set in. For a while, the European Union teetered on the brink of collapse. Meanwhile EU citizens sought refuge in the UK as economic migrants and, rather bizarrely, house prices in central London soared. Elsewhere in the UK they froze or dropped, reflecting the true state of the economy. And all the time there was growing disbelief and widespread anger that bankers were still receiving bonuses that would support minor fiefdoms, when it was widely believed they were actually a major cause of the economic crash. Citizens across the globe felt disillusioned, insecure and dispirited about their futures. How had this happened? Who was responsible? What would happen next? What would the future hold? The questions reverberated.

This worldwide financial crisis that erupted in 2008, as if from nowhere, swept quickly around much of the developed world like a tornado; unexpected and unwelcome, a bolt out of the blue. At least that was how it was experienced by the majority of ordinary citizens who did not have access to knowledge that the major banks and governments possessed. Initially it was hoped that this was a blip, that things would quickly return to normal; there would be a brief period of belt-tightening and then it would be back to business as usual.

This did not happen. Instead, many European economies, along with markets worldwide, slipped relentlessly into recession. Companies that had been household names for decades started to falter and collapse, alongside confidence in worldwide economies. The general public was left with a residue of fear, anxiety and helplessness as redundancies, cutbacks and wage freezes became commonplace. Financial worries and uncertainty became part and parcel of the fabric of life.

In the UK, a culture of thrift emerged, as we adopted wartime values, at least on the surface. We took pride in our make-do-and-mend strategies, sought out bargains, baked our own bread, made cupcakes and assiduously hoarded discount vouchers. There was much talk about the failure of capitalism and what might replace it. We considered ourselves to be victims. Most people did not feel any personal responsibility for the sad state of the economy. It was the fault of the government, the banks, the greedy, immigrants, those out of work, the pensioners or all of the above. We sought a simple target on which to pin the blame. It was easy, as the bankers fitted the bill rather nicely. They won hands down.

It is interesting, in retrospect, to observe how we interpreted these circumstances in ways that supported our personal stories. In the growing – and sometimes booming – economies of the preceding decades, there was a general belief that success was achieved through a combination of individual hard work, entrepreneurship, productivity and creativity. We – both as individuals and as a cluster of disparate groups, companies and cultures – created success. However, once the tables had turned and we were facing tougher times, there was a different story. The recession, it seemed, was nothing to do with us; it was not of our making. It was 'them', the rich, the greedy, the privileged, the EU, the bankers, the governments who were responsible. We, the general public, were merely victims.

Six years on, the resentment expressed towards bankers and other high earners is still palpable. Bankers present a convenient scapegoat for a general public that is still searching for answers.

Meanwhile, in many workplaces, employees, ranging from senior to junior, continue to feel under the cosh, in spite of increasing claims of an economic recovery. Some board directors questioned the strength of the recovery; they were feeling the pressure from shareholders who wanted to see healthy returns. Equally, their senior executives attempted to maintain sales in a nervous market and staff at all levels were concerned about job security and maintaining their living standards. This climate created a breeding ground for fear. Constant pressure to perform trickled down from shareholders, managers and clients; there was more pressure to deliver, with reduced resources. People felt worn down, regardless of their seniority in the organization. Even managers who tried to protect their staff from the worst political fallouts could get caught up in the crossfire.

The economists' explanation

Economists described these economic upheavals in a different language, but their sentiments were broadly similar. There was general agreement that this was the worst decline in economic activity since the 1930s. The consensus was that the crisis was triggered by a complex interplay of problems within the international banking systems. When the US housing bubble burst, it caused the values of securities tied to US real estate pricing to plummet, damaging financial institutions globally. Questions regarding bank solvency, a decline in credit availability and damaged investor confidence had an impact on global stock markets, where securities suffered large losses during 2008 and early 2009. Economies worldwide slowed during this period, as credit tightened and international trade declined. Governments and central banks responded with unprecedented monetary policy expansion and institutional bailouts.

Many root causes for the financial crisis have been suggested. The Levin–Coburn[5] report found that 'the crisis was not a natural disaster, but the result of high-risk, complex financial products; undisclosed conflicts of interest; and the failure of regulators, the credit rating agencies, and the market itself to rein in the excesses of Wall Street'.

Critics argued that credit rating agencies and investors failed to accurately price the risk involved with mortgage-related financial products, and that governments did not adjust their regulatory practices to address 21st-century financial markets. The 1999 repeal of the Glass–Steagall Act of 1933 effectively removed the separation that previously existed between Wall Street investment banks and depository banks. In response to the financial crisis, both market-based and regulatory solutions have been implemented or are under consideration.

Of course the crisis did not stop with the financial institutions: it quickly spread its tentacles wide, affecting all aspects of society. It has been argued that a range of other factors also contributed to the climate of fear and uncertainty: the rising costs of oil consumption and falling house prices, competition from lower-cost countries and/or moving manufacturing to the East, the polarizing effect of digital technologies, the changing roles of public–private partnerships and what this entails for employees. None of these factors operated in isolation: they created a systemic process of knock-on effects that were difficult to predict or stop.

The widespread residue of fear in the workplace

The recession has changed many of us. We are more fearful and fear is highly contagious; it spread rapidly as the recession deepened. According to The Poverty Site, within the UK unemployment among the young peaked at

22 per cent.[6] Equally, many of those who were in work felt uncertain about their future employment prospects. Within all manner of organizations both large and small there was, and to an extent still is, considerable unease and distrust of government figures that suggest an economic recovery. Both the public and private sectors have experienced savage cuts in staffing levels. Redundancies, part-time working, high unemployment and lower wages are common. There is still considerable uncertainty about future employment prospects. These factors fed into the workplace and we will explore their effects in Chapters 4 and 5.

Fear and uncertainty also impact on health. According to the *British Medical Journal*, the downturn and the policies of austerity have also had an effect on the mental health of populations that have been affected by recession. With surprising candour, the *BMJ* states that it tries not to get involved in party politics but 'where there is evidence that a policy is harming health, we must speak as we find'. New research published in the *BMJ* highlights the 'associated harm' of recession.[7] Building on previous smaller studies, Shu-sen Chang and his colleagues have examined data from 54 countries to explore the link between the 2008 global economic crisis and increased rates of suicide.[8] By comparing the number of suicides reported in 2009 with the number expected based on trends before the crisis (2000–7), they identified over 4,000 'excess suicides'. Increased suicides were most apparent in Europe and the United States, and in men rather than women. The authors of the study looked for and found what they called a specific 'dose response', a relationship between increased suicide rates and increase in unemployment, especially in countries where unemployment levels before the crisis were relatively low.

The *BMJ* report continues: 'So governments can, if they choose, ameliorate the serious danger to mental health from unemployment, the brunt of which in almost all countries examined by Chang *et al* was borne by young men.' This is not an isolated finding, as a similar study concluded that 'being unemployed was associated with a two- to threefold increased risk of death by suicide, compared with being employed'.[9] Of course, these findings raise questions about whether or not it is the responsibility of the government to create more jobs as an antidote to potential mental health problems and suicide rates. This does not seem to be a topic that governments are keen to address.

However, there is a much bigger issue here, one that is looming on the horizon, which will potentially blow the whole issue of employment, mental health and suicide sky high.

The nature and availability of jobs are changing radically and we have no real strategy to deal with this. As Eric Schmidt, executive chairman of Google, warned at the World Economic Forum in Davos on 23 January 2014:

Recent advances in artificial intelligence and mobile communications have also fuelled fears that whole classes of clerical and research jobs may also be replaced by machines. While such upheaval has been made up for in the past by new types of work created by advancing technology, some economists have warned that the pace of change is too fast for employment levels to adapt. There is quite a bit of research that middle-class jobs that are relatively highly skilled are being automated out. The problem is that middle-class jobs are being replaced by service jobs. It is pretty clear that work is changing and the classic nine-to-five job is going to have to be redefined. Without significant encouragement, this will get worse and worse.

Schmidt is not alone in his pessimism. The philosopher and computer scientist Jaron Lanier has spent his career pushing the transformative power of modern technology to its limits. But then he started to reflect on the effects that technology is having on our lifestyles and our brains – and he changed his mind:

> In the past, a revolution in production, such as the Industrial Revolution, generally increased the wealth and freedom of people. The digital revolution we are living through is different. Instead of leaving a greater number of us in excellent financial health, the effect of digital technologies – and the companies behind them – is to concentrate wealth, reduce growth and challenge the livelihoods of an ever-increasing number of people. As the protections of the middle class disappear, washed away by crises in capitalism, what is left in their place? And what could replace them?[10]

So this is the working climate that we and our children are likely to inherit. It is little wonder that, as we will see in Chapters 4 and 5, employees are nervous about the future and fearful of their prospects. This is the backdrop of fear that we will be discussing throughout this book – and these are the issues that we need to address if we want to move towards a psychologically healthy workplace. In the next two chapters we will explore the nature of fear in more detail.

Notes

1 BBC News, 23 January 2009

2 Paper given at the Market Research Society Annual Conference (2009): *Under the Skin: Credit-crunched, recessionary times: Implications for the UK and its banks*. Research carried out by Truth Consulting in conjunction with HSBC Bank

3 Campbell Keegan Ltd have carried out research on consumer financial attitudes and behaviour at regular intervals between 1983 and the present day, and in particular during the period from 2008 to 2010. The recurring consumer themes during this time were: the sense of fear, unpredictability and paralysis; seeking simplicity and the re-emergence of traditional values, safety and predictability; the cult of blame

4 Lehrer, J (2009) *How We Decide*, Canongate

5 Levin–Coburn report [online] www.levin.senate.gov/imo/media/doc/supporting/2011/PSI_WallStreetCrisis_041311.pdf

6 www.poverty.org.uk/35/index.shtml

7 Godley, F (2013) Austerity, Suicide and Screening, *British Medical Journal* [online] www.bmj.com/content/347/bmj.f5678

8 Chang, S, Stuckler, D, Yip, P and Gunnell, D (2013) Impact of 2008 Global economic crisis on suicide: time trend study in 54 countries, *British Medical Journal* [online] www.bmj.com/content/347/bmj.f5239

9 Blakely, T A, Collings, S C D and Atkins, J (2003) Unemployment and suicide: Evidence for a causal association? *Journal of Epidemiology & Community Health*, 57, pp 594–600

10 Lanier, J (2013) *Who Owns the Future?*, Allen Lane

Perspectives on fear

03

In time we hate that which we often fear. **WILLIAM SHAKESPEARE,**
ANTONY AND CLEOPATRA

Exploring the boundaries of fear

This book is about fear in organizations, but before we launch into the organizational territory, we need first to dip a toe into the ways in which fear manifests itself and explore some of the many faces of fear, just as we explored the economic climate that provided the context for the financial backdrop in the previous chapter. The different aspects of fear that we touch on can be equally relevant both within and outside organizations. Essentially, fear is an emotion without borders, which makes it difficult to pin down and define. Like a prism, its colour changes as our view shifts.

Writing, and indeed talking, about fear is a bit like herding cats. As soon as you pin one fearful thought down, another pops up unexpectedly in a different area of the mind. Fear is slippery, Machiavellian and coquettish, sometimes our friend, sometimes our enemy. 'Fear is a kind of unintentional storytelling that we're all born knowing how to do,' says TED author Karen Thompson Walker. 'Our fears focus our attention on a question that is as important in life as it is in literature: what will happen next . . . How we choose to read our fears can have a profound effect on our lives.'[1]

As we move through this chapter, allow yourself to make connections with fear in different areas in your life, either in the present, past or future and either within or outside the organization where you work. Try to feel the fear physically and emotionally. Put that feeling into words. What does it mean to you? Do you feel in control of it? Does the feeling of fear make you feel uncomfortable? Can you easily switch it off? Do you have an automatic, bodily response when you feel fear? How would you describe it? As we go through this chapter, and indeed the rest of this book, try as best you can to understand how fear influences your behaviours, especially in a work context, and try to identify your automatic and habitual behaviours when faced with fearful situations at work. As you become used to examining your response to fear, you will also become used to choosing how you will respond to that fear, and this will increase your behavioural choices.

Now, as you read the story below, try to experience the different aspects of fear as they unfold and, as you do so, try to make connections with your own personal experiences and feelings.

Fear and the unexpected

Imagine you are strolling through the park with your partner. It is a bright and beautiful day, one of the first days of spring. The flowers are bursting forth in vibrant colours of blue and yellow. The birds are chirping and you are feeling relaxed and happy. You have packed a picnic and are searching for a place to lay your blanket, so that you can spread out on the grass. You are laughing and joking with your partner as you choose the best spot to picnic. Suddenly, from nowhere, a man appears from the undergrowth alongside the path. He looks dishevelled and panicked. Then you see that he is holding a knife in his right hand. He has spotted you. He yells and runs towards you. What do you do? In all probability, you run as fast as you can until you find someone to report the incident to – and where you will feel safe.

However, in practice, the question 'What do you do?' is largely irrelevant. It suggests that your rational mind will assess the situation, evaluate the options, quickly devise a strategy and implement it as quickly as possible. Chances are this will not happen. Our rational minds are too slow to react in such situations. Instead of considering the options and weighing up the likelihood of the man launching an attack, you will almost certainly succumb to your body's instinctive, protective strategies. The body's 'fight or flight' mechanism will cut in and attempt to save you from whatever real or imagined danger threatens you.

First you will become highly sensitized to visual and auditory cues. Second, your priorities and goals will change: hunger, pain, thirst will be suppressed. Third, your information-gathering systems will become focused on the perceived threat. Fourth, some simple thoughts, such as 'This is dangerous' will pop into your head. Fifth, any past memories of similar situations will be triggered. Sixth, you might well scream or yell – or alternatively you might become paralysed by fear and unable to make a sound. Seventh, your brain will be racing to work out what is happening and to guess what will happen next. Eighth, your learning systems will be activated and then ninth, physiological systems will get to work and you will act. These stages will happen at the speed of light and the fear mechanism will be activated, prompting you to fight or flight.[2]

Later, assuming that you survive the ordeal, you may think back and find yourself unable to remember exactly what happened. From which side of the path did the man emerge? What was he wearing? How old was he – 20? 30? 40? Does your partner have the same recall of the details? How, exactly, did you escape? As you mull on the incident over the next few days, you may ask yourself, 'Am I really sure he was going to attack us? It all happened so quickly. Could he have been trying to escape from someone who was chasing *him*? Did I overreact? I was frightened out of my wits – was my judgement impaired?'

Recreating fast-moving events that occurred when we were extremely frightened is very difficult; it is one of the most challenging aspects of court cases for prosecuting lawyers. How is it possible to rely on the evidence of a witness who was in a state of acute fear when the alleged offence occurred? Cross-examining such witnesses is notoriously difficult because they are literally *'not themselves'* at the time. According to leading QC, Nigel Rumfitt, 'Juries are told to make allowances for memories being rendered inaccurate by sudden, unexpected and frightening events. The effects of fear may explain discrepancies between honest witnesses who appear to see different aspects of the same event.' Indeed fear at work can have a similar effect by distorting our judgement, restricting our ability to think 'straight' and can prevent us from speaking lucidly.

This *not-one-self-ness* can be brought on in a variety of ways. It is not restricted to extreme life-or-death situations. Fear, ranging from mild through to extreme, can trigger rapid physiological changes in our bodies, including the way in which we view and interpret the world around us. Indeed, these bodily changes can, in extreme situations, ensure our physical survival by making us temporarily 'superhuman' – as we will discuss later in this chapter.

The role of fear

So, although fear gets a lot of bad press, it is nonetheless a vital part of our survival mechanisms. Without fear, human beings would have died out long ago. In fact, they would probably not have evolved in the first place. We might assume that bodily reactions to different emotions are the same, or at least that they overlap, but this is not the case. Fear mechanisms provoke very specific physiological responses, which differ from those of other similar human emotions. This is no accident. It means that our bodies can react in precisely targeted ways that will maximize our chances of getting out of a dangerous situation alive, and preferably with a minimum of damage. In times of danger, speed is often of the essence. When we do not have time to make decisions, fear mechanisms can take over without consulting us.

Fear is the body's primeval response to perceived threat. As such it is a protective, adaptive response. The way in which the body prepares itself to deflect or defeat threat is quite remarkable and involves a transformation in our body that rivals that of Clark Kent morphing into Superman. For instance, if you are preparing to give an important presentation, feeling nervous, your body will automatically gear itself up to provide you with the necessary resources.

The physiology of fear

So how does fear actually work, and can our body 'sense' fear and decide what to do when we are – or feel that we are – in danger? How does it know what to do, often instinctively, without our conscious involvement? We are all familiar with the fear response – the 'fight or flight' mechanism that kicks in when we are in real or perceived danger, or when we feel under emotional or existential threat. Actually, 'fight or flight' is not quite an accurate description. Like many theories that subsume a great deal of data into one explanation, it has turned out to be an oversimplification.[3] It is more accurate to say that there are at least four types of defensive reaction, each with a suite of physiological responses optimized to handle a different category of threat. When danger is far away – or at least not imminent – the instinct is to freeze (like a deer in the headlights). When danger is approaching, the impulse is to run away. When escape is impossible, the response is to fight back and when struggling is futile, the instinct is to become immobilized in the grip of fear. So, although it is less snappy, a more accurate description of 'fight or flight' would be 'fight, freeze, flight, fright'. Each of these responses has a cluster of physiological reactions, optimized to handle different types of threat and triggered by the autonomic nervous system. These fear responses are, in part, an energy conservation device. They allow us to live our lives using limited energy, while keeping large amounts of energy in reserve. However, if a predator jumps out of the bushes, we can, in a split second, increase our physical resources and scale a wall we would have thought impossible.

Fear in practice

The body is very pragmatic in the face of fear. It does not excessively worry about whether or not the fear response is embarrassing or proportionate. It simply acts. When humans – and indeed other creatures – feel physically threatened, a very sophisticated system of instinctive mechanisms cuts in, which is designed to protect us, and which is largely outside our control. This includes increases in heart and lung rate, constriction of blood vessels in many parts of the body, contraction of the heart, musculature and respiration rate, a general effect on the sphincters of the body, paling or flushing, and relaxation of the bladder, in addition to many more effects. In this way the blood distribution is centralized to maintain a good blood supply to the heart and brain and to create a protective circulatory response to stem severe blood loss (as might be expected from an attack by a predator). In addition, the body creates elevated levels of glucose, and chemicals such as adrenalin and the stress hormone, cortisol, are released into the bloodstream, causing certain physical reactions. There is a redistribution of blood from the digestive tract to the muscles, sharpened senses, dilation of the pupils, and much more.

Fear can take two routes in the brain. The first route travels from the sensory input regions – our eyes, ears and nose – into the amygdala, hypothalamus and straight to the body, which immediately starts priming itself to escape. A second route has fear stimuli travelling more slowly to the frontal cortex where they are assessed and evaluated in terms of the actual threat. For instance, walking down a dark alleyway at night, I might see something moving out of the corner of my eye. Is there someone hiding in the shadows, about to jump out and mug me? I am immediately on high alert. After another look, once my information has travelled the second, slower, route via my anterior temporal cortex, I can see the object. It is just a tomcat. My frontal cortex now reassures me. There is no need to worry. My fear subsides and my pulse and breathing return to normal. My blood sugar starts to fall and normal blood flow returns to those organs that are not essential for a quick getaway.

While key areas like the amygdala and the cortex play a large part in all our emotions, a whole set of brain mechanisms is called upon. Fast reactions to certain emotion-inducing stimuli are imprinted in the circuitry of our brains. Curiously, small babies do not express fear until some of the fear mechanisms are in place; they have not yet had a chance to learn fear responses. It is also interesting that many of our phobias are directed towards things that would, in our ancestral pasts, have posed a real threat: snakes, spiders, open spaces, crowds of people or heights. Professor Robert Winston suggests that this might be a primed survival response, which is no longer useful.[4] It is a timely reminder. However much we want to present ourselves as 21st-century beings driven by rational choice and inhabiting a technological world, we still carry within us our prehistoric past.

Fear is arguably the most powerful emotion in our repertoire and real fear results in these massive changes in the body's systems, which control blood flow. The extraordinary power of fear makes sense in evolutionary terms. Our ancestors developed a wide range of impressive faculties like language and consciousness, but they were rarely safe from predators or other dangers. Fear assisted and enabled our survival. Given the dangers of the world, our ancestors did well to develop such effective survival mechanisms. For instance, they could run like the wind, or they could freeze. Depending on the situation and their previous experiences, they selected their strategy – or simply allowed their body to decide for them.

The feeling of fear

Fear is such a wide-ranging and complex emotion, with tendrils reaching into all aspects of our lives, that it is nearly impossible to pin it down. Fear was there in the mists of time before Homo sapiens walked on two legs. It is here now, when a newborn baby emerges, covered in blood, and the mother looks on anxiously.

Sometimes fear is a constant gnawing in our stomach. At other times it roars like an angry tiger. We grit our teeth – feel the fear and do it anyway – and we are euphoric when we succeed, when we manage to tame fear for a little while. We may feel fear in the face of very tangible threats such as the policeman pulling us over for speeding. At other times fear simmers and it is hard to pin down exactly why we feel fearful.

You may laugh and say, 'Fear, what fear? I don't have any fear. This is all an exaggeration.' Of course, you may be right. Who am I to say? But if so, you are very unusual. Most of us experience fear of different types and intensity on a fairly regular basis but we are skilled at concealing our fear – sometimes to the point where we do not even recognize that we are fearful. Instead, we call what we are feeling anxiety, worry, concern, fretting, bother, nervous, to make the feeling more palatable. Or we keep silent. Fear has many euphemistic names. Facing fear can feel a bit like staring into the sun.

How fear works

Fear mechanisms have developed and become honed over millennia, so it is hardly surprising that they are so complex and sophisticated – and that they serve us so well. However, while it is still useful to have the 'fight or flight' mechanism at the ready, just in case a roving lion escapes from the zoo and is looking for a tasty meal, the risk of being savaged by a lion is pretty low. This does not mean that the emotion of fear has become redundant. Fear has become more generalized, in the sense that it can be triggered in many different situations nowadays, not just when it is a matter of life or death. Of course fear can still be experienced as extreme, but it may also be perceived as low-level and continuous, or associated with particular situations. Fear can also be a state of mind, which is self-generated, irrespective of the environment.

Psychologists are still learning about the *ways* in which our emotions influence us. However, current thinking is that there is some degree of hard-wired emotion-specific physiological patterning linked to major emotions such as fear and anger. With the exciting new developments in neuroscience, which are giving us a much greater understanding of how our brains work, we are learning that our bodies and our brains are much more adaptable than we originally thought. We may eventually realize ways in which we can develop, control and hone our emotions in order to broaden our emotional repertoire.

Fear is contagious

According to Daniel Goleman, the author of *Emotional Intelligence*, both *stronger* emotions and *very negative* emotions are more contagious than supposedly less intense emotions such as surprise, sadness, pity or jealousy.[5] Certainly fear is up there among the strong and negative emotions. You may have experienced fear contagion as the herd instinct kicks in. Fear is easily and unconsciously communicated to others and it causes the recipient to convey similar symptoms of fear, often without awareness. For instance, a person perceiving another's fear will unconsciously make a fearful face.

The classic example of contagion is in the financial markets. If the markets drop, traders quickly become anxious. If they plunge, there are widespread fear and panic as traders rush to dispose of risky assets at almost any cost. As we saw in the 2008 global crisis, financial activity was only loosely related to the value of the stocks. Although they might deny it, traders are generally influenced more strongly by their peers than by the actual state of the markets – unless of course they are experienced contrarians. We hang on to the illusion that we are individuals who can make our own decisions. The reality is that we more commonly run with the herd and this favours a collective blindness to risk and uncertainty. In organizations that are undergoing restructuring or a programme of redundancies, contagion can be particularly dangerous, as fear spreads rapidly by word of mouth and levels of fear soar dramatically, sometimes to the extent of undermining organizational stability.

In his fascinating book, *Thinking, Fast and Slow,*[6] the Nobel laureate in economics, Daniel Kahneman, provides many examples of 'herdiness'. One of my particular favourites is the Florida effect.

The study was carried out with university students, who were asked to assemble four-word sentences from a set of five words (for example, *finds, he, it, yellow, instantly*). For one group of students, half the scrambled sentences contained words associated with the elderly, such as *Florida, forgetful, bald, grey* or *wrinkle*. In the other group there were random words. The students were then asked to construct sentences from these words.

On completion, the students were asked to move to another lab. This was the real – but secret – purpose of the experiment. Surreptitiously, the time they took to cover the distance was monitored. Lo and behold, students who had made sentences from words with an elderly theme walked down the hallway significantly slower than the others. When the students were told about the purpose of the study, they refused to believe that they had been influenced in this way without their awareness.

When our tendency to herdiness is combined with highly emotional states such as fear, our judgement can become seriously impaired. All emotions have the potential to be contagious, and fear, because it is one of the most powerful of emotions, can trigger the most extreme of reactions.[7] Given half an opportunity, fear can quickly and effortlessly spread through a crowd, a party, a school or an organization, and can spread from individual to individual, often without our conscious awareness.

This is the fear response doing its job, which is to get us away from possible danger as quickly as possible. Of course, this state of arousal can be expressed in different ways, such as anger or violence. Our emotions are never completely discrete.

The Hillsborough disaster

Fear responses have evolved slowly and physiological mechanisms that developed to protect hunter-gatherers living on the plains are not always appropriate in contemporary urban life. On 15 April 1989, Liverpool were due to play Nottingham Forest in the FA Cup semi-final at Hillsborough Stadium in Sheffield. Fans were streaming excitedly into the stadium, anticipating a great game and a win for their team. However, a combination of decrepit turnstiles and poor crowd control resulted in severe congestion. Fear and panic quickly spread through the crowd as people tried unsuccessfully to escape. Ninety-six people died.[8]

What role did fear play in this tragedy? Fear is an invaluable part of our armoury for survival, but given our current lifestyles, it is sometimes not appropriate for the situation we find ourselves in. It is not always fit for purpose. The fear mechanism gives us the strength, the focus and the energy to escape from danger. It enables us to run very fast, as our forebears did. However, these fear mechanisms developed at a time when we were living on the land – not in crowded cities. To run faster than your adversary was therefore a life-saving skill. In contemporary life, the fear mechanism is sometimes ill-adapted to our needs. The football fans did not have the chance to escape. There was no way out. The fear responses kicked in but they could not utilize these skills because they were trapped.

Distortion of fear

As we touched on earlier, fear is not always proportionate to the degree of risk. The 'fight or flight' mechanism can become corrupted, so that the degree of fear is grossly disproportionate to the risk. On the one hand, an individual who is reckless may ignore risks at their peril and put themselves or others in danger. Conversely, they may have a tendency to exaggerate the risks in everyday life so that generalized fear becomes out of proportion to the real risks. At the extreme, individuals become fearful of all manner of things which pose no serious threat. Fears such as these can become crippling to the point where they affect daily functioning. If we are so afraid of events that might happen – but haven't yet done so – that we become consumed with anxiety, then fear constrains our life and we feel out of control.

As Daniel Goleman explains in *Emotional Intelligence*, fear conditioning is the name psychologists use for the process whereby something that is not intrinsically frightening becomes so by association.

Ordinarily, when someone learns to be frightened by an experience or self-generated anxiety, the fear slowly subsides with time. This seems to happen through natural relearning, as the feared object is encountered again in the absence of the further fear. For instance, as children we learn that most dogs are not dangerous and most adults are safe. However, there are situations when the fear response is being constantly reinforced so that the body does not have the time or ability to recover. Repeated exposure to the perceived threat reinforces and amplifies the original fear, sometimes to the point where the individual can no longer bear to be in the fearful situation.

This process may occur in the workplace, for instance when an individual feels that, because of a particular incident or ongoing incidents, they feel they are no longer physically or psychologically safe. Going to work therefore becomes increasingly stressful. The individual is overwhelmed with fear and may show symptoms of post-traumatic stress disorder (PTSD).[9]

Superhumans

Normally, the fear response is dormant or operates at a low level. However, under certain circumstances, especially where the individual or someone nearby is in danger, people have become 'superhuman', if only for a short period of time. Typically this occurrence is triggered by a sudden, extreme and unpredictable event, such as a car crash, which results in a life-threatening situation with one or more victims.

In these situations, the rescuer instinctively rushes in to help, without consciously assessing the risk or determining whether or not they can realistically help the victims. They are driven by fear and the human desire to do what they can, fuelled by adrenalin. Their autonomic nervous system kicks in and, focusing solely on the task at hand, they attempt the near-impossible. Sometimes they fail, but sometimes they succeed against all the odds in spectacular fashion. There has been much debate about whether these claimed rescues are really superhuman feats: holding a car up while a child is rescued from under its wheels, for instance, or instinctively steering a car away from danger – often without being aware of doing it until afterwards. Typically the rescuer has little recall of what he or she did.

Jeff Wise in *Extreme Fear*[10] describes an incident in which a man was driving along the highway in his pickup truck. Suddenly the truck in front of him accelerated, spun its wheels and jerked out onto the avenue. The man, Boyle, saw a shower of red sparks flying up from beneath the chassis of the truck. Then he saw that the truck had hit a cyclist and that the rider was pinned underneath the truck. He was badly injured. Without stopping to think, Boyle ran to the truck, reached under the chassis and lifted it. After several attempts, he managed to hold the truck up long enough for the boy to be pulled free. Afterwards, he was unable to explain how he did it. The Camaro that Boyle lifted weighed 1350 kg, whereas the biggest bar-bell that Boyle had ever dead-lifted weighed only 320 kg.

If this was a one-off event, we might dismiss it as hyperbole, and undoubtedly many of the stories of superhuman strength are fictitious, or at least elaborations. However, there are enough plausible reports of such incidents to suggest that we can summon up such superhuman strength in extreme situations. As we rarely find ourselves in such situations, it is hard to imagine how powerful the effects of fear can be on our physical speed and strength. However, we can throw more light on this area by examining the body's response to extreme stress under controlled conditions.

Vladimir Zatsiorsky, a professor of kinesiology at Pennsylvania State University, has studied the biomechanics of weightlifting extensively. He makes the distinction between the force that our muscles are able to theoretically apply, which he calls 'absolute strength', and the maximum force that they can generate through the conscious exertion of will, which he calls 'maximal force'. Normal individuals can only summon about 65 per cent of their absolute power in a training session, while a trained weightlifter can exceed 80 per cent. However, under competition conditions, a trained athlete can improve as much as 12 per cent above that level. This is not a fixed level. The more intense the competition, the higher it can go, as the brain's centres progressively remove any restraint against performance.[11]

It is therefore no coincidence that world athletic records tend to get broken at major events like the Olympics, where the stakes are highest, the pressure is greatest and the fear of failure sky-high. Of the eight gold medals that Michael Phelps won at the 2008 Olympics, seven were world records. In addition, when he crossed the finish line in the men's 100-metre butterfly in 50.58 seconds, breaking the previous Olympic record, three of the other seven swimmers who finished after him also came in ahead of the previous record.

However, it seems that there is a limit to how fast and how strong fear can make us. Zatsiorsky's work suggests that, while fear can certainly help us to get closer to our absolute power level, there is no way in which we can exceed it.

The brain is the last frontier in terms of our understanding of the human body, and we have yet to understand the mechanisms by which the brain is able to muster great reserves of power which, under certain conditions, can make us superhuman. It is possible that an ability to exceed our normal strength is linked to an inability to feel pain, at least for the duration of the crisis. Under extreme fear and stress, whether this is in a sporting event, rescuing a child trapped under a car, or giving an important presentation, it seems that we can suppress the pain – at least at the time. We just do what needs to be done.

Using fear to our advantage

Therefore, in spite of its bad press, fear is not all bad. If we can learn to control or steer our fear, rather than being overwhelmed by it, we can sometimes use it to our advantage; to improve our performance and make a difference to our lives. While low levels of anxiety can actually help people stay alert and focused, as anxiety rises, so levels of performance start to drop off. However, it is possible to shape our response to fear over time. Practice in appearing to be fearless can make individuals *feel* and *act* fearlessly. Social psychologist Dr Amy Cuddy recommends that 'we fake it until we make it'. According to Cuddy, changes in posture – making ourselves bigger and more expansive – improve our feeling of fearlessness, as do 'holding a silence', acting powerfully and being sparing in speech. Cuddy concludes that 'bodies change minds just as minds change bodies and tiny tweaks can make big changes'.[12] Fear can be a force for change – positive or negative. We are all familiar with fear that stops us doing something we would really like to do, whether it is a sporting challenge, making that difficult phone call or starting a new job. Often we cannot easily predict whether the fear will improve our performance or inhibit it. Fear may even prevent an individual from taking on the task in the first place. It takes courage and determination to face up to fear and this is not helped by our ambivalence about it. Often, we cannot quite make up our minds about the extent to which fear is real or how much of it is the bogey man leaping out from our long-forgotten childhood.

But, when we choose to take the risk – to feel the fear and do it anyway – and we have succeeded in whatever task we have attempted, we feel that we have grown in strength and stature through conquering our own fear. We feel a strong sense of achievement, which is life-enhancing and can generalize to other activities. Next time it will be easier. We will expand on the concept of feeling the fear and doing it anyway in relation to the workplace, in Chapter 5.

Fear in the workplace – and elsewhere

We have touched upon fear in a variety of contexts, not simply within the workplace, because as individuals we move constantly between different environments; we are the same individuals but our behaviours must change to fit the new environment. This is both a constraint and a liberation. There is much to worry about. There are worries about the economy, our job prospects and those of our children. We may be fearful that we will be made redundant and, as we focus on these possibilities, the fear grows and multiplies like a many-headed monster. Whether we acknowledge or deny our fear, and regardless of its source, many of us drag it behind us like a ball and chain. Even if we feel no fear today, it is rarely far away, however much we suppress its existence. Fear is such an elemental and powerful aspect of our lives that we avoid facing it, if possible.

In the next two chapters, we will elaborate on some of these aspects of fear at work and examine ways in which we can both begin to reduce our fear and to manage it to our advantage. Having painted some of the broad-brush strokes of this book, it is time to focus in on aspects of fear within the workplace.

Notes

1 https://www.ted.com/talks/karen_thompson_walker_what_fear_can_teach_us

2 Furnham, A (2012) *50 Psychology Ideas You Really Need to Know*, pp 60–1, Quercus

3 Wise, J (2009) *Extreme Fear: The science of your mind in danger*, p 64 Macmillan

4 Winston, R (2003) *The Human Brain*, pp 37–40 Bantam Press

5 Goleman, D (1996) *Emotional Intelligence*, Bloomsbury

6 Kahneman, D (2011) *Thinking, Fast and Slow*, Farrar, Straus and Giroux

7 Meyer, A (2013) Don't let them smell you sweat, *Psychology Today* [online] www.psychologytoday.com/blog/c-is-cognition/201307/don-t-let-them-smell-you-sweat

8 BBC 12.09.2012, Hillsborough papers: Cameron apology over double injustice

9 *British Journal of Guidance & Counselling*, 32, (3) 2004, pp 265–7 Special issue: Special symposium on bullying at work

10 Wise, J (2009) *Extreme Fear: The science of your mind in danger*, Macmillan

11 Wise, J, Extreme Fear blog, *Psychology Today* [online] www.psychologytoday.com/blog/extreme-fear. See also Zatsiorsky, V, (2006) *The Science and Practice of Strength Training*, Human Kinetics

12 http://blog.ted.com/2012/06/28/what-we-tell-ourselves-with-our-body-language-amy-cuddy-at-tedglobal-2012/

Cultures of fear within organizations

04

" In organizations, real power and energy are generated through relationships. Patterns of relationships and the capacities to form them are more important than tasks, functions, roles and positions. **MARGARET WHEATLEY, 1992**

The long tail of the recession

The past five years of austerity have been very tough for many employees around the globe. It has been a time of cutbacks and insecurities. Fear, anxiety and uncertainty are spectres that have haunted many workplaces and sectors of society across Europe and further afield. These fears are not just a consequence of the downturn; they will not disappear as the recession finally lifts and prosperity returns. They are inherent within modern-day working practices. Short-term contracts, home working, virtual offices, unpaid internships, regulatory environments and the increasing automation of job functions that used to be carried out by human beings are all here to stay. Surviving and thriving, particularly in work cultures that are challenging, rapidly changing and increasingly demanding of our time and energies, require a degree of resilience that many of us do not naturally possess and which we never thought we would need.

This chapter examines changes in working practices in countries around the globe within the last decade. In particular it highlights the widespread culture of fear within many workplaces and the impact of fear on organizational life. We explore the evidence provided by major international studies on employment, which consistently shows high levels of employee disengagement within many workplaces.

The end of a job for life

A few years ago I was carrying out exit interviews with staff who worked for an oil company. They had just been made redundant and my job was to talk with them, as an outside researcher, and obtain their feedback on the process of redundancy. Was it handled appropriately by their line manager? Could the process be improved? Might the company help them find another job? Historically the company was described by staff as 'like a family' – which of course had its benefits and drawbacks. These were tough oil workers, resilient, their own men. As I made the journey up to Scotland to meet with them, I reflected on the interviews to come. Would the men be difficult? Resentful? Would they dislike being interviewed by a woman? Would they clam up on me?

In fact, the interviews *did* turn out to be difficult, but not for the reasons I was anticipating. The men were very keen to talk. In fact, they talked with little prompting, about their feelings of being rejected, the shock of being discarded, how they had given their all to the company, how they had signed up to the promise of a job for life and had been let down. It was heartbreaking to listen to them describing their sense of shame, rejection and abandonment. Most of them had wives and families. They adopted traditional male roles within their families and they believed that it was *their* responsibility to provide for them. Their inability to do so, because they had been made redundant, made them feel impotent. They found it hard to discuss these worries with their families because they regarded it as a sign of weakness on their part. So, given the opportunity to talk to a researcher in confidence, someone who was an outsider and non-judgemental, they took the opportunity. It was not difficult to get the men to talk. Indeed, it was difficult to get them to stop. Their anger, fear and resignation just spilled out. In particular I remember Gareth, who was distraught about his redundancy. 'I have given my life to this company,' he said. 'I have worked weekends without pay. I have come in during the night when there were problems. I even missed my daughter's wedding because I had to work.'

Whatever we may think about prioritizing work over your daughter's wedding, it was obvious that Gareth had a very strong sense of duty and attachment to the company that had employed him for all of his adult life. He also had a very clear notion of the psychological contract he believed he had with his employers. It involved a secure job until he retired, in exchange for exceptional loyalty. However, it was clear that the terms of the psychological contract, as perceived by Gareth, were very different from those perceived by his employers. How does this expectation gap between employer and employee arise?

When Gareth was first employed, the norm within his company, as with many large companies at the time, was a job for life. However, over the decades, as organizations became more fluid and more driven by shareholder profits, as they merged and consolidated, as staff came and went and company loyalty was diluted, a job for life became increasingly anachronistic. The job-for-lifers found themselves in a psychological work climate that no longer valued continuity, history or loyalty. Times have moved on and flexibility, reducing costs, responding to market conditions, being lean and change management are valued more than continuity and embedded knowledge. Often in this process we lose valuable skills. Equally important, we lose loyal employees and a whirlwind of fear and anxiety streaks through the organization on the coat-tails of redundancies. Those who remain are riddled with uncertainty. The pace of change will continue to accelerate and unless we can adapt to new working conditions, we too will become redundant.

The uncertain future

For many of us, fear of the unknown, of not being able to plan for our future, is an ongoing concern. In 2008, certainties were shaken to the core by the economic crash. This had not happened for over half a century and the ongoing economic crisis still clouds the future. Even now, we cannot predict what will happen to jobs, to levels of employment, to the ways in which our societies will develop or what the economic prospects for the next generation will be.

Fear lurks in the shadows and has many faces: 'the fear of loss of face, prestige, position, favour, fortune or job'.[1] Uncertainty still dominates the present, in spite of the green shoots of recovery that we hear about from governments and business leaders.

Symptoms of fear in the workplace

Organizational life has inevitably felt the knock-on effect of the downturn and the unease that accompanies it. Redundancy, high unemployment and lower wages are common. Many companies that were household names have disappeared. Fear is rife throughout many contemporary organizations, both in the private and public sectors, yet fear is a taboo subject. In some organizations voicing fear is tantamount to admitting weakness, ineptitude, lack of stamina and inadequacy. Fear may be all-pervasive but never spoken. In this context, showing fear is arguably the worst mistake an employee new to the organization can make.

Is this why there is so little mention of fear in mainstream organizational literature? Sociologist Barry Glassner, in his updated book, *The Culture of Fear*, cites crime, drugs, minorities, teenage mothers, killer kids, mutant microbes, plane crashes and so forth as sources of fear. There is no mention of fear in organizational life. Glassner was talking about the United States, but in a global world organizational fashion travels easily.[2]

Within this climate, many organizations have become frightening places. Fear may be concentrated in particular departments or functions, for example, where outsourcing is anticipated or where performance is considered to be weak. Alternatively, fear may be widely spread when the organization as a whole is performing poorly on the stock market and job cuts or takeovers are rumoured. In volatile markets, it is difficult for employees to evaluate whether or not the perceived threats and job insecurities are real or imaginary, so rumour is rife. This lack of certainty fosters a climate of contagious anxiety, which quickly spreads throughout the organization. Regardless of whether or not the fear is well-founded it *becomes* real, because employees come to *believe* it to be real. Of course this in turn affects people's behaviour, and cycles of overlapping mistrust are created: fear of redundancy, restricted contracts, increased workloads (with related stress), reduced workloads (leading to fear of job loss), takeover fears, anxiety about performance targets and so on. In this way, downturns can become self-fulfilling. Employees at all levels in the organization tend to become more cautious, worried, risk-averse and, as a result, less productive. In becoming so, they may inadvertently contribute to the very situation they seek to avoid. Business psychologist and coach Chris Welford, of Sixth Sense Consulting, identifies five telltale signs of a fear-based culture:

- There is a preoccupation with status and conformity and where rules have precedence over common sense.
- Distinct in-groups exist and there is little opportunity to cross the boundaries between them.
- Everything is measured but nothing is questioned.
- Appraisals are only ever one-way.
- The accent is on pace but short-term gain is known to be at the long-term cost.

Exploring fear within organizations is like catching eels. There is always the danger of trying to pin down the ephemeral, of assuming that all workplaces are frightening and threatening environments. *All* managers are unreasonable. *All* employees are fearful of losing their jobs. Clearly this is as absurd as saying that all workplaces are welcoming, inclusive and joyous places and there is never any stress, conflict or tantrums.

It can be useful to view organizations along a loose continuum. At one end are organizations with hierarchical structures that are, predominantly, individualistic, results-driven, rigid and demanding. At the other end of the spectrum sit organizations that see themselves as supportive of staff, that espouse and prioritize 'human values' of cooperative and flexible working, an emphasis on work–life balance and so on. Organizations – and departments and individuals within them – are in constant flux along this continuum, and arguably many organizations could increase staff productivity through greater engagement and support of their workforces.

Of course, the reality is never so neat. Within these stereotypes there are inevitably differences according to department, function, the mix of people who work in the department and the various pressures that they are under, as well as the influential managers who steer them. And, perversely, some of the most hostile work environments I have encountered have included people who viewed themselves as benign! Anger, jealousy and fear were alive and well, but covert; they were only visible to the initiated. The casual visitor saw only brightness and light. Every organization is unique and evolves over time and in line with internal and external pressures. In hard times, the overall economic climate may swamp the cultural differences between organizations.

How can we gauge fear?

When we talk about work environments as a potential source of fear, there are judgements to be made. Is a degree of fear helpful? Do employees experience the fear as stimulating or frightening? Does it excite, tantalize and encourage them to stretch themselves and produce excellent work? Would they even call this feeling 'fear'? Is 'challenge' a more appropriate term? And then, how do we deal with the differences between employees in their capacity and willingness to handle fear? What about employees who feel anxious at work, who are fearful of speaking up or challenging their manager? Should they just keep their heads down, rather than taking the risk of speaking up and possibly being criticized or penalized?

Our response to these questions will, to a large degree, reflect how we personally deal with stress and anxiety, as well as reflecting any measurable level of that fear. Although we are talking about *the culture of fear within organizations*, we need to bear in mind that fear is not a fixed entity, either in an individual or a culture. We inevitably interpret fear in the context of our personal situation: our past experiences, our abilities, our character, our drives and ambitions, as well as the environment in which we are working. At the end of the day, it is our *feeling* of fear that is the barometer. And each of us has different settings on our barometer.

The effects of fear on organizational life

A fearful working environment quickly becomes debilitating and demotivating. This in turn encourages conformity and not sticking one's head above the parapet. Then, in an attempt to reduce their own anxiety – and fearful of chaos – senior managers may introduce *greater* controls and *more* performance measurement within the organization, which can set up a spiralling cycle of fear and paralysis. The result of these overlapping processes of control is often an overly rational approach to management. This is frequently justified on the grounds that if we can control what is happening in the organization and if procedures and protocols are religiously imposed then somehow all will be well. Control is employed as a method of attempting to conquer fear. However, this attempt at lockdown is often counterproductive. We can compare this to a car attempting to stop suddenly on a wet road. The driver's instinct is to brake, but braking results in the car skidding, the driver becoming out of control and the car crashing. Instead, the driver must fight his/her instincts, go with the car and drive into the skid. In fast-moving work situations we often cannot control what is happening. Sometimes the best we can do is to go with the flow and improvise, using our past experience and our instincts.

The tendency to do what we have always done

In times of crisis within organizations, we need to remember the old adage: 'If you keep on doing what you've always done, you'll keep on getting what you've always got.' Rather than locking down, we need to do something different; to be contrarian, to view the situation in a different way, to experiment with a different approach, to improvise. The medic and guru Deepak

Chopra explains why upping the control over employees is likely to achieve the opposite result to the one we'd hoped for:

> Everyone is faced with similar fears, yet only those people who cannot admit the threats hiding inside [themselves] cope with them by resorting to control . . . a controlling person appears to be free from fear; that is the façade that control presents to the world. We put a high value on seeming to be in control of our lives, which further promotes the ego's belief that its controlling behaviour is working.

Following the leader

Not surprisingly, in a fearful working climate, employees tend to mirror the behaviour of their managers. Management over-control in organizations generally has the effect of discouraging risk-taking among employees, squashing initiatives and dispelling creativity and novel thinking. This can be disastrous, as these are just the qualities that are most needed in times of recession, in order to kick-start the economy and foster innovation. Rather than conformity, what *is* needed is people who can think and act in different ways.

What effect does all this shutting down have on employees who work in these organizations? As a general rule, fearful, mechanized approaches to organizational life diminish us as human beings. We start to feel used, resentful, undervalued and disillusioned. As we are more controlled and more mechanized in our work, so we become increasingly disengaged and frightened: not only frightened of losing our job, but also of losing our sense of identity, the pride in doing a good job, our ability to support our family and to maintain our status in our work community.[3] We also lose a sense of trust in the organization we work for and question whether the management has our interests at heart. Are we just a cog in the wheel? The classic response in this situation is to withdraw emotionally, to close down. We become numb and while we may become overtly compliant we are internally removed, so that we don't feel the fear. In doing so, we contribute less but, perhaps more importantly, we also feel as if we are lesser people. As Searle *et al* point out, we need to understand how to repair trust. This is a topic that we will cover in more detail in Chapter 11.

Alternatively, some employees may become mavericks, deliberately sabotaging the organization in minor ways as an expression of their anger. Working to rule, not going beyond the minimum work requirements or not helping colleagues or managers with feedback are just some of the passive-aggressive tactics employed. I am not suggesting that structure and procedures within organizations can be dispensed with; down that road lies chaos. I *am* suggesting that the over-structuring of procedures and practices within the workplace explicitly or implicitly encourages thinking *inside* the box. If we are interested in increased productivity, innovation and a committed workforce, we clearly need a lot more thinking *outside* the box as well. We will expand on this area in the next chapter.

Fear undermines performance

Feeling fearful, threatened or undermined at work can have a major effect on our work performance, as well as on our mental and physical health. Fear impacts on our relationships with our colleagues and managers. It impacts on our confidence and on how we make decisions, and can distort our decision-making. It influences the way we talk, how we hold ourselves, what we say and the way we say it. It influences how our workmates see us and how they behave towards us. Fear has a huge impact on our sense of satisfaction at work. And, of course, we are not two different people, the 'worker' and the 'non-worker'. This is particularly true in the current climate in which many of us are expected by our bosses to be always available. We bring fear home with us and it impacts on our home life and our relationships, our decisions about where we live, whether we decide to move house, what to spend our money on and so on. We have well-established evidence that ongoing stress and fear can lead to mental or physical illnesses. This in turn impacts on both our home and work lives.

Workplace productivity at an all-time low

When we examine countries that seem culturally diverse, we may discover a surprising similarity; that is, they have low and/or dropping workplace productivity. In particular, the remarkable productivity growth that has enabled the US to become the wealthiest country on earth has slowed considerably in recent years. According to a report in the *Wall Street Journal*,[4] the productivity of US workers has grown at an average annual rate of about 2.5 per cent since 1948, but has averaged only about 1.1 per cent since 2011, which is less than half the historical rate. Even more concerning, the productivity of US workers declined in the first quarter of 2014 at the fastest pace in six years. Meanwhile, the OECD has warned that low productivity is a threat to Australia's future,[5] and the UK Royal Economic Society has described UK employment as 'a mystery'.[6] GDP per hour in the UK remains lower than at the beginning of the recession in 2008. Falling production is not a feature of all economies, but it is prevalent enough for us to question why there are such differences between economies and if there is something to be done about the low levels of productivity.

Dr George Madine, a leading UK expert in employee engagement, resilience and well-being, has conducted extensive research within a variety of workplaces, in order to understand these differences in productivity and to explain why productivity in some countries is at such an all-time low. He expands on his findings below:

The UK is one of the countries that is most affected by low productivity. The government has linked future pay rises to improved performance yet they have not fully understood why performance is low; their preferred explanation being a lack of capital expenditure in the recession. As a consultant in the field, I was able to conduct research which indicated that this does not appear to be the main cause of low productivity. My work was designed to help managers understand the causes and use that knowledge to get the necessary increase in performance they need to fuel the recovery.

The challenge is to get ever-busier managers to see that certain of the strategies and processes they are employing to increase productivity are actively fuelling the reduction of productivity. In May 2012 the Chartered Institute of Personnel Development (CIPD) published a paper entitled 'Emotional or transactional engagement – does it matter?'[7] The answer is one of the underpinning problems. Since 2008, the majority of workplaces have had radical restructuring with many downsizing, with dramatic effects on the level of emotional engagement. Altering the type and amount of work is also know to switch emotional to transactional engagement.

Depending on the metric used, average earnings have fallen between 8 and10 per cent in this period, challenging the reward employees actually get from their work transaction. The problem is compounded by flatlining, a state of enhanced negative sensitivity to change. Unless these issues are addressed, improvements in productivity cannot be addressed by capital investment alone.

I talked with 28 companies, large and small, in the public, private and third sectors, talking with both employees and managers. The trigger to involvement was often poor staff engagement. In the course of the study managers and employees (approx 200) were seen on a one-to-one basis, to appraise and to develop strategies to address poor performance and engagement. Redundancies had a particularly damaging effect on the psychological contract between employee and employer. Employees understood the reasons for redundancies, but reacted strongly to the way in which they were implemented. This was especially true among women, given that they suffered a disproportionate level of redundancies because they were mainly part-time staff.

(Abridged version of Dr George Madine's article in the *Association for Business Psychology Quarterly Newsletter*, summer 2014)

Studies on mental health in the workplace

Fear in the working environment is nothing new and researchers have been monitoring this topic for decades. There is ample anecdotal evidence and a growing body of academic evidence, going back several decades, on the effects of fear in organizational life. Numerous studies have been designed to shed light on how employees' perceptions of the workplace affect their engagement with their work and their commitment to their employers – and ultimately their behaviour and performance on the job. For instance, Ashkanasy and Nicholson,[8] among others, cite downsizing, 'hyper-competition' and decreased job security as sources of stress and fear within organizations.

More recently, Martin Knapp and his colleagues explored mental health promotion and mental illness prevention and put forward the economic argument for improved mental health care both inside and outside the workplace.[9] Given that mental health is the largest single cause of disability in the UK, the economic cost to employers is huge. The Chartered Institute of Personnel and Development (CIPD) estimates that mental health-related sickness costs £8.4 billion a year, and 36 per cent of sickness absence in the UK can be attributed to mental health conditions.[10] There is clearly a strong economic argument for trying to reduce fear, anxiety and stress within the workplace as an *economic* imperative, even if it is not considered to be a health priority.

Furthermore, an individual with a mental health condition can have an impact on the workplace, just as the workplace has an impact on the individual. The working environment may be changed in a variety of ways; for example, the emotional climate, productivity, reaching targets, interactions with customers, difficulty making decisions and finding it difficult to learn new tasks may all be negatively affected by one employee, although it is estimated that only 15 per cent of mental health problems are caused directly by the workplace.

Fear within large organizations worldwide is on the rise, as we will see in the workplace studies, and this has had a direct knock-on effect on the well-being of staff, their health, levels of absenteeism, presenteeism and staff turnover, as well as undermining productivity, creativity and innovation within the organization. Over the past 20 years there has been a general downward trajectory in sickness rates, from 178 million lost days in 1993 to 131 million days in 2013, according to figures recently published by the Office for National Statistics.[11] In 1993 the average worker lost about 7.2 days a year in sickness. In 2013, the average was 4.4 days, according to ACAS.[12] On the face of it, you might think that reduced sick leave is a good thing; that it is indicative of fewer employees taking time off and claiming to be sick when they are not. However, in practice, there is a trend – described as 'presenteeism' – for employees to go to work even when sick.

Presenteeism is a big issue in many organizations. The CIPD states that:

Presenteeism has reached epidemic proportions as 93 per cent of employees come into work despite being ill, new research has shown. Presenteeism remains a concern, with a third of organizations saying they have seen an increase in employees coming to work ill over the last year.

You might wonder why presenteeism is such an issue and why, indeed, it is so prevalent in the first place. It is generally thought to be driven by fear. Employees are frightened to take time off, even when they are ill, for fear that they will lose their job. This theory is supported by the fact that presenteeism increases when jobs are at risk and it is more common among white-collar workers. Presenteeism often leads to low morale and low engagement. So what lies at the root of this behaviour? According to the organizational psychologist Sharon De Mascia, it is due to a combination of work and personal factors, including 'having to catch up with backlogs of work', time pressures, lack of resources, job stress, job insecurity, long working hours and inflexible sickness absence processes. What is *not* said may be most interesting. According to studies that we will examine later, fear is often the core factor at play. Both absenteeism and presenteeism are taken to be symptoms of ill health within the organization and both affect productivity.

The work environment impacts on individuals in a variety of ways, including job design, management style, leadership style, pay and conditions, work environment, respect shown and opportunities for development and learning. Some business leaders have taken these issues on board and are actively attempting to manage mental health in the workplace. As Dr Paul Litchfield, Chief Medical Officer of British Telecom, puts it:

> Businesses that don't take mental health seriously will not survive in the 21st century. The global economy is changing fast and the capabilities that companies require now centre more on innovation, communication and emotional intelligence than just the more straightforward requirements of strength, dexterity and intellect that characterized previous eras.[13]

Studies on workplace climate and trends

In recent years, a number of annual studies have monitored workplace trends around the world. Recent research indicates that in spite of, or perhaps because of, greater control on working practices, coupled with recessionary pressures, fear within organizations is on the rise. The studies vary in their focus and scope, but the overall themes emerging are consistent and show a picture of a depressed, anxious workforce. We will examine the key findings from three significant studies on workplace attitudes and trends.

The UK Government Skills and Employment Survey 2012[14]

This government-backed research was led by a team from the London Institute of Education and Cardiff and Oxford Universities. It was funded by the Economic and Social Research Council and involved face-to-face interviews with 3,000 workers aged between 20 and 60. It came to the conclusion that work fear in the UK is at a 20-year high and British employees are feeling more insecure than at any time in the last two decades. For the first time, public sector workers feel less secure than those in the private sector.

The main findings of the study are as follows:

- After five years of recession and slow growth, the workforce is more fearful and working harder than before.

- 'Work intensification' (rife in the 1990s) has grown again. Speed of work and pressure of tight deadlines have risen to record highs.

- Job-related stress has gone up. Happiness at work and job satisfaction have fallen.

- Just over half of employees are worried about losing job status, ie reduced pay, less say in how they do their job, demotion to less interesting jobs.

- Almost a third of staff are anxious about unfair treatment at work, including being dismissed without good reason, discriminated against or victimized by management.

- One of the most notable results is the degree to which fearfulness has increased in the public sector, probably reflecting spending cuts and austerity imposed since 2010.

These findings are quite sobering. We might expect a high degree of concern, given that the economy has only relatively recently started to emerge from a deep recession. However, what is surprising is that levels of concern about job losses were significantly higher in 2012 than in 1986, when just over one in five employees was afraid of losing their job and becoming unemployed. Unemployment in 1986 was over 11 per cent compared with around 8 per cent in 2012, according to statistics from the Work Foundation.[15] In spite of this, concern about job loss was higher in 2012 than in 1986. People are more worried now, although they probably have less reason to be.

Responding to the survey, Peter Cheese, the chief executive of the CIPD, commented:

> Too many recent and spectacular failures – from the banking crisis to public scandals like that affecting the MidStaffordshire NHS Trust – are almost entirely born of problems of culture. Although profoundly different in many ways, they have common roots in issues of trust, empowerment and engagement. What's good for people is good for business – and if we can embrace that trust to build cultures in which people want to work and are unified by a common purpose, we can not only prevent catastrophes, we can truly achieve more sustainable economic growth.[16]

The Towers Watson Global Workforce Study[17]

The biennial Towers Watson Global Workforce Study (GWS) is one of the largest studies of its kind. It is designed to shed light on how the views of employees affect their engagement in their work, their commitment to their employers and, ultimately, their behaviour and performance on the job. As such, it provides insight into the elements of the work environment that help shape employee behaviour and performance.

The study includes a statistically validated definition of *sustainable engagement* at work. Certainly the nature of the study, as a two-yearly review of organizational life, gives it considerable weight, by virtue of the fact that changes can be observed over time. Back in 2012, the GWS surveyed 32,000 employees across 29 key global markets. Findings from this study described 'a recession-battered workforce' with increased anxieties, new priorities, and highlighted a desire for security among employees. Job mobility was at a decade-long low and the study identified a 'disturbing' lack of confidence in leaders and managers.

The most recent study, published in 2014, covered over 30,000 full-time employees working in large and mid-sized organizations across a range of industries in 26 markets around the world. Among many of the interesting findings that emerge from the study, certain themes leap out:

- There is a clear relationship between high levels of sustainable engagement and improved operational and financial results. However, the Towers Watson 2014 GWS indicates that 40 per cent of the 30,000 full-time workers who participated in the study are 'highly engaged', while 19 per cent are 'unsupported', 17 per cent 'detached' and 24 per cent disengaged'. In total, more than 18,000 people are 'detached', 'unsupported' or 'disengaged'. This reflects a huge waste of human resources.

- In 2012, employees across the study, in recessionary as well as growth economies, had expressed some level of concern about financial and professional security, their stress on the job, their trust in their company's leadership, the support they received from their managers and their ability to build their careers. All these factors remain relevant for attraction, engagement and retention in 2014.

- In 2012, businesses appeared to be at a critical tipping point in terms of their ability to maintain employee engagement over time. In 2012, the authors of the study summed this up as follows:

A surprisingly large number [of organizations] don't appear to be keeping pace in terms of how they're managing and supporting the very people assigned to execute the work on the ground. Put starkly, they are running 21st-century businesses with 20th-century workplace practices and programmes and the cracks in the foundations are starting to show in both small and large ways.

The 2012 study highlighted the finding that personal financial security is taking precedence over almost everything. In 2012, approximately 4 out of 10 respondents claimed that they would trade a smaller salary increase or bonus for a guaranteed retirement benefit that does not rise or fall with the market. In 2014, workplace fundamentals like base pay and job security remain at the top of the wish list when deciding to join or leave an employer.

Perhaps the most telling conclusion from the Executive Summary of the GWS, when contrasted with the findings of its simultaneous global employer study – the Talent Management and Reward survey – is that job security is being overlooked by employers as being of key importance to employees:

Stress and anxiety about the future remain common. 36 per cent of the overall sample complained about excessive pressure on the job. 51 per cent worried about their future financial state.

In 2014, there are continued doubts among employees about the levels of interest and support from management and suboptimal confidence in leadership, both of which matter for sustainable engagement. In 2014, under half (45 per cent) of the respondents agreed that their organization's senior leaders have a sincere interest in employee well-being. More worrying, given the importance of managers in creating a positive work experience, was the finding only half (54 per cent) of respondents believed their direct supervisors remove obstacles that hinder the day job. And in 2014, less than half of employees (42 per cent) think their employer provides opportunity to advance their careers and a similar number (41 per cent) think they need to leave to advance.

The 2014 study concludes that attracting and retaining employees are now largely about pay, job security and opportunity for advancement. Engaging employees day to day is, in addition, about the effectiveness of leaders and managers. However, employees' aspirations for competitive pay, job security, effective leadership and management and opportunity for advancement are in sharp contrast to their experience. There is a long way to go before most employees feel that their work environment lives up to their expectations and inspires them to give their best.

The Gallup 'State of the Global Workplace' study 2012[18]

The Gallup study, a worldwide study of employee engagement and well-being, examined levels of engagement among more than 47,000 employees in 120 countries around the world. The overall results indicated that 13 per cent of workers worldwide are 'engaged'. In other words, about one in nine employees worldwide is emotionally connected to their workplace and feel they have the resources and support they need to succeed. However, 63 per cent are not engaged; that is, they are emotionally detached and likely to be doing little more than is necessary to keep their jobs. A further 24 per cent are actively disengaged, indicating that they view their workplaces negatively and are liable to spread that negativity to others.

This study, completed in 2012, reflects similar themes to those that emerged from two previous Gallup studies. They also show broad similarities with the findings from both the Towers Watson study and the UK Government Skills and Employment Survey. While the percentage of those who claim to be 'not engaged' is relatively stable, it is depressingly low, at 63 per cent of the workplace in Table 4.1 below.

TABLE 4.1 Levels of engagement at work (Gallup 2012)

	2009–2010	2011–2012
Actively disengaged	27%	24%
Not engaged	62%	63%
Engaged	11%	13%

The authors of the Gallup study conclude:

Employee engagement will become an increasingly important concern for countries and organizations seeking to boost labour productivity as the global economy continues its rapid pace of change . . . In other words, the need to build highly engaged workplaces will become more important than ever.

Gauging 'reality'

It is clear from these three studies that lack of engagement at work is a major problem in terms of a wide range of variables including engagement, productivity, physical and mental health, resilience, trust, innovation and many more. When fear levels are high, it is difficult for employees, both junior and senior, to accurately gauge the emotional climate. Reality can become distorted. Employees become less effective at evaluating whether the perceived threats and job insecurities are real or imaginary. Fear *becomes* real because people come to *agree and believe* that it is real; this is part of the contagious power of fear.

Fear as a management tool

There are instances in which senior management may subtly instil anxiety in staff as a way of keeping them compliant. In one such situation Campbell Keegan was commissioned to carry out research among oil workers in Aberdeen. There was conflict between the staff and management at that time and our job was to identify the concerns of the workers and establish how the problems could be resolved. To do this, we carried out a series of group discussions with the oil workers. Among other issues, it turned out that they were particularly concerned about letters from their company that had been sent to their home addresses while they were out working on the rigs. The letters threatened the men with dismissal if they did not sign up to the new contracts.

The workers regarded this as provocation on the part of management, because they knew the letters would be opened by their wives in their absence. The wives would worry and put pressure on their husbands to sign up to the new deal. Some workers even suspected that the letters had deliberately been sent to the men at this time.

Having finished the research sessions, I returned to London and arranged a meeting with the oil company management. During the meeting, I mentioned that the oil workers were concerned about the timing of the letters and suspected that it was deliberate.

'Well, yes,' explained one manager, 'we *wanted* the wives to put pressure on their husbands to sign. We deliberately sent the letters when they were on the rigs.'

Fear and anxiety are not only *by-products* of the stresses and strains within organizational life. On occasion, they can also be carefully chosen tools, used to try to ensure compliance.

However, I do not want to suggest that oppression is always a one-way street from management to staff. As the Sufi scholar Idries Shah put it in a rather tongue-in-cheek way:

Almost every day I am reminded of Saadi's reflection that there is no senseless tyranny like that of subordinates. We can all tyrannize each other, if we so choose. Or we can choose to cooperate!

These studies present a depressing picture of 21st-century working life. Perhaps the greatest surprise is the consistency of the findings across many different countries and workplaces: fear appears to be embedded within many workforces. In this chapter we have concentrated on the studies and data that have emerged to support the view that fear is endemic in the workplace. In the next chapter we will focus on the experiences of those individuals who are working within environments that they feel to be threatening or frightening, or where they feel that silence is the only viable response.

Notes

1 Trans V (1998) The role of the emotional climate learning organizations, *The Learning Organization*, **5**, pp 99–103

2 Glassner, B (2010) *The Culture of Fear: Why Americans are afraid of the wrong things*, Basic Books

3 Searle, R, Hope-Hailey, V T and Diez, G (2012) Who do you trust? Understanding how to repair lost trust, *OP Matters*,**15**, May

4 Prescott, E and Ohanian, L (2014) US Productivity Growth Has Taken a Dive, *Wall Street Journal* [online] http://online.wsj.com/news/articles/SB1000142405 27023035194045793505431649848818

5 OECD's 2014 Going for Growth: Avoiding the low-growth trap, *OECD* [online] www.oecd.org/about/secretary-general/oecd-2014-going-for-growth-avoiding-the-low-growth-trap.htm

6 The UK's Productivity and Employment Mystery, *Royal Economic Society* [online]www.res.org.uk/details/mediabrief/4571391/THE-UKS-PRODUCTIVITY-AND-EMPLOYMENT-MYSTERY.html

7 Emotional or transactional engagement – does it matter? *CIPD* [online] https://www.cipd.co.uk/hr-resources/research/emotional-transactional-engagement.aspx

8 Ashkanasy, M and Nicholson, G J (2003) Climate of fear in organisational settings: Construct definition, measurement and a test of theory, *Australian Journal of Psychology*, **55**, (1) pp 24–9

9 Knapp, M, McDaid, D and Parsonage, M (2011) *Mental health promotion and mental illness prevention: the economic case* 1597, Department of Health, London

10 Presenteeism reaching epic proportions, finds survey, *CIPD* [online] www .cipd.co.uk/pm/peoplemanagement/b/weblog/archive/2013/05/07/presenteeism-reaching-endemic-proportions-finds-survey.aspx

11 Sickness absence in the labour market [online] www.ons.gov.uk/ons/dcp171776_353899.pdf

12 Sickness absence downward travel continues, *ACAS* [online] www.acas.org.uk/index.aspx?articleid=4768

13 'Mental Illness in the 21st Century – an Increasing Challenge for Europe' Co-hosted by the Interest Group on Mental Health, Well-being and Brain Disorders, and the Stephen Hughes MEP Initiative on Depression and the Workplace European Parliament, 29 May 2013

14 The Skills and Employment Survey 2012, *Cardiff School of Social Sciences* [online] www.cardiff.ac.uk/socsi/ses2012

15 Unemployment is bad for your health, *The Work Foundation* [online] www .theworkfoundation.com/Media/Press-Releases/1884/Unemployment-is-bad-for-your-health-new-report-shows-how-men-suffer-double-whammy-from-joblessness

16 Peter Cheese, chief executive of the CIPD, on engaging with employees, *Scunthorpe Telegraph* [online] www.scunthorpetelegraph.co.uk/Peter-Cheese-chief-executive-CIPD-engaging/story-19121621-detail/story.html

17 Towers Watson Global Workforce Study 2014 [online] www. towerswatson.com/en/Insights/IC-Types/Survey-Research-Results/2014/08/the-2014-global-workforce-study

18 State of the Global Workplace, *Gallup* [online] www.gallup.com/poll/165269/worldwide-employees-engaged-work.aspx

Feeling fear at work

05

No passion so effectively robs the mind of all powers of acting and reasoning as fear. EDMUND BURKE

The hidden fear at work

It is all very well to talk about fear and mistrust in the abstract, to look at the statistics that show the rising levels of fear within organizations across much of the developed world and to monitor the effect this has on productivity and employee engagement. But what do employees actually *feel*? How do they brace themselves as they walk in the door to their office or warehouse or meet up with their manager? Indeed, how do the managers or the directors feel? Fear affects the everyday behaviour of all employees at work. It feeds into absenteeism and presenteeism (and has a direct impact on work output). In this chapter we examine what it feels like to work in an environment we perceive to be threatening in some way, where we are constantly looking over our shoulder, where we expect to be criticized or demeaned or where we are overloaded with work that we are unable to complete. In the extreme, we may feel the threat of dismissal or redundancy hanging over us. How do these perceived threats affect our work behaviours and performance and how does working in such environments affect our happiness and self-esteem?

Managing people is often difficult. It is a skill that takes time to hone but it is an essential part of organizational life. The basis of management is communication but when there are mistrust and suspicion, communication suffers. As W Edwards Deming, the US statistician and consultant, expressed it back in 1987, 'The fundamental problem in American business is that people are scared to discuss the problems of people.'[1] This hasn't changed much in recent years and it isn't restricted to the United States. We are still scared to discuss 'the problems of people' in an open, constructive way. It is easier to ignore, to backbite, to moan, to mutter under our breath, rather than address the issues head-on.

Although it is rare for an adult in Western culture to publicly admit to feeling fear at work, this doesn't necessarily mean that he or she is not frightened. It just means that they don't talk about it. We are taught from childhood that fear indicates weakness, and weakness, in turn, is seen as indicative of lack of character, unreliability, someone who cannot be trusted to do the job or who is 'just not up to it'. We carry these patterns from childhood with us all our lives and replay them in organizational life. For these reasons most employees avoid expressing fear – although it does not stop them feeling it.

If we feel fearful at work, but are unable to express our concerns or discuss the issues that bother us, how can we begin to improve the situation? How do we go about reducing fear in the workplace without even mentioning the 'f' word or making people feel *more* anxious and under threat in the process? It is easier to address these issues peripherally rather than head-on. We will start by looking at some of the symptoms that are indicative of a fearful workplace – although they may not be immediately recognized as such by the workforce.

While reading this interview with Naomi, try to put yourself in her shoes. Is she confident? Is she happy? What is she displaying and what is she concealing? What are her strategies for survival in a cut-throat working world?

My name is Naomi. I am 30 years old and I work for a large management consultancy. At one level it is a 'people business', because the role of outside consultants is inherently nebulous and hard to measure. But it is also very much about systems and processes. For a large organization to call in specialist consultants, especially where there are big plans for change – it is a big thing for staff. It can mean that 'things happen' to employees. Often this is the result of much bigger issues, macro issues, such as a changing competitive environment, a new set of financial regulations, a changed political alignment. The job of the outside consultant is to act as a non-emotionally invested change agent on behalf of the highly emotionally invested seniors within the organization. The cost is justified in terms of the experience, training, and intellectual capital of the consultant team.

Yes, people do feel that they have to be the best. It's a battlefield. You have to win. Strength and resilience – if you don't have them, you won't survive. People want to be superstars and there are lots that are super-bright; you feel that you have to go further than anyone else. It can be incredibly tough. We have some amazing performers.

How do I survive? Um, I think, for me, I do it by avoiding – or not allowing people to see – my human side. Friendship, warmth, social interaction, humour, affection, reliance or malleability, I avoid them. I had to learn it the hard way. In my previous role (in a different organization) I tried to befriend the colleague that I was having difficulty with. It backfired badly.

With a recent project, I felt I needed to report a director. It was a really hard decision to make but I could see that his practice was inappropriate and even disreputable, and I had to do it, even though I worried that I might get caught in the crossfire. I am more circumspect and less open these days. I am extremely careful to avoid any mixed messaging, inconsistency or, in particular, weakness. I have learned to project a stronger, more inscrutable front. I never want them to see me struggling. I've learned to be very slow to trust people in my work. I bide my time and I am forensic in the detail of my reports. I avoid any impetuous or emotional responses.

Being tough and avoiding the display of soft or weak (human) characteristics clearly tallied with the competitive culture that Naomi inhabited, a culture in which intellectual and presentational strength wins. And, in an overarching culture where the remit is effectively inhuman (advice based on the careful marshalling of data about outside macrofactors, not 'felt' experiences) these traits stand employees in good stead as they become more senior. Displaying fear is taboo. Competitiveness is a driver that is both encouraged and nurtured. At its most sour, this can be actively divisive – which is ironic, given the mantras around project teams and team spirit that are also verbalized in consultant organizations.

In Naomi's world, fear exists at the personal level. The fear is not so much related to the work, or even the workload – which can be considerable – but is almost literally primal, a fear of defeat in the battle for superstar status, the winning pitch, the ultimate contract, the bonus or the directorship. Relationships between employees are almost always therefore subjugated to personal effectiveness and successful acquittal in front of clients. Notionally, an individual succeeds at the expense of others within the organization.

Recognizing fear and mistrust in organizations

If fear is hidden – and even talking about fear is a taboo subject – how do we even begin to address the issues? As ever, the devil is in the detail. A while ago, I attended a talk on positive psychology. The speaker described an experience she had had some months earlier. She had been talking to a group of employees about change in the workplace and how fear was affecting work performance. She mentioned several studies that had found that levels of fear and anxiety in the workplace were at an all-time high. A member of the audience put his hand up and said:

> I don't think fear and anxiety are issues in my company. Morale is OK – well, I think it is – and the job gets done. But we do have some problems. We are losing some of our best people and we don't know what we need to do to persuade them to stay. And people don't take the initiative; they do what they are asked to do but they won't go the extra mile. We have endless meetings – I can spend all my day in meetings – but at the end of it, I'm not sure what we have achieved. No one seems to want to take things further so it all fizzles out. We have no new ideas and if someone does come up with something new, people are often cynical or disinterested.

I recognized these symptoms. They are grounded in fear. In my early years as a consultant, I had sat through endless meetings where lots of people talked and nothing really happened. It was disheartening, often depressing. I remember once spending three hours discussing the quintessential baked bean! It took me the first hour to realize that the purpose of the meeting was simply to look busy and 'be seen'. And here we still are, many years on, without much progress, still too frightened to challenge behaviours that are time-wasting or counterproductive. In fact, rather than moving on, the evidence suggests that fear in the workplace is much greater now than it was two decades ago. Fear has many symptoms, such as listlessness, indifference and lazy organization. Fear continues to thrive in workplaces and is all the more effective because we refuse to face up to it.

Until we can recognize the symptoms of fear, it is difficult to contemplate the cure. Of course this is not an exact science, but neither is it beyond the ability of most of us to recognize when a fellow employee is uncomfortable or scared. We have each had years of experience in interpreting human communication on a day-to-day basis and most of us do it passably well. Focusing on people's speech and body language, actively listening to what they mean as well as what they say, watching other employee groups interact and, above all, interacting honestly with our own work colleagues, all provide a huge amount of knowledge and understanding. I will expand on this area in Chapter 11 because I believe that effective human communication is the lynchpin for developing profitable, healthy, productive and innovative organizations.

Patterns of fear and distrust

So, let's go back to the symptoms of fear in organizations. How can we tell when employees are frightened or even terrified? The list of symptoms is almost endless. The following are just a few of the behaviours that can indicate fear in a work context:

- absence, lateness;
- presenteeism;
- not contributing in meetings;
- poor morale, little interest in their work;
- short-term thinking;
- defensiveness, reluctance to admit mistakes;
- obsessing about rules, rigid interpretation of guidelines, over-management;
- management through fear;
- criticism of co-workers, blaming others;
- blanket criticism of management: 'us and them';
- passivity: reluctance to do work or doing it mechanically;
- some topics are out of bounds, especially those that are politically sensitive;
- appearances are everything: staying at the office longer than your boss;
- stealing the ideas of others and not recognizing their contributions;
- managers discourage lateral communication across departments/work groups;
- having your credibility questioned;
- not getting the recognition you deserve.

These symptoms often coalesce so that a number of common patterns of fear behaviour emerge. The behaviours described above are by no means comprehensive, but they may help to identify particular patterns of fear that are manifest in your own organization. In addition, we need to be conscious of the context in which these symptoms arise. Criticizing a colleague in earshot of a manager will create a very different result from a quiet word over a pint. Likewise, one-off lateness is usually forgivable, whereas persistent lateness suggests a problem.

Indications of a disengaged workforce

Some indications are particular to the events happening within the organization – mergers or downsizing will create specific concerns – but there are also indications that are common to most organizations. Ryan and Oestreich[2] ask four key questions which help move us towards a deeper understanding of how fear operates within organizations:

- What issues does fear conceal in organizations?
- Why don't people speak up?
- What does this mean for results and morale?
- What behaviours trigger mistrust in relationships and how does this mistrust become ingrained in organizations?

Organizations are evolving entities so there are no definitive answers to these questions, but they provide an excellent backdrop for evaluating the current state of health within an organization and they can offer some steers as to how to go forward.

Classic symptoms of disengagement

There are certain patterns of behaviour that are indicative of employee disengagement and often these are common across a wide range of organizations.

Good people are leaving

In a fearful workplace, those who *can* leave, typically do so. Why would they stay in a work environment that is unduly stressful, where they cannot achieve what they are capable of, where they are inhibited by managers who are more interested in control than creativity, where toeing the party line provides more kudos than new ideas? In organizations where there is no encouragement or benefit in going the extra mile, people leave. As a result, the organization loses the people it most needs to keep, the individuals who have the skills, enthusiasm and drive to move the organization into new pastures and foster a healthier, more productive work environment.

People are scared to speak out

Kish-Gephart *et al* (2009) point out that the most noticeable aspect of fearful organizations is the unwillingness of people to speak out, to disagree, to have healthy debate, to criticize, to offer suggestions or thoughts without feeling the need to defend their ideas.[3] Often this reluctance to speak is highlighted when a manager sets up a meeting to explain changes, new procedures or protocols to be implemented. Employees file dutifully into the room, sit down and listen respectfully until the manager has finished. At the end, he or she asks, 'Are there any questions?' People look a bit shifty but no one says anything. The manager doesn't ask again, but thanks the staff and makes a quick exit. Relief that the meeting is over, that there has been no overt drama, is etched on his or her face. As soon as the manager leaves, conversation bursts into life. The masks of neutrality are abandoned. The energy in the room rises palpably. The employees clearly have lots of opinions that they have no trouble expressing to their peers.

What stops people speaking out? In general it is because they fear repercussions. Regardless of their role or seniority in the organization, in situations where individuals feel under threat, their automatic response is to withhold, to stay silent. It can also be a form of passive resistance: '*Don't think I'm going to make it easy for you*' or '*I'm not going to let you know what I'm thinking.*'

There are many reasons why people will not speak out critically. There is the fear of losing one's job, being overlooked for promotion, being excluded from important meetings or not being consulted about key decisions, losing credibility or a specific project, losing face. Milliken *et al* found that the most frequent reason for remaining silent was fear of being viewed or labelled negatively. Speaking up, the study concluded, may take away the employee's ability to have influence within an organizational setting.[4]

However, lack of communication can equally damage valued relationships and result in two-way communication breaking down and employees refusing to discuss job-related issues. By encouraging people to speak up and finding out what they are reluctant to talk about, we have an opportunity to learn how fear prevents all of us from doing our best at work. If we are afraid to ask for an honest opinion or we are afraid to give one, suspicion and distrust grow. Developing a more open climate in a fearful organization is not easy, but it is an essential element of change towards healthier organizations. Put simply, if employees feel that they cannot speak out, if they cannot be heard, then they will not contribute fully.

Assumptions create realities

Some employers may believe that their employees are inherently dishonest, lazy or disinterested; that they have to be monitored to ensure that they work effectively. When these assumptions are entrenched, they can easily *become* realities, as employees decide that there is no point in making an effort. In this way, employers and employees together create a stuck and dysfunctional environment, with each side suspicious of the other. Ryan and Oestreich, in their excellent book *Driving Fear Out of the Workplace,* offer the following warning:

> Think about the assumptions that underlie your [institution's] vision, mission and values. Typically these documents assume the best about the intentions and capabilities of both customers and employees. Next, take a look at the policies, practices, systems and structures of the organization. Very frequently these are based upon negative assumptions. They assume that people will lie about sickness absences, abuse telephones or copy machines with excessive personal use, put themselves rather than the customer first when they control their own scheduling, or produce low-quality products or service unless they are supervised. It is this misalignment that causes people to believe that their leaders say one thing but truly believe something else. Instead of the trust, respect and creativity talked about in the public documents, people see an organizational culture characterized by mistrust, bias and control.

Doing the minimum work demanded

Employees carry out their job in a mechanical fashion. They do not attempt to improve the way things are done or suggest alternative working practices. In some cases they may have made suggestions in the past that were rejected by their managers, so they decided to do what was required in terms of their job spec, but no more. In a sense this can be seen as a form of passive resistance.

Endless meetings that achieve very little

Going through the motions is a typical response in an organization driven by fear. Sometimes the greater the time spent in meetings, and the more meetings people attend, the less effective the organization. Typically, in this scenario, the real purpose of the meeting, as far as employees are concerned, is to protect their positions, to ensure that they are not criticized and that there are no repercussions. The classic stance of a going-through-the-motions employee is 'I need to be seen to be here, and appear compliant, but I intend to contribute very little.' No one is prepared to put their head above the parapet. As a result, everyone involved in the session is frustrated and huge amounts of time are wasted. Nothing gets done and there are no improvements.

People never know what's coming next

One of the most difficult aspects of working in fear-ridden environments is that employees never know what to expect. Communications do not flow freely, rumour is rife and the information employees do receive is often partial, out of date or exaggerated. Suspicion abounds and too many decisions are made based on irrational fears and preconceptions. These fears are stopping people doing their jobs with enthusiasm. Research carried out by Mozy,[5] which included 550 IT decision-makers and 1,250 office workers across the United States, UK, Ireland, France, Germany and the Netherlands, describes decision-makers as 'relying on popular buzzwords to secure buy-in' to their choices of strategy, rather than convincing their stakeholders with arguments based on real business benefits. Decision-making was fuelled more by fear than logic. According to the Mozy study, innovation is being held back, as 84 per cent of employees harbour irrational fears and 37 per cent of workplace projects have been blocked by company management due to fear.

Therefore, in this climate, if a couple of managers are let go without explanation, or organizational changes are announced, or jobs are re-structured, the immediate assumption is that disaster is looming. In the absence of information we fill in the gaps – and not in a positive way. As the consultant Dawn Lennon puts it, 'We create doomsday stories to prepare ourselves for the worst, but they only drive us into an unhealthy state of living in fear.'[6] So we end up with an institutional fear of trying new things at work, and this applies to employees at all levels of the organization. The Mozy report concludes: 'Leaders in business and technology need to be enablers, not road-blockers, if they want their companies to succeed in difficult economic circumstances.'

Guerrilla tactics

Employees who feel downtrodden and undervalued may become mavericks and resort to subversion as a means of restoring their sense of self-worth. Recently I was copied in on a round-robin email that provided tongue-in-cheek advice on how to deal with 'the dreaded procurement' (what used to be called 'purchasing' within large organizations).

Fred (a pseudonym), the author of the email, was a small supplier. Procurement was a large department in a large organization. Fred was clinging on to his self-esteem in the face of what he saw as the sheer absurdity of procurement procedures – which he was obliged to follow if he wanted to make a living. He dealt with the contradiction through ridicule and through sharing his experience with other small suppliers. It was a satisfactory tool of retaliation and it raised his status with his colleagues. The following is an excerpt from Fred's email:

> The trick (when filling in voluminous procurement forms) is to think of things that might go wrong that won't, and then itemize them and tell them (procurement) how you know they won't go wrong, eg risk of not meeting the key milestones of the project (work to timetable), risk of child protection issues (no children involved), risk of snow (summertime), risk of train delays (fly) etc etc.
>
> Although these things are totally tedious, I get perverse amusement by thinking of the doom and gloom on every aspect of the project and then using the right language to say 'It won't happen.' It's nonsense, but they believe it shows how competent and comprehensive your proposal is. It plays into the fears and insecurities of procurement people who lie awake at night needlessly. You need to agree with them that the world is a really scary place but you can make it all better. Personally, I'm quite comfortable with procurement people lying awake at night. So they should.

In the preface of their book, Ryan and Oestreich sum up their hopes for the future of organization life as follows:

> We see this as essentially a hopeful time, full of opportunity and potential . . . If the current state is one of extraordinary flux and change, it also brings the problem of fear centre stage and into the spotlight. In turn this means that the possibilities for learning and progress are even better.

Sadly this has not happened in many organizations. The possibilities for learning and progress may have been there but, too often, these possibilities have not been grasped. Ryan and Oestreich could not have anticipated the global turmoil, the social, organizational and technological changes that have revolutionized workplaces in the last couple of decades. As I write, in 2014, the levels of fear within many organizations have not reduced. On the contrary, many have risen significantly.

The growth of mistrust

It is telling that most of the employees interviewed for this book did not want to be identified, nor would allow their company to be named. They were afraid that they would be penalized if they were seen to be criticizing their company, particularly to outsiders. James (not his real name) agreed to talk to me, but only once he was convinced that the interview would be anonymized.

I was at X (a corporate law firm) for a long time. I was a corporate lawyer and I witnessed a complete turnaround in the organization during the last couple of years I was there. As an organization, X used to be very benign. If you asked them what its purpose was, they would have said, 'employees, customers'. Shareholders would have come somewhere lower down the list and therefore, during my career, I had many different opportunities. I was sent to Rome for two years so I could develop my career and they could keep me in the organization – and I was looked after. It was a patriarchal type of system. Now – the poor things – the shareholder is the only thing that matters. Technology means that the analysts want everything *now*. They don't want to know about next year. It's data, not understanding. My hypothesis is that we have gone back to the mill mentality, where you drive the workers and they are just a resource. It is no longer the kind of model – the Unilever and the Cadbury, the Quaker mentality – of looking after the workers. The whole thing has gone back to being very capitalist, exploitative. It's like going from a patriarchal culture to a bullying culture. The word bullying was never used in my time in the organization. Suddenly, people at the top are seen as bullies. This coincides with the explosion of the differential between people's remuneration – what the people at the bottom get and what people at the top get. They are so driven by money – that whole thing is just escalating. These attitudes are exacerbated by the throughput of employees. They are not at the top for very long. An old university friend of mine became a partner at X. He said, 'A third of us are culled every year.'

Bullying at work

Fear comes in different guises. There is the generalized fear in which employees feel that they will be heavily penalized for minor misdemeanours or mistakes, where they have an expectation that they will be put on the spot, criticized, found wanting and ultimately overlooked or, in the extreme, made redundant.

Then there is one-on-one bullying and harassment in which an individual or group is systematically picked on, criticized, ignored or belittled in some way. These behaviours may be covert and persistent, but they are almost always undermining, especially in situations where the individuals being attacked feel they cannot report the offender for fear of repercussions.

There is no statutory definition of workplace bullying in England and Wales, although ACAS defines it as 'offensive, intimidating, malicious or insulting behaviour, an abuse or misuse of power through means that undermine, humiliate, denigrate or injure the recipient'. It can be persistent or an isolated incident. Whatever the tactics employed, harassment and bullying generally have the effect of making the target feel a wide range of emotions, including anger, frustration fear, stress, humiliation, loss of self-confidence and isolation. These feelings, in turn, can lead to job insecurity, illness, absence from work, problems at home and even resignation.

According to Anthony Sakrouge, head of the employment team at the legal practice Russell-Cooke, bullying allegations are increasingly common in employment litigation. The pressure on managers to meet performance targets and get the best out of staff, which increases in a tough economic climate, is only one reason for the steady growth in workplace bullying allegations.

Sakrouge explains: 'The manager accused will often have been given the task of improving results quickly or having been hired into the organization for that purpose. They may even have been told that one or more team members need to be 'managed out' of the organization . . . The performance management process will often be handled very clumsily, even by organizations (such as law firms) that might be expected to know better.'

Bullying and harassment can be one-off or ongoing and they take many forms, such as:

- spreading malicious rumours or insulting someone;
- racial, gender, age or disability slurs;
- undermining a competent worker by overloading them with work or constantly criticizing them;

- ridiculing or demeaning someone – picking on them or setting them up to fail;
- copying memos that are critical about someone to others who do not need to know;
- exclusion or victimization;
- overbearing supervision or other misuse of power or position;
- preventing individuals from progressing by intentionally blocking promotion or training.

However, bullying is not a simple issue. People who rise to senior positions need to be fairly robust characters in order to do their job effectively. Managers are often unaware of the effect their behaviour is having on those around them or of the impact they have merely because of the senior position they occupy. Managers accused of bullying may well have themselves been subjected to tough treatment in the past and regard this as character-building. Those who are prepared to put in very long hours and to work under pressure may assume that it is valid to ask the same of their staff. They may believe that a pressured environment is justifiable where the rewards for success and the potentials for failure are very significant. In an ideal world, managers would be trained to understand the different strengths of each staff member and make the most of these, while supporting them in developing their skills – but we rarely experience an ideal world.

Lutgen-Sandvik and colleagues describe the overwhelming evidence that being persistently abused at work negatively affects all aspects of the targeted workers' lives, not just their work lives. They suffer from a number of physical ailments that they directly associate with being bullied, including gastrointestinal problems (eg irritable bowel syndrome), insomnia, weight gain and loss and musculoskeletal problems. Medical research suggests that bullying is associated with chronic stress, high blood pressure and increased risk of coronary heart disease. The targets' emotional health suffers as well. They reported experiencing depression, elevated anxiety and anxiety attacks, which they linked with being abused at work.[7]

Bullying as a cultural issue

The bullying does not only affect the bullied. Bystanders play complicated roles in organizations that have problems with bullies. Whether or not it is acknowledged, other workers are generally aware of what is going on. They may be frightened that they will be the next victim. They may feel guilt if they do not intervene and depressed at their own powerlessness.

Nonetheless, bystanders can impact the bully–victim relationship and are of great importance to the general office reaction to bullying in the workplace.

Workplaces where bullying is left unchecked have the potential to become impoverished over time. There is a familiar pattern: the brightest and most talented leave, taking their skills to a new employer. Those who can, follow – and so the talent pool gradually evaporates.

Given the many different definitions and understandings of workplace bullying, it is difficult to pinpoint its exact prevalence rate. A 2007 study, carried out by the Workplace Bullying Institute in the United States, involving 7,740 US workers, found that 13 per cent of employees had reported experiencing workplace bullying in the previous year. In addition, a further 24 per cent of employees reported that, while they had not experienced bullying in the past year, they had been victimized at some point in their working life. Another 12 per cent reported that they had witnessed workplace bullying or victimization, but were not the direct victims. In all, 49 per cent of employees sampled reported having been affected by workplace bullying. Extrapolating from these statistics the Bureau estimated that around 71.5 million US workers are or have been affected by workplace bullying or aggression.[8]

Bullying and aggression are often broken down into two types: direct, where the bully attacks the target face to face, and indirect, where the bully spreads slanderous comments or stories. Both of these approaches have negative effects on the victims, the perpetrators of bullying and the organizations in which they work. Regardless of whether the bullying and victimization last a month or many years, the consequences can be catastrophic. Victims often suffer long-term, sometimes permanent, psychological occupational impairment.[9]

Workmates, regardless of their level of authority, rarely know how to handle the situation. Managers may be shocked or frightened. Lutgen-Sandvik and her colleagues stress the importance of naming what is happening as workplace bullying. They also emphasize the usefulness of providing information to those who are being bullied, but if these strategies do not work, then sacking the employee who is bullying others is the only viable option.

While individual bullying and humiliation can occur in any workplace, they are much more likely to be prevalent in organizations in which generalized fear is rife and employees are afraid to rock the boat, where they fear that complaining could lose them their job. By contrast, in organizations that are more open, where people feel supported and more confident in general, bullying tends to be less tolerated. Employees feel better able to stand up to bullies because they know that this sort of behaviour is not accepted within that organization. In this way, the power of the work group can protect the individual.

Cyber bullying

Sadly, the opportunities for bullying in the workplace are greater now than ever before, thanks to modern technologies. Cyber bullying is convenient and the victims are easily accessible. ACAS[10] highlights the fact that cyber bullying in the workplace is on the rise and is becoming as prevalent as non-electronic forms of bullying. It also has the advantage, from the perspective of the bully, of being more discreet and hidden from prying eyes.

ACAS references a recent study, 'Punched from the Screen', which was carried out by a team of occupational psychologists from the University of Nottingham's Institute of Work, Health and Organizations in conjunction with Sheffield University.[11] Of the 320 people who responded to the survey around eight out of ten had experienced cyber bullying in the previous six months. Until recently the impact of cyber bullying has mainly been focused on younger people rather than adult workers. This is changing. The researchers suggest that it is time for employers to tackle cyber bullying in the workplace head-on, given that the problem will undoubtedly increase with the growth of communication technologies.

Indeed, cyber bullying at work is already as widespread as non-electronic forms of bullying, due to the prevalence of email, texts, web posting and the myriad of communication tools available. It could take the form of receiving an offensive email or being humiliated, ignored or gossiped about online. Between one in seven and one in five people had experienced this kind of bullying on a weekly basis, which, according to the researchers is comparable to figures reported for non-electronic bullying.

The same study mentioned by ACAS claimed that the effects of cyber bullying were worse than those of non-electronic forms, with some respondents showing greater mental strain and lower job satisfaction than in cases of traditional bullying. However, the effects of *witnessing* cyber bullying were not as great as for conventional bullying, possibly because the impersonal and remote nature of cyber bullying made it harder for onlookers to empathize with the victim.

When we think about bullying we tend to think of it in simplistic terms: the stronger individual or group bullying the weaker. And we impose a 'goodies and baddies' model on the situation. Sometimes this is accurate but often the situation, particularly within an organizational setting, is far more complex than this. We have layers of power within the company, we have degrees of knowledge within different parties, and there are vested interests and alliances. Distinguishing truth from falsehood is almost an impossible task, not least because truth itself is slippery.

The complexities of whistle-blowing within an organizational context

Whistle-blowing is frequently discussed in the media, accompanied by a debate on the pros and cons of speaking out about organizational irregularities. It is easy to come away with a simple picture of rights and wrongs. The reality is often much more complex, as this example illustrates.

My name is Julia. I was caught up in a situation, a really complex incident at work. It involved whistle-blowing and upward bullying, which is quite unusual. A senior manager was accused of bullying one of the board members. It was also claimed that the directors covered it up. It was a really difficult situation because the people you would normally have put in place to investigate such an accusation were themselves being accused. So it was really messy. We ended up with external lawyers coming in to investigate because it was at such a senior level. But, you know, the expectation when you have a situation like this is that it is the junior person who is the victim – and that isn't necessarily so. I feel that in this case, the lawyers just leapt to conclusions. They bought into everything the junior manager was saying, without any critical faculties. I think they lacked objectivity. They came at it with a presumption that the guy was guilty. They didn't take on board the context or what the task had been.

We don't know who the whistle-blower was, of course. That's anonymous. I still don't know who it was, so you have accusations from a whistle-blower of poor behaviour by a very senior manager and the people he reports to are the directors. And what you don't know is whether or not this is malicious.

The problem is you don't know if this is another member of staff who feels aggrieved and is using this as an opportunity to dump on this guy. The man who is accused is brusque and he's very direct, so he may rub people up the wrong way. I am sure he was critical in some ways but he had been brought in to sort out people who weren't performing in a department where everybody had been allowed to 'chug along' not doing a good job for years. So they didn't like it and they got all uptight. He said, 'What's your problem?' and they certainly didn't like that.

I am sure he could have done it more sensitively – I am now working with him to try to get him to understand how it feels from the other side and how to get messages across in a more effective manner. I don't think we helped him enough. It was his first really senior role. In retrospect, it's clear that he needed more support from the business to deal with those personnel issues.

I suppose that what I learned was that bullying is complex and this guy was being bullied by staff accusing him of being bullying. It is really complicated. What it comes down to is the real challenge of how you set forth these objectives, how you train people to manage those roles and objectives and how you create a culture that is sufficiently empowered that people don't actually become malicious.

Looking back, I see that we put someone in to reorganize the department who had no experience of doing it and no training. He was left to do it on his own. He did it. He has done the job. The collateral damage is that he himself became very stressed by it because he didn't really know what he was doing and he was on the receiving end, but he also had to recognize that he hadn't been doing a very good job, which is never a nice thing to learn.

I think, for me, one of the most difficult things to figure out was 'Who is the victim?' We usually like it to be nice and neat – goodies and baddies – but in this case, the victim could have a variety of roles. He could be the perpetrator of some aspects of the situation. On the other hand the person who looked like the underdog could be controlling things: the tyranny of the weak.

When fear stimulates, energizes and motivates us

So far we have concentrated largely on the negative effects of fear in the workplace because, in the current work climate around the world, fear has become largely endemic and acts as a depressing and supressing force, as we saw in the research studies we examined in Chapter 4. The large majority of these studies have highlighted the negative effects of fear in the workplace.

However, fear is not necessarily a negative force. Fear also has the potential to be challenging, exhilarating and life-affirming (as we discussed in Chapter 3) in relation to sports, to emergencies that require superhuman endeavour and to self-selected challenges such as speaking in public, even though it might be a personal nightmare. It is hard to find studies that demonstrate how fear can enhance performance in the workplace. I believe this is because of the predominant view that workplace fear is always a negative emotion. There is something of an anomaly here. Why are the benefits of fear, as in 'feel the fear and do it anyway', espoused in sports or daring challenges, whereas fear in the workplace is considered largely negative? There so little talk about positive fear at work; what might it be?

Most work fear involves two components. First, it is usually invoked by someone other than the employee, often a manager or supervisor. Second, the employee is not wholly autonomous in the situation. This is very different from an individual undertaking extreme sports or being superhuman in the way we discussed in Chapter 3, where the individual *chose* to take part in a fearful act because they sought the sense of danger, exhilaration and adrenalin or because he or she was rescuing a boy from a car crash. In these latter cases, the individuals made a personal choice. *They* were in charge. In this situation, and also in the case of dangerous sport, it is frightening but exhilarating, especially in retrospect. Fearful situations that we choose and which we can, to some extent, control, help us to grow and build our capacities. As Mark Twain put it, 'Courage is resistance to fear, mastery of fear – not absence of fear.' Fear often inspires action; it forces us to do *something* and sometimes that something turns out to be the right move – but we can rarely be sure until afterwards. Fear also builds confidence. When we do something that scares us, we become stronger. However, it is important to find a balance. Moderate levels of fear can help us to grow in confidence, whereas high levels of fear can be counterproductive in that they can inhibit our abilities.

What is the equivalent in a work context and why should we court fear? Fear gets a lot of bad press, but it has a number of benefits at work. It keeps us alert and on the edge. It hones our survival instincts which, in many workplaces, is essential. Fear is also a sign that we are stretching our abilities, confronting our demons in the workplace, speaking out and taking risks. Just as exercise builds up our muscles, so confronting fear builds up our confidence, power and stamina. In this sense, fear can be a positive force in the workplace because it helps us to grow as individuals and as contributors to the organization. Nonetheless, it is important that we monitor the level of fear that we embrace. Research studies[12] show that fear is often ineffective in achieving behavioural change. Moderate fear makes us feel more alive: it hones our senses and activates our adrenalin. However, high levels of fear can have the opposite effect. We can become frozen, unable to carry out the task that we are attempting.

Differences in how people respond to fear in the workplace

As we discussed in Chapter 3, fear is a complex and quixotic emotion. It is difficult to predict how an individual will react to a stressful or fearful situation at work. Individuals may become visibly upset, freeze, express anger, walk away, fight back and so on. An incident may greatly upset one employee, whereas a similar incident will barely register with a colleague. How can managers handle this variability? There is no simple way of dealing with this and there are no clear ground rules. Human beings are endlessly variable in their responses and, as a manager, the most useful strategy we have is to develop and hone our human skills. Empathy, resilience, expressing trust, listening, humour (where appropriate) and above all awareness are invaluable skills to develop within the workplace – as well as outside. We will further expand on these skills in Part Two of this book.

We will never eliminate fear and mistrust from organizations. They are embedded in the human psyche and they serve a useful purpose in ensuring our psychological survival. However, we can become more discriminating about when and with whom we need to be fearful and mistrustful and whom we can trust. This requires us to build greater perceptual awareness so that we can choose our allies. We will expand on this in Chapter 11.

In summary, fear within the workplace is an ongoing issue. It can never be totally eliminated; fear is endemic to the human condition and, indeed, a degree of fear can enhance performance. However, widespread fear within organizations is counterproductive on an organizational and individual level. It is the responsibility of all employees within an organization to be alert to the destructive signs of fear in individuals, departments and the organization as a whole. It is, in particular, the responsibility of senior management to root out pockets of unhealthy fear, bullying and intimidation. Of course, it goes without saying that senior managers have both the greatest scope for creating fear and also the greatest ability to reduce it. Consequently, they must bear the major responsibility for ensuring that they preside over an organization where fear is managed appropriately.

Notes

1 Quote taken from Ryan, D and Oestrich, D (1998) *Driving Fear Out of the Workplace*, John Wiley & Sons

2 Ryan, D and Oestrich, D (1998) *Driving Fear Out of the Workplace*, John Wiley & Sons

3 Kish-Gephart, J, Detert, J, Klebe Trevino, L and Edmondson, A (2009) Silenced by Fear: The nature, sources and consequences of fear at work, *Research in Organizational Behaviour*, **29**, pp 163–93

4 Milliken, F, Morrison, E W, Hewlin, P F, An Exploratory Study of Employee Silence: Issues that employees don't communicate upwards and why, *Journal of Management Studies*, **40**, pp 1453–76, doi: 1111/1467-6486.00387

5 Irrational fears and the cloud, *Mozy*, May 2013 [online] http://mozy.co.uk/blog/wp-uploads/2013/06/Mozy-Fears-US.pdf

6 Dawn Lennon [online] www.dawnlennon.com

7 Lutken-Sandvik (2014) Bullying in the workplace: How bullying affects employees, workgroups, workforces and organizations: The widespread aversive effects of toxic communication climates

8 Workplace Bullying Institute [online] www.workplacebullying.org. For more detailed discussion of the causes, symptoms and remedies of bullying in the workplace, the following book is recommended: *Bullying in the Workplace* (2014) edited by John Lipinski and Laura Crothers

9 Pamela Lutken-Sandvik [online] www.ndsu.edu/pubweb/~lutgensa/

10 Cyberbullying in the workplace is on the rise, *ACAS* [online] www.acas.org.uk/index.aspx?articleid=4023

11 Punched from the screen – workplace cyber bullying becoming more widespread [online] www.nottingham.ac.uk/news/pressreleases/2012/november/punched-from-the-screen---workplace-cyber-bullying.aspx

12 Soames Job, R F (1988) Effective and ineffective use of fear in health promotion campaigns, *American Journal of Public Health*, **78**, (2) pp 163–7

Over-control and manipulation in the workplace

06

> *In the economic sphere an act, a habit, an institution, a law produces not only one effect, but a series of effects. Of these effects, the first alone is immediate; it appears simultaneously with its cause; it is seen. The other effects emerge only subsequently; they are not seen . . . It almost always happens that when the immediate consequence is favourable, the later consequences are disastrous, and vice versa. Whence it follows that the bad economist pursues a small present good that will be followed by a great evil to come, while the good economist pursues a great good to come, at the risk of a small present evil.* **FRÉDÉRIC BASTIAT**

The power of control

We live in an era in which control is a dominant theme within most large organizations. There is a culture of monitoring: rules, regulatory compliance, performance measurements, policies, governance requirements, health and safety and more, as illustrated in Boyne's (2002) paper on statutory frameworks in relation to performance within local authorities.[1] This framework, which contains 14 dimensions of organizational performance, was applied to the indicators set for local government from 1993/94 to 2001/02.

Few of us would argue that regulations and performance measures are unnecessary. However, we cannot always anticipate the outcomes of imposed regulations and regulatory compliances. In this chapter, we will examine some of the unintended consequences of such regulations and question the wisdom of target cultures that are not regularly reassessed to ascertain their appropriateness within changing organizational needs and conditions.

To an extent we feel comfortable with regulations. They make us feel safe. We know our place and we can gauge our performance. But what happens when control becomes out of control, when meeting targets becomes the goal rather than fulfilling the task itself? When the desire to control is excessive for the needs of the task, it is worth questioning our motives for imposing these controls and perhaps heeding the warning signs. The need for control should be proportionate to the task in hand. Where we find high levels of control of systems, protocols and restrictive behaviours, which are disproportionate to need, we have to ask, 'Is this control necessary or is it a symptom of a generalized level of fear – and our attempts to control this fear?' Over-control is one of the most obvious symptoms of fear in the workplace.

As I mull on this prevalent culture of control and read Bastiat's wise words, I realize that each generation has to find the same self-evident truths. The law of unintended consequences was obvious to Bastiat, but in today's organizational cultures it is far from obvious, as we will see later in this chapter.

In the same vein, it is interesting that in the 1970s the political theorist Herbert Marcuse argued that, in modern technological societies, so-called 'free institutions' and 'democratic liberties' are used to repress individuality, to disguise exploitation and limit freedom and the scope of human experience.[2] This sort of language sounds delightfully quaint today, but maybe both Bastiat and Marcuse had the right end of the stick. Maybe the self-imposed constraints of contemporary organizational life prevent us from seeing the obvious: that order is necessary in organizations to keep things on track, but humanity, creativity, improvisation, collaboration and passion are also essential if an organization is to survive and thrive.

Control and order

In many organizations, we have created working environments in which control is confused with order. Clearly, order is normal and necessary in organizations. Control, on the other hand, is more ambiguous. None of us would argue against control, where appropriate, but it has a dark side. It can imply locking things down, being inward-looking, avoiding new ideas and off-the-wall thinking. Control can suggest that, without strict managerial structures and interventions, staff would be chaotic. In turn, the thought of incipient chaos brings rampant fear; most management teams are more frightened by chaos than anything else. So the way to prevent chaos is to further tighten up the managerial controls.

Wikipedia offers an interesting definition of organizational control:

Control of an undertaking consists of seeing that everything is being carried out in accordance with the plan that has been adopted, the orders that have been given, and the principles that have been laid down. Its object is to point out mistakes in order that they may be rectified and prevented from recurring.

Stafford Beer, professor at Manchester Business School, takes a similar tack when he says, 'Management is the profession of control.'[3] There is an interesting contradiction here. Fear and its doppelganger, control, are held up as the ideal management tools. However, increasingly, within organizations, we find that control is hard to find. Is it really possible to control organizations any more, in an era of virtual working lives? Was it always just a fiction?

My experience in fast-moving contemporary organizations is not predominantly about control and 'seeing that everything is being carried out according to plan' or even 'pointing out mistakes to be rectified'. At least as important as control, in my view, is the ability to adapt to the situation that we find on the ground. Often this requires that we improvise; adapt our strategy and adopt an approach that fits in with the situation as it emerges. We need to try and create conditions that are most conducive to the current, often-changing, frequently chaotic situation. Clearly organizations differ considerably but, as a broad generalization, in workplaces today employees have to be fast-moving, quick-thinking and agile – and this often takes precedence over control. Indeed, in many cases, this desire for control can, yet again, be seen as a futile attempt to combat fear: 'If we can control our environment then fear will be thwarted.' But, as Margaret Wheatley puts it so well:

We have created trouble for ourselves in organizations by confusing control with order. This is no surprise, given that for most of its written history, leadership has been defined in terms of its control function.[4]

However, in a world that is increasingly unpredictable, in which our responses within organizations need to be faster and more flexible, control is likely to be less important than agility.

The Industrial Revolution

The Industrial Revolution, around 1760–1840, saw dramatic changes in working practices. Factories were established, tasks became mechanized and jobs broken down into their component parts. The workers each took their place in the production line and performed repetitive tasks from the beginning to the end of their shift. The mechanization of work processes was clear for all to see and there was pride in the efficiency and modernity of factory working. By implication, the workers became cogs in the machine. It was an efficient, if tedious and often dangerous, way of working which, in some industries and some countries, has not changed much, even today. By the 1920s, the adaptation of workers to machines was taken for granted. Managers then turned their attention to ways of increasing the efficiency and productivity of their workforces – and this was applied equally to machine and human. Control was needed in both areas and so control became accepted as the lynchpin of organizations. In essence, this model of control has not changed greatly in more than a hundred years.

The Hawthorne experiments

We come back to the Hawthorne experiments that we briefly touched on in the preface of this book. It was in the early 1920s that the famous experiments were initiated at the Hawthorne Works, a Western Electric factory just outside Chicago in the United States. The factory housed some 35,000 female staff who worked on a production line making components for telephones; there was a huge demand at that time. If you recall, the overall aim of the study was to identify those factors that would increase or decrease productivity. In particular, the researchers wanted to find out if workers would become more productive in more brightly lit conditions, and then if lower levels of light would reduce productivity.

They made the light brighter and, indeed, productivity increased. They concluded that more light meant greater productivity. They then experimented with lowering the light. Surprisingly, productivity went up again. Over a number of years, a wide range of changes was made to the working conditions in the factory and, it seemed, whatever the researchers did, productivity increased.

After much further experimentation and a great deal of controversy that still rumbles on today, Henry Landsberger, who analysed the data in the 1950s, concluded that the findings could be explained by the 'observer effect'; that is, if you are observed, your behaviour will change. It seems that it was the *attention* given to the staff that produced this change, rather than the change in the lighting. This phenomenon became known as the Hawthorne effect. It is now an established psychological principle: we change our behaviour when we are aware that we are being observed. The Hawthorne experiments marked the beginnings of industrial psychology, which has now morphed into a range of different psychological specialisms such as occupational psychology, health psychology and positive psychology.

Most importantly, these experiments heralded the beginning of a process in which workers came to be viewed – at least in part – as subjects to be monitored and controlled. To an extent this mentality still persists in many large organizations. Performance targets and the multifarious range of controls that organizations impose – and arguably need to impose – operate as mechanisms to monitor staff and to ensure order and control.

The processes of management control and manipulation in the workplace are, in many ways, vastly more sophisticated today than they were in the 1920s, in that we have more effective tools for monitoring and measuring employee performance. However, our *thinking* about how these tools can be usefully applied, what they are actually monitoring and the effects of monitoring itself on employee performance, is often less sophisticated than Frédéric Bastiat's thinking on these matters in 1850.

The unintended consequences of target culture

We are all familiar with target-driven cultures. Many of us are subject to performance targets in our working lives, or as patients, parents, drivers and so on. As citizens, our data is incorporated into a wide range of targets set by government departments, health services, commercial organizations and very many more bodies that we are completely unaware of, but which nonetheless impact on our lives. Targets are usually quantitative measures that provide information to help organizations assess their progress and keep on track. You might think that this is a fairly uncontroversial process. Why then has there been so much criticism of target culture over recent years?

There is nothing intrinsically wrong with targets. The problem lies in the ways in which they are employed and how they are interpreted. They are often used naively, in both the private and public sectors, with insufficient thought given to their purpose, how the implementation of the targets will, in itself, affect performance, and with scant attention paid to reviewing the targets in the light of ongoing changes in conditions or requirements in the workplace. Poorly thought out and badly applied, mechanistic targets have fostered organizational cultures that are toxic. We will examine the effects of some of these targets and explore how inadequately considered targets can lead to unintended and sometimes lethal consequences.

Targets are useful for monitoring performance, for encouraging staff to focus on objectives and to plan for the future, while at the same time being reductionist, static and linear – unlike the employees whose behaviour they may be monitoring. Targets may remain constant even as organizational or client needs evolve, or even change rapidly, so that employees may be locked into irrelevant targets that no longer serve their purposes. Quantitative-based targets are, by their nature, crude measures. As the sole indicator for gaining a broad understanding of the complexities of dynamic work environments, they are inadequate. This is not necessarily a problem, provided we recognize the limitations of the targets we set. Perhaps the most important limitation is that, if employees cannot meet the specified target, or if they do not support the targets because they believe them to be unattainable, irrelevant or counterproductive, then the targets will fail to achieve their purpose, which is generally to measure and/or improve staff performance and organizational objectives.

How targets can distort staff initiatives

The levels of control that managers may impose on staff, in terms of required procedures and behaviours, often hamper staff initiatives, as does the widespread adoption of 'target culture' itself. Employees may be subject to strict protocols that are quantitatively monitored and inadequately reviewed. As we will see, in some instances this has led to appalling situations in which 'the system' dictates working practices regardless of need or, indeed, common sense.

It is not only performance targets that can skew working practices in ways that can be unproductive, unfair or even dangerous. Reinhard Sprenger, a management consultant and author of *Trust: The best way to manage*, describes the mechanism of bonus systems and incentives as 'institutional mistrust'. He interprets these measures as management saying 'I don't believe you are willing to work! I don't regard you as a partner capable of entering into an agreement.' According to Sprenger, this is why so many management systems fail. 'They take people's motivation and throw it back in their faces,' he says. 'They are really saying, "We don't trust you."'[5]

Underpinnings of fear

These strong drives to measure and control – the rules, regulations, regulatory compliance, performance measures, policies, governance requirements, health and safety and so forth – are rooted in fear. We are frightened of being caught out, exposed, found lacking as employees and as human beings. Fear lies at the root of our obsession with control. Therefore, beyond a certain point, increasing the levels of control on staff will not result in greater staff compliance. It will simply drive up fear and further reduce the ability of staff to function effectively.

Instead of simply increasing control as a means of improving productivity and innovation, I suggest that we need first to review our approach to control itself and second to delve back into our roots and rediscover human ways of interacting in the workplace that are more constructive, and that play to our strengths as human beings. This is an area that we will come back to in the second part of this book.

Target culture within the UK police service

The UK police service is an organization in which targets have historically dominated, although theoretically it is no longer driven by them.

Campbell Keegan was commissioned to carry out a study for the police service,[6] part of which was to explore target culture. This was quite a daunting brief. We had not worked with the police service before but it was an exciting challenge. Could we really teach the police something they didn't already know? We immersed ourselves in the police environment and conducted intensive research with police officers and with the general public, in three diverse geographical areas within the UK. For our purposes here, I will focus purely on the effects of *targets* on police behaviour.

Since 5 March 2009 the only national police target set by the UK government has been to increase public confidence in the police service by 15 per cent.[7] Why then is the police service still driven by targets? The main reason is that senior police officers need to monitor crime rates in order to demonstrate their effectiveness – targets provide evidence of the officer's worth. So the situation is rather more complex than it initially seems. Essentially we are right back in the bosom of fear; fear of failure, of not performing, of not being promoted. Proof of successful performance insulates officers against these criticisms.

The effects of performance targets on police behaviour

Targets inevitably affect staff performance. What would their purpose be otherwise? However, at the stage where the targets are implemented, it is very difficult to predict exactly what these effects will be. Within the police study, three significant effects of performance targets were evident. Each of these had an impact on police officer behaviour.

1 What gets measured gets done

Currently, if a crime is not defined as a *priority* within a particular police force and/or it is not measured by a target, then it is less likely to be detected and less likely to be addressed. In this sense, '*A crime without a target may not exist.*'

A poignant illustration of this effect was the way in which drugs were viewed in one area in which we conducted research. It was clear that drugs were a problem in this area. We had accompanied drug squads on raids, in which they had busted down doors and arrested drug dealers. Nonetheless, the mantra within the particular Basic Command Unit (BCU) was 'There are no drugs in X.' I kept hearing this statement – followed by a laugh – and eventually I cornered one of the officers I had been shadowing. Reluctantly, he explained. 'We have no drugs in X. If we had drugs, we'd need a drug squad, but we can't afford a drug squad. And if we did have a drug squad, we'd have targets, but we wouldn't be able to meet the targets because there is no way of controlling the drugs. Drugs are at the root of most crime here, but there is nothing we can do about it.' Therefore the most pragmatic solution to the problem of drugs was to deny their existence.

In this way performance targets can influence both the definition of crime and also whether or not that crime is considered worthy of prioritizing. Targets are insidious. They occupy no moral high ground and can work just as effectively against crime reduction as for it.

2 Targets that undermine professional judgement

Police officers called to a domestic dispute generally have two choices. They can arrest the suspect, charge him or her, and take them into custody, even if this is against the wishes of their partner (who may have initially called the police). Arresting the suspect probably means that they will spend a night in jail, will be absent from work, possibly get a criminal record as well as suffering other repercussions. In this instance, the police officer will have followed the rule book, met the target, but will probably not have exercised much professional judgement.

Alternatively, the officer could talk to the offender and the complainant, consider the context in which the incident occurred, evaluate the severity of the potential crime, establish if it was a first call-out, seek assurances of no repeat incident – and then make an informed judgement about whether or not to charge the offender on this occasion. However, going down this route makes the police officer vulnerable. There is a victim, there is a crime and there is a suspect, but there is no tangible outcome. The officer must log the incident as an 'unsolved crime' and this will not look good on his record or on the BCU targets. In this way, performance targets can act as a disincentive for the officer to use his/her judgement and to take responsibility for solving what might be a relatively minor problem. However, the 'safe' option is for the police officer to arrest the suspect and charge him/her with assault. In situations where the officer feels vulnerable, he or she is much more likely to opt for the safe option and arrest the suspect.

Emphasizing *rules*, rather than *principles*, encourages a mechanistic response. Officers cannot easily utilize the experience, skills, intuition and knowledge they have honed over years of dealing with the general public. Given that most of our judgements involve emotional, bodily, as well as intellectual, input, aren't we missing a trick here? As John Kay puts it, 'By downplaying genuine practical knowledge and skill in pursuit of a mistaken notion of rationality we have in practice produced wide irrationality – and many bad decisions.'[8]

3 Meeting the target may not solve the problem

A group of teenagers hangs out in a patch of wasteland near a high wall. On the other side of the wall is a showroom for a Mercedes-Benz dealership. A collection of expensive cars is regularly parked in the forecourt of the dealership. At some time during the evening, a group of drunken teenagers starts throwing bricks over the wall. The bricks hit the cars and cause damage. This happens irregularly, roughly once a month. Each time the police are called by local residents. Sometimes the officers catch one or two of the young people, but this does not deter the others for long. After a while, the trouble starts again. This goes on for some months. Both neighbours and police officers are frustrated, as indeed is the dealership. Then a senior officer decides to investigate the site. He walks around the wasteland and the forecourt of the dealership and then asks, 'Why are all these discarded bricks lying around?'

No one knows. The senior officers insrtuct the juniors to clear away the bricks. Over the course of the next few weeks there are no attacks on the cars. The senior officer had asked the obvious question, one that no one else had asked. He had realized that the attacks weren't premeditated but were the impetuous actions of bored, rebellious teenagers. Remove the bricks and you remove the temptation. Of course it is probable that the teenagers would find another site, or do something equally antisocial, but it did break that particular cycle of repetitive criminal behaviour. Quick-fix responses, in which police officers were repeatedly being called out to caution or arrest a few teenagers, contributed to police targets but did not provide a long-term solution to the vandalism. However, the senior officer, by redefining or flipping the problem, had turned the situation into a creative problem-solving exercise, which *did* solve the antisocial behaviour, at least locally.

Personal judgement vs procedures

I have tried in this chapter to explore the benefits and drawbacks of performance targets, while at the same time presenting them in ways that demonstrate their potential. Targets serve purposes. Applied to simple goals, they may be *good enough* to assess the effectiveness of achieving those goals, or to gain some measure of productivity. However, targets can also offer an illusion of control, which evaporates on closer inspection.

More often than not fixed targets – at least as the sole method of evaluating – do not serve the purpose they ostensibly set out to serve. This is particularly true when we are dealing with complex situations, where outcomes are unpredictable and evolving. Traditional targets are too static, too unforgiving. They are unable to take account of the iterative processes of exploration, reflection and experimentation that are necessary when steering complex decision-making. So what to do? Do we abandon targets? Or do we look for alternative or complementary approaches?

Complex decisions demand a variety of perspectives. Experienced staff can make judgements that take account of particular factors that may not be obvious to managers. We need to find better ways of motivating staff in large organizations, so that we can tap into their expertise and varied experience, ways that encourage them to integrate experience and innovation, especially in situations where there is no rule book.

A working environment in which we feel fearful, mechanized and over-controlled diminishes us as human beings. As we become more constrained, so we become more disengaged or frightened, not only of losing our job, but also of losing our sense of self and our pride in doing a good job. We also lose a sense of trust in the organization we work for – and its management. The classic response in this situation is to withdraw emotionally, to close down. We become numb or brittle, so that we don't feel the fear. In doing so, we contribute less, but we also feel as if we are lesser people. Alternatively, some employees deliberately sabotage the organization in minor ways, as an expression of their anger. Working to rule, not going beyond the minimum requirement, or not helping out colleagues or managers with feedback are just some of the passive-aggressive tactics adopted.

What role should targets play?

So, coming back to what we might do about targets: there are no easy answers but somehow we need to reintegrate common sense and experience. We need both in equal measure. Targets are aids, not solutions. We have invested too much faith in abstract measures. Conversely, we have placed too little faith in human beings. Investing in employees, valuing opinions and acquired knowledge – our own and that of other people – and using our judgement, past experience and intuition will give us more holistic perspectives.

While targets may seem straightforward, they frequently trigger unintended consequences. Paradoxically, the targets themselves may be met, but they might not have achieved the goals they were designed to achieve. As Mark Scoular, chief inspector within the London Metropolitan Police, explained at the height of the targets debate within the police force, targets may be met, but this does not necessarily mean less crime:

> We no longer target criminality; we target how many stop-and-account forms we get during a shift . . . I fail to see how, with current key performance indicators, we are doing anything but fudging the real picture.[9]

So why are targets still ubiquitous throughout government and other large organizations, if they are inadequate for the job they were designed to do? Quantitative targets appeal because, superficially, they appear straightforward, easy to apply and, on the surface, it seems easy to assess their effectiveness. They are comforting, promising certainty. Targets make a messy, contradictory world appear simpler, apparently more comprehensible. They allow us to reduce productivity to numbers – or so it seems. And of course, they act as psychological protection: 'I followed orders.' Targets reduce fear, at least on the surface.

When we fail to meet the targets set, the response is often not to question the appropriateness of targets as a measurement tool, but to seek better, more precise or more comprehensive targets. Over the years, a great deal of effort has been expended on improving the efficacy of target systems, but with limited benefits. Essentially this is because the perfect target is an illusion and it is an illusion that has had some disastrous consequences for organizations, their employees and for the people they attempt to serve.

The best way to illustrate this contradiction between the promise of quantitative certainty and the reality is through examining some of the unintended consequences that can result from management performance targets, imposed in good faith, but adapted to the situation on the ground.

Targets that hinder, targets that help

Although targets, whether qualitative or quantitative, are not in principle bad, they can become bad (or unhelpful) if they are poorly designed, rigidly enforced and inadequately monitored. When meeting a target becomes prioritized over the task it is designed to support, then there is a problem. In these instances, the target has become an end in itself. It becomes reified, fossilized. Such targets often promote a blame-and-reward culture rather than a learning culture. In too many cases, this use of targets corrupts the organizational goals and purposes and can even undermine the whole ethos of the organization.

As social scientist Alfie Kohn points out in his punchy and provocative book *Punished by Rewards*,[10] manipulating people through setting targets or by offering them incentives seems to work in the short term, but ultimately fails and even does lasting harm. According to Kohn, people actually do *inferior* work when they are enticed with money, grades or other incentives. As he demonstrates in his book, the more an organization relies on incentives, the worse it gets at achieving its purpose successfully and efficiently.

Psychologist and researcher Joanna Chrzanowska reinforces this point:

Targets are a current 'taken for granted', as many people work with an implicit behaviourist model [of punishment and reward] in their minds about motivations. Ironically, the behaviourist model does work but largely in the negative – failing to meet targets is, in general, a de-motivator.[11]

Trust and the impact of targets

Onora O'Neill's 2002 Reith Lecture,[12] which addressed issues of trust and the effect of organizational targets and accountability, sums up this issue very succinctly:

I'd like to suggest that the revolution in accountability be judged by the standards that it proposes. If it is working we might expect to see indications – performance indicators! – that public trust is reviving. But we don't. In the very years in which the accountability revolution has made striking advances, in which increased demands for control and performance, scrutiny and audit have been imposed, and in which the performance of professionals and institutions has been more and more controlled, we find in fact growing reports of mistrust.

Since O'Neill's lecture, I would hazard a guess that performance monitoring has doubled or trebled. Clearly the problem does not lie with targets themselves, but in their application. Properly constructed targets, which are reviewed on an ongoing basis and which are treated as diagnostic tools rather than ends in themselves, can make useful contributions to improving productivity, health and happiness within organizations. When targets are used in this way, they act as signposts for the journey, but they are not destinations. They can be flexible. If the particular targets are not working, that is, if they are not helping individuals and organizations to achieve their aims, then they can be modified – ideally by the people who are themselves subject to these targets.

The word 'target' is often taken to imply 'quantitative': the *percentage* of crimes that have been successfully solved this quarter, the *number* of patients that have been seen in a hospital outpatient service within a specified time, *how many* cold calls an operative is expected to achieve each hour. It does not have to be like this. Just as targets can be flexible, they can also be qualitative. Professor Tim Blackman describes the constructive use of targets in which:

> targets are not regarded as reliable or valid ends in themselves but are re-framed as tracers picking out the key features of change as it happens. Employees become agents of change, alert to the feedback messages that these tracers send, modifying their own behaviour with the understanding that outcomes are *co-produced* between themselves, colleagues and customers, with the resources each brings to the interaction.[13]

This is quite a different and more flexible definition of target from that described previously. Unfortunately, the word 'target' has itself become contaminated through association with a variety of organizational disasters. Indeed the word initially conjures up an image of the firing line. Targets have become the scapegoat of management literature, often without a true understanding that it is the way in which targets are conceived, set up and used that is to blame, not the targets themselves. It is, after all, *people* who design and implement targets. The targets themselves are innocent.

As a broad generalization, simple targets are appropriate for simple objectives. However, few objectives in today's complex, multifaceted organizations are simple. John Kay in his delightful book *Obliquity* sets out to convince us that complex goals are best achieved indirectly. He explains:

> In general, oblique approaches recognize that complex objectives tend to be imprecisely defined and contain many elements that are not necessarily or

obviously compatible with each other, and that we learn about the nature of the objectives and the means of achieving them during a process of experiment and discovery. Oblique approaches often step backwards to move forwards . . . Problem solving is iterative and adaptive, rather than direct . . . High-level objectives are typically loose and unquantifiable – though this does not mean it is not evident whether or not they are being achieved . . . The criteria of achievement are constantly redefined by great achievers.

Kay gives fascinating examples of how, in complex situations, oblique approaches can achieve greater success than direct approaches. He cites Picasso, who was commissioned to draw a picture of a cockerel. However, if Picasso had drawn a realistic cockerel it would be unremarkable. Instead, he drew a cockerel which looked nothing like a cockerel although it captures the aggression and character of a cockerel better than any photograph.

Targets in practice: Machiavellian manipulations

Some years ago we were commissioned by a vehicle rescue organization to help them steer an upcoming culture change programme. 'Putting Customers First' programmes were very fashionable at that time. This study proved to be a great illustration of the skills and ingenuity of the patrols – but not in the way that you might imagine.

As a start, we interviewed board members as well as a diverse cross-section of employees gathered from different levels of seniority, job functions and experience. Finally we spent time shadowing service patrols that were sent out to rescue stranded motorists and, it was hoped, sort out their vehicle problems. We accompanied the patrols for several days, as the service engineers rescued stranded motorists from hard shoulders, towed them home, repaired vehicles and such like. It was all good fun. One of the great advantages of this type of ethnographic research is that you are, on the one hand, a novelty and therefore it is usually fairly easy to engage with the employees you are shadowing. On the other hand, you quickly become one of the crew, so that employees forget that you are *actually* there to observe and note their behaviour.

At that time, the vehicle recovery organization had implemented a customer pledge, backed by TV advertising. It guaranteed to send out a service patrol that would reach a stranded driver within the hour. This marketing goal was linked to employee targets, which in turn fed into the staff bonus scheme. Simultaneously, competitor rescue organizations were introducing their own pledges; they promised waiting times that were less than an hour. Competition became fierce.

Does it sound reasonable that recovery services should measure their performance in terms of the speed with which they arrive with the motorist? It is likely that it does. Isn't every motorist's wish, when they break down, that the rescue service arrives as quickly as possible? Well, that is not exactly true. Every motorist wants their car repaired and on the road again as quickly as possible. Quite a different thing.

The target that senior management had set did not take account of wily human nature. Human beings are endlessly inventive – and sometimes Machiavellian. A target can become a barrier to be circumnavigated, especially when it is unattainable. With the best will in the world, service patrols could not always get the appropriate rescue vehicle to the stranded motorist within an hour. For instance, if the vehicle needed to be taken to a garage for repair, then a tow truck was required. However, tow trucks were in short supply; they were not always available in the area and patrols could not magic one up, so they had to wait until a truck was available. The service patrols were mindful of their bonuses and the advertising claims of the company. This put pressure on them to achieve the unachievable. With a bit of lateral thinking, the solution proved to be surprisingly straightforward. If the appropriate rescue vehicle was not available, then an alternative vehicle, which *would* arrive within the hour, could be sent out to the motorist, *regardless of whether or not it had the equipment needed to deal with the problem*. So, a mechanic on a motorbike might be sent to a motorist who needed a tow truck. The target was met, but the hapless motorist might have to wait an additional hour or more before the necessary tow truck arrived because, of course, the irony was that the tow truck couldn't be called until the motorbike mechanic had arrived and called in for back-up. This could mean an even longer wait for the motorist than it would have done if no 'fill in' vehicle had been sent. This reminds me of an ancient Sufi tale I once heard. As Idries Shah tells it:

Someone saw Nasrudin searching for something on the ground.

'What have you lost, Mulla?'

'My key,' said the Mulla. So they both went down on their knees and looked for it.

After a while the other man asked: 'Where exactly did you drop it?'

'In my house,' he replied.

'Then why are you looking here?'

'There is more light here than inside my house.'

The tale illustrates the human tendency to opt for the easy, rather than the most effective, option. So too, calling out the mechanic on the motorbike provided the illusion of helpfulness but ultimately it delayed the unfortunate motorist even longer. A target which was designed to improve customer service therefore had the effect of delivering poor customer service. Corruption of targets is symptomatic of the law of unintended consequences that can cut in when employees are put in a situation in which expectations of their performance is high, but they are unable to carry out the task successfully. They are afraid of being singled out and of admitting failure for fear of the consequences, so they seek a plausible solution which will protect them. Fear of putting their head above the parapet resulted in major impacts on customer care.

Targets at their worst: failures of the Mid Staffordshire NHS foundation trust

Being stranded with your car by the side of the road is inconvenient, but generally not life-threatening or fear-provoking. However, the effects of ill-conceived or badly monitored targets can be much more serious, and indeed life-threatening. Between 2005 and 2009 a scandal erupted within the Mid Staffordshire NHS Foundation Trust hospital in the UK, which would be difficult to believe if it had not been so thoroughly investigated after the event. It transpired that patients were routinely neglected and left sobbing and humiliated by staff at the Trust, where at least 400 unexpected deaths were linked to appalling care. Bullying, patients left in their own excrement or having to drink water from flower vases, buzzers not being answered, a 20-year-old who died from a ruptured spleen after he was not properly examined, and many more such instances eventually emerged, to the shock of the general public. Why did no one speak out earlier? A doctor explained, on assurance of anonymity: 'There are the usual whistle-blower consequences. You're going to have to continue to work with people afterwards. You would feel that you could be putting yourself in harm's way.'

As extraordinary as it sounds, an independent inquiry found that managers at Mid Staffordshire NHS Foundation Trust stopped providing safe care for their patients because they were preoccupied with government targets and costs. How is this possible in the UK in this day and age? It is truly shocking that numbers of staff in the Trust behaved in this way, but it does illustrate how poorly thought out and badly applied mechanistic targets can foster organizational cultures that are often riddled with fear. If we treat people like robots, if they are driven by targets and not allowed to make judgement calls, if they work in an environment where staff suppress empathy and do as they are told, lo and behold we succeed in dehumanizing them. Human beings are very adaptable. In general this is a benefit, and it is one of our most useful skills, but we are also capable of adapting in negative as well as in positive ways – and the Mid Staffordshire hospital was one such situation.

The Mid Staffordshire Trust scandal has become a notorious example of toxic targets occurring in in the UK. Four hundred deaths were linked to poor care at the Trust. The government report on the scandal blamed 'over-reliance on process measures, targets and striving for Foundation status at the expense of an overarching focus on providing quality services for patients'.

Sir Ian Kennedy, Chair of the Healthcare Commission on the Mid Staffordshire NHS Foundation Trust Review of 29 April 2009, which investigated the case, described 'a story of appalling standards of care and chaotic systems for looking after patients'.[14]

How *did* this situation come about?

It is hard to believe that the hospital staff were evil or that they intended to harm patients. I think it is reasonable to assume that they wanted to do their best for them. How is it possible, then, that performance targets could instil such a degree of compliance that no one questioned what was happening? I cannot fully answer that question. My supposition is that it was a mixture of fear and compliance with what had become cultural norms; that these factors induced a degree of myopia and mechanistic adoption of the rules. Such environments are contagious and new staff modelled the behaviours of established staff, believing it to be normal and expected. These cultural norms framed the way in which staff interacted and behaved, in spite of the fact that the norms were seriously detrimental to patient care and would be rejected by the world outside the hospital, if it was aware of it. Equally, targets played a very strong part. If you have any doubts that ill-considered and badly monitored targets can have destructive effects, you need look no further than this case. Mid Staffordshire NHS Foundation Trust may be an extreme example, but sadly it is not unique.

You may doubt how this situation came to be, and ask, 'Why did no one speak out? How is it possible that an institution that was set up with the clear purpose of helping the sick and dying could become so distorted in its practices?' At the very least this example serves as a case study on groupthink, a psychological term that refers to the process by which members within a group begin to form quick opinions that match the group consensus and override their own views. The extreme of this effect is mass hysteria.[15] To help prevent another such tragedy happening elsewhere, we need to understand how, and under what conditions, performance targets can create a contagious mindset that works against both the aims of the organization and the good of the employees, patients, customers or clients.

Mike Williams, an ex-CEO of an NHS Trust (now an academic), described to me the difficulties of dealing with conflicting performance targets during a norovirus epidemic at the NHS Trust hospital where he worked. Hospital staff were required to juggle waiting time targets and simultaneously manage targets for emergency admissions. However, they could not reduce patient demand by cancelling elective patients for fear of breaching other targets and they were not permitted to close the hospital although the staff were also catching the virus, which put further pressure on resources. The fear of breaching targets, even in an emergency situation, meant that common sense could not prevail. A common theme in situations in which targets are sacrosanct is that target mentality is so strong that it overrides all common sense.

You might say, 'Well, the targets were wrongly set in the first place. If the targets had been patient-focused, if the goal had been "better care for patients", then these awful consequences would never have happened.' There is some truth in this, but it is a dangerous path to follow because the underlying assumption is that 'if only we can find the perfect target and stick with it, all will be fine'. This assumes a static, predictable world. Few if any of us work in that type of environment nowadays and certainly hospitals cannot be static and predictable organizations. Fear of missing targets is a powerful driver. Targets can give us tunnelvision. They can encourage a myopic perspective in which meeting the target becomes more important than almost anything else. Carrying out the task that the target is meant to ensure become peripheral.

Situations change. Life is messy and complex, particularly in fast-response environments such as hospitals, and it is likely to become more rather than less so, as expectations of response times are accelerated through modern communications. A great many decisions in life are essentially qualitative. Increasingly we are required to react, communicate, and think more quickly and in an improvisational manner within organizations as well as outside them. Targets can only ever be steers, useful for pointing us broadly in the right direction. If we believe that targets on their own hold the answer to efficient and effective organizations, then we are on course for disaster.

And we could do worse than follow the advice of Frédéric Bastiat, so generously passed down to us from 1850. And if I might be so bold, I have adapted Bastiat's words to fit the current century:

> When considering performance targets, we need to remember that they produce not only one effect, but a series of effects. There is the immediate effect, which is often anticipated and seen. Then there are the other effects that may not be seen initially. They can emerge later and in unexpected ways. Often, when the initial consequences of the targets are favourable, the later consequences may be problematic or even disastrous. The only way to avoid this is to constantly monitor the effect of the targets and whether or not they are achieving the desired result. If they are not, then they need to be adapted or abandoned.

Notes

1 Boyne, G A (2002) Concepts and Indicators of Local Authority Performance: An evaluation of the statutory frameworks in England and Wales, *Public Money and Management*, **22** (2) pp 17–24

2 Marcuse, H (1972) *One-dimensional Man: Studies in the ideology of advanced industrial society*, Routledge

3 Beer, S (1994) *Decision and Control: The meaning of operational research and management cybernetics*, John Wiley & Sons

4 Wheatley, M (1999) *Leadership and the New Science: Discovering order in a chaotic world*, ReadHowYouWant

5 Sprenger, R (2004) *Trust: The best way to manage*, Cyan Books

6 Citizens and Institutions of the Future: Rethinking interaction of the police and the public, *Campbell Keegan* [online] www.campbellkeegan.com/images/RSA-NPIA%20Symposium%20revised%2017.12.09.pdf

7 www.community-safety.info

8 Kay, J (2010) *Obliquity: Why our goals are best achieved indirectly*, Profile Books

9 Police target forms, not criminality, *The Telegraph*, July 8 2007

10 Kohn, A (1995) *Punished by Rewards: The trouble with gold stars, incentive plans, As, praise and other bribes*, Houghton Mifflin

11 Joanna Chrzanowska's material can be found at her website www. qualitativemind.com

12 O'Neill, O (2002) *A Question of Trust: The BBC Reith Lectures 2002*, Cambridge University Press

13 Blackman, T, Targets or Tracers? The role of numbers in public policy, *Radstats* [online] www.radstats.org.uk/no079/blackman.htm

14 Mid Staffordshire NHS Foundation Trust Public Enquiry [online] www. midstaffspublicinquiry.com/

15 Janis, I L (1982) *Groupthink*, Houghton Mifflin

Organizations in crisis

07

> *There cannot be a crisis next week. My schedule is already full.* **HENRY KISSINGER**

Organizations in transition

Working life in many large organizations is in a state of crisis. As we saw in earlier chapters, several major studies from around the world have shone a light on high levels of employee disengagement from their work and the working environment. Meanwhile, managers are often struggling to maintain existing structures, protocols and procedures in the face of organizations that are increasingly complex, fluid and unpredictable. In this chapter we discuss some of the difficulties that contemporary organizations face, including the role of leadership in fast-moving cultures, the balance that needs to be struck between hierarchical and emergent management styles, the role of consultants, short-term CEOs, 'stuck' organizations and the influence of 'corporate psychopaths' within organizations. In spite of the obvious fact that many large organizations can no longer be run as they used to be, with a strict hierarchical structure, a pecking order of control and an expectation of climbing the greasy pole, some of the traditional assumptions about organizations still hold sway and this causes confusion. Should employees follow the traditional path to promotion through steady, dutiful compliance or should they attempt to stand out, take shortcuts and cultivate influential bosses? These times of change have produced some seismic shifts that challenge long-established norms and practices. It can be difficult for employees at all levels to adapt to new times.

Clutching at old straws

We are all familiar with traditional, hierarchical organizations and many of us work in them. In its archetypal form, the board acts as the steer and overseer of the organization. Power resides within the board and it trickles down the organization from top to bottom, as do formal communications. Hierarchical organizations are tried and tested, and we know our place in the pecking order. However, such organizations can become stuck. The rigid structure inhibits the free movement of ideas, opinions and thinking. Practices can more easily become fossilized because there are few conflicting perspectives. Employees from different tiers in the organization are likely to have limited contact and even less opportunity to mix with those who are much more or much less senior. As a result, there is a tendency for staff to become siloed within their own particular department, function or level. The case of the Co-operative Group, which we will discuss later, illustrates some of the disastrous effects of resistance to change within large organizations.

Many workforces have become increasingly dispersed, peripatetic and isolated as a result of changing working patterns and the need for fast-turnaround projects. Working from home – or on holiday – working weekends, managing virtual teams and late nights are now standard practice in many working environments. In the midst of these changes, how can organizations best leverage the skills and performance that great individuals and teams are able to offer? What are the unique challenges involved in working with remote colleagues and displaced teams and what are the benefits?

According to a survey that was carried out by the US firm Knightsbridge Human Capital Solutions, 92 per cent of respondents viewed teams as critical for organizational success, although only 23 per cent believed that their own teams worked effectively.[1] This suggests that the *concept* of team working is seen as beneficial but there is a lack of understanding of how to get the best out of a team.

There are a number of possible reasons why teams may have limited success. For instance, many of us have not yet learnt the subtleties of different communication media and, in particular, matching the medium with the message. Too often we underestimate the importance of face-to-face human communication. It is more convenient and cost-effective to communicate virtually and there are an increasing number of virtual methods to choose from for day-to-day purposes. However, we need to choose the medium which is best suited for the task. For example, when communication is important, delicate and potentially ambiguous, you cannot beat face-to-face communication, for the simple reason that you can understand so much *more*: both verbally and non-verbally. Of course this is expensive and time-consuming, but it is a lot cheaper than a project that goes wrong because of inadequate communication. It's a question of choosing the best communication medium for the task, rather than just using the habitual medium.

Everyday conversation, by its nature, is emergent, in that we cannot predict how it will go. It involves verbal and non-verbal content, so we need to be reasonably adept at interpreting both. It is also clear that that hierarchical communications – up and down the official channels – are increasingly giving way to fast, local and improvised communications. Often there is no time to defer to seniors. Decisions will have to be made *in the moment* and employees will not necessarily have the experience or expertise.

Bringing in the consultants

Organizations are hierarchical (to varying degrees) and steered from the top, with power concentrated in the senior management team, who may be frightening and remote from the rest of the workforce. In this context, bringing in the management consultants is often an acute source of fear and anxiety among employees. At its worst, the change programme they adopt is created and delivered from on high, and staff wait passively to be told what to do. Employees may feel infantilized and unable to contribute to changes that are pertinent to their work responsibilities. This is rarely the intention of senior staff. They may aim to be inclusive and communicative, but they are often themselves fearful of the changes and of facing up to anxious staff who lack trust in the management.

Change programmes that sweep through organizations have had varied degrees of success in revitalizing organizational cultures and have often provoked resistance and cynicism in the workplace, especially if employees have previously lived through several change programmes and feel that these programmes did not live up to their promise.

Some management theorists, such as Ralph Stacey,[2] have argued that top-down change programmes are increasingly out of step with much of contemporary organizational life and the ways in which we now work, with semi-autonomous work teams, discrete departments, home-based, peripatetic working and so on. Perhaps it is time to view organizations in different ways and to approach organizational change differently as well.

The hierarchical model has been with us for so long it is almost part of our DNA. How do we change it? Can we adapt it? Besides, what do we adopt instead? The very notion of 'the organization' being challenged sounds almost absurd. Does it mean that employees from the CEO to the workers on the shop floor have to learn to adapt, as do customers and investors, even though we do not know what we are adapting towards? It is hardly surprising that this period of transition is causing considerable unrest at all levels of organizational life.

Arguably, the last decade has thrown up more disasters within long-established organizations than we have seen since the great depression of the 1930s. The banking sector, in particular, has been pilloried as stories of greed, arrogance and incompetence have seeped into the public domain. Many large organizations have felt the need to reinvent themselves and this has often been a painful process for staff. What organizational leaders need and expect from employees has moved on, as technology changes the nature of the workplace and as the traditional relationships that employees had with their co-workers are renegotiated.

As we examined in Chapter 5, fear, anxiety, covering your back, keeping your head down, playing by the rules, not speaking out, compliance, working to rule, and all the multifarious forms of passive resistance that thwarted employees become expert at, dominate the workplace. This is such a waste of resources, time and good man/woman power. Surely in the 21st century, with all the vast understanding we have of what motivates people, what makes work engaging, and how we can get others enthused about their work, we can do better.

Breaking the culture of fear

Repeatedly we come back to the core theme of this book. That is, we need to find ways of reducing debilitating fear within organizations. To a large extent, senior management has a responsibility for developing a healthy, relatively low-fear culture. However, in the current climate of uncertainty, high stress and unpredictability, many senior managers may feel as fearful and vulnerable as more junior staff. Consequently, they can feel unable to support junior and middle-level staff and may even avoid contact with them for fear that they will be blamed for the working climate.

The psychologist and business coach Chris Welford from Sixth Sense Consulting asks:

> Why are so many managers still more comfortable with a coercive rather than a supportive and coaching style of leadership? Perhaps the consequences of fear are not fully understood. Maybe it's not widely appreciated that fear is the number one enemy of creativity and that the anxious mind is rigid and limited as it seeks to solve a problem in more or less the same way, time and time again.

Perhaps some leaders confuse superficial compliance with real progress, but fail to notice the corrosive effects of passive aggression or the exaggeration of the strengths in those that lead to the point that they become weaknesses.

Breaking the culture of fear and threat within an organization might involve no more than a change of chief executive. I have experienced fear-based tactics in large government departments and watched staff bloom as an overbearing and narcissistic leader moved on. In a further education college, I have seen an executive team pull together and take an institution from average to outstanding as the new principal gave them time, space and overall trust. Adults are merely children with wrappers on! The way we function in organizations is a direct consequence of how we experienced our formative years and how we are now treated. If early scripting was to please others, that's what people will do, even to the detriment of themselves and the organizations they work for.

An aggressive boss who operates from a position of fear will just bring out the worst in people. If we were taught to avoid mistakes, the situation is no better. Desiring perfection in themselves, some people work harder and harder to tolerate no less than perfection in others. If we have been taught that other people cannot be trusted, our shrewdness will be bent into paranoia. And if we survived by retreating into our own worlds or quietly rebelling, that's what we will do too. Fear can make people into extreme versions of themselves and mostly these extremes are not helpful. When we are relaxed, we have choices but when we are frightened we seem to have none.[3]

Leadership in uncertain times

So, we come back, having ventured briefly into alternative models of organization and perspectives on work to ask: How does change happen and to what extent can it be controlled? As we have seen, many large organizations are in crisis as they struggle to maintain existing structures and protocols while at the same time trying to adapt to a more fluid, emergent and uncontrollable world. We have talked a good deal about the pressures on employees within contemporary organizational life, but what about the specific pressures on senior managers and other business leaders? They have never been greater. The demands from shareholders are rising inexorably. The speed of expected media response is also accelerating: as soon as another organizational crisis hits the news, senior executives are called upon to defend themselves in public. How can leaders cope with this level of uncertainty and change and what hope is there of building psychologically healthy workplaces?

Organizations that are operating in fast-moving markets need to be flexible and agile. Many are trying to carve out territories within highly competitive markets and speed is of the essence. Hierarchies slow down communications but they do provide structure. Remove that structure and there is a risk of chaos. Can organizations retain both the speed and flexibility while retaining control? It is a difficult balance to achieve.

In the *Journal of Applied Behavioural Science* James Krantz, a leading voice in organizational change, writes:

> A consensus is emerging that contemporary organizations are in critical need of leadership with compelling vision. Often this leads to an overemphasis on the personality or character of the leader. Although most people clearly need to coalesce around a shared purpose in today's organizations, the same conditions that make vision so prominent also make the huge emphasis on the leader inappropriate. Increasingly, complex, turbulent environments have made highly centralized, bureaucratic hierarchies obsolete and require our understanding of effective leadership to shift from the leader alone to the context in which leadership can be exercised. People's heightened interdependence and need to exert authority and leadership at all levels call for a focus on systemic leadership capacity, for focusing only on top executives as the sole source of organizational leadership hinders the confrontation of the more troubling, deeper, problems contributing to the contemporary crisis in leadership."[4]

As David MacLeod, author of *Engaging for Success*, puts it:

> To lead engagingly, CEOs have to open up. Command and control leadership is much easier. It just happens to be less successful in the long run. Yes, in a crisis you need command and control but the whole point is to stay out of crisis.[5]

Ken Starkey, a professor at Nottingham University Business School, also highlights the conflict between the expectation and the requirements of leaders to know, to predict, to lead – and the difficulties of doing so in an unpredictable world. Admitting ignorance is a risky stance and quite a sea-change for many managers. Starkey asks:

> What are the three hardest words for a business leader to speak? Probably 'I don't know.' Business leaders are encouraged to exhibit confidence, competence and omniscience, but this leads to only two possible outcomes. They can fake it: pretend that they are right because they know that the admission of uncertainty and weakness can be a career killer. Or, they can believe their own hype, convinced that they are right and know better than everybody else. This is where we now stand. A model has evolved whereby the leaders of business and

finance, abetted by an elite group of economists, have convinced themselves that only they know the way the world should work.[6]

Improvisation in leadership

To function effectively in a rapidly changing organizational world, we need to let go of old certainties. We need a more flexible, more emergent way of working together, which does not limit us to established ways of thinking. We need to be able to improvise, to experiment and to adapt to the situation in which we find ourselves at the particular time, place and mindset.

Adopting a stance of improvisation and flexibility involves a sharp departure from the position of expertise that business leaders have traditionally adopted, but are now questioning, Confessing that 'I don't know' exposes the leader to suspicion. We like certainty. Should a leader be leading us if he or she doesn't know? Leaders who appear vulnerable make us feel nervous and of course fearful. We have to find our own security – or rather we have to live with uncertainty.

Douglas Griffin in *The Emergence of Leadership* expands on this theme.[7] 'Traditionally leaders are supposed to be knowledgeable, authoritative and certain,' he says, 'but, in the current world, it is impossible to maintain that stance.' Working life is not only about fixed, learned skills or knowledge. Increasingly it is about acting authoritatively, making the appropriate or 'good enough' decisions in an uncertain situation, where there is insufficient information and too little time to gather it. Informed improvisation is the name of the game.

Situations move on and we have to adapt to the emerging situation. At the same time, groups tend to recognize the leader role in those who have acquired a greater spontaneity, a greater ability to deal with the unknown as it emerges from the known. And, as Nitin Nohria, the dean of Harvard Business School sums up, we also need leaders who can demonstrate moral humility and an approach to leadership in which the starting point is our lack of knowledge.[8]

In many spheres of working life, we simply cannot 'know'. Paradoxically, it is almost impossible nowadays to have up-to-date information because there is so much of it – and it is constantly changing. Information flows as if from an open tap and, for many purposes, information is just the starting point. Making sense of it, analysing, interpreting, connecting, predicting are often what makes information useful, and, as often as not, this requires the complex, ingenious machinations of the human brain.

And of course then there is the problem that we no longer have time to think. Few of us have the luxury of mulling on work issues, thinking about them from different perspectives, incubating our thoughts, delaying judgement, sleeping on it. These are invaluable human abilities that are too easily ignored because we simply do not have the time nowadays in a work context to think creatively and explore alternative approaches.

Make time. Prepare your mind. Think creatively

Our brains need time and rest – sometimes. If we want to create a psychologically healthy workplace for ourselves and our colleagues, a place in which we can explore and develop ideas, we need to make time to reflect, to play with ideas, to look at things differently, to merge and challenge our ideas, to elevate or dismiss them and so on. Ideally we would do this with other people, sharing our thoughts and building on the ideas of others. Woodrow Wilson said, 'Originality is simply a fresh pair of eyes.' Louis Pasteur said, 'Inspiration is the impact of a fact on a well-prepared mind.' We need to restore that simple vision.

Tucked away on a top shelf, I have a book I cherish called *The Creative Behaviour Guidebook*.[9] It was written in 1967 by Sidney Parnes, a professor of Creative Studies at the State University of New York College at Buffalo. It is a treasure trove of practical exercises designed to encourage the development of innovative thinking. I bought it as undergraduate when I was embarking on my thesis, 'Training People to be More Creative'. I dutifully dragged my student subjects out of the pub twice a week for six weeks and subjected them to an array of tasks with the aim of improving their creativity. Lo and behold, it worked. Their scores on a questionnaire purporting to measure 'creativity' did indeed rise throughout the course of the training, although it was never quite clear if my teaching or the local cider contributed more. *The Creative Behaviour Guidebook* is a wonderful book, not least because it includes the following quote from the psychologist and educational reformer, John Dewey:

> An idea is a method of evading, circumventing or surmounting through reflection of obstacles that otherwise would have to be attacked by brute force.

Sadly, nowadays, creativity is too often squeezed out of organizational life. External pressures, lack of time and tramline thinking reinforce the current obsession with measurement within organizations, which in turn encourages us to think in linear, mechanistic modes, rather than fostering creative thinking. We have had the fashion for slow food. I would like to instigate a movement for slow thinking.

Revolving CEOs

The historical notion of organizations as immutable things, slowly evolving entities that frame the activities of the workplace, is no longer relevant – but we are struggling to create viable alternatives. Hierarchical organizational models have traditionally been slow to evolve. However, one of the advantages of slow evolution is that senior executives have time to implement and see through processes of change. Conversely, the disadvantage may be that the CEO and/or the rest of the board are very resistant to any change or that the board is split in terms of future strategy. Currently, among large organizations, there is a shift towards short-stay CEOs.

A study reported in the *Harvard Business Review* of 356 US companies between 2000 and 2012, conducted by Professor Xueming of the University of Texas, measured the value and volatility of stock returns and the strength of relationships within two groups – employees and customers. He concluded that the answer to corporate life, the chief executive, the universe and every kind of performance is 4.8 years.[10] You might question whether life can ever be so simple. Nonetheless Professor Xueming argues that 4.8 years is the optimal tenure for a CEO. Currently the average tenure for a Fortune 500 CEO is indeed 4.6 years, so it's pretty close. The reason why CEOs allegedly have a five-year peak is interesting. The argument goes as follows. While the CEO is in charge, the strength of his or her relationship with employees continues to improve. However, as the CEO becomes more established, he or she relies on colleagues for insight and market intelligence, and so the ties with customers and employees are weakened and the consequence is a dropping-off in performance.

I am not sure that I buy this argument. Many experienced CEOs who have historical, practical and intuitive knowledge of their organization are quite capable of maintaining a grip on the changing market conditions, sometimes over decades. We also need to remind ourselves that it is not so much the time spent as CEO that is relevant, but what is achieved in that time. Think of Sir Alex Ferguson, the longest-serving and most successful football manager of modern times, or Paul Walsh, one of the longest-serving and most successful CEOs in the FTSE 100, or Arsène Wenger or Sir Martin Sorrell. Good managers transcend averages.

Conversely, we might argue that 4.6 years is too short a time to instigate and bed down necessary changes within an organization and that it will inevitably lead to short-termism. In fact, many CEOs do not reach the 4.6 year average and nowadays companies should expect their CEOs to exit before they planned. According to the *Wall Street Journal*,[11] 80 per cent of CEOs of S&P 500 companies have been ousted before retirement. On a related tack, analysts point out that, in poorly performing companies, external hires who replace most, if not all, of the senior executive team will produce the best results, which helps to explain the turnaround of Lloyds Bank.[12] It is perhaps worth reflecting on the effect that such rapid turnaround of CEOs and other senior staff can have on employees as a whole. In times of general staff insecurity, as is common at present, the disruption of senior staff members and the associated restructuring are likely to cause considerable staff insecurity and unease, which will undermine productivity.

While we are still at this stage of reassessment and of reinventing the notion of the organization, some fear and chaos are inevitable. It is easier for smaller organizations to experiment. They do not have to carry the weight of time and tradition, of established structures, behaviours and expectations and shareholders that are writ large in the organization's history. For larger organizations, it can be very painful, especially if management boards cling on to traditional organizational models, even when they are no longer appropriate to their needs.

The stuck organization

The Co-operative Group was set up in Rochdale, in the north of England, in 1844. It was based on a set of high principles and ethical values such as helping people to help themselves, democracy, equality, solidarity, social responsibility and caring for others. Its strapline is 'Here for you for life'. The Co-op Group incorporates a range of businesses, including banking, pharmacies, travel, funeral services and legal services, and it is owned and run by its members. Over the years, it has become a national treasure. However, the Co-op Group had become mired in history to the point where it struggled to survive, as the modernist and traditional camps within the management board slogged it out in a fight that nearly lead to the group's demise. The Co-op Group, which includes the Co-operative Bank, simply could not sustain a business model that was tenable in the current era.

At the end of 2013, there was a shock announcement. The Co-op Group unveiled losses of more than £2.5 billion and was accused of 'reckless' deal-making and 'shocking' debt. Lord Myners, a former City minister, was para-chuted into the mutual to reform its corporate governance structure. He was tasked with overhauling the Co-op Group, but he quickly realized the extent of the task he had taken on. In particular, he found himself being bullied by some of the Co-op's diehard traditionalists who were vociferously opposed to change. He described the Co-op as 'not a democratic organization' and viewed it as 'having been captured by a group of insiders'.

Lord Myners wasn't the only one to have felt the fury of the diehards. Euan Sutherland, the chief executive who had joined the Co-op in May 2013, resigned just 10 months later, claiming that the organization was simply 'ungovernable'. He too had been verbally attacked. Colleagues say he encountered 'remorseless rudeness' from the board members, most of whom were highly resistant to any reform. 'The senior officials talk the talk but in practice they won't do it,' said Sutherland before he resigned. The experiences of Sutherland and Myners laid bare the power struggle within the group which pitted traditionalists, who want to see democratic powers retained, against modernists who argued that if members resisted change, the financial consequences for the group would be dire.

Meanwhile, in May 2013, the Reverend Paul Flowers, a Methodist minister and deputy chairman of the Co-op Bank, resigned in disgrace, hav-ing been caught taking illegal drugs in the light of concerns about excessive use of expenses. Flowers was filmed spending hundreds of pounds on illegal drugs days after being questioned by MPs on the Treasury Select Committee over the Co-op Bank's dismal performance. It emerged that debts racked up in boom time had come home to roost. In addition, the series of boardroom disputes was troubling the Co-op's consortium of lending banks. 'Nobody wants to be the person who pulls the plug on the cuddly old Co-op but at some point bankers have to start behaving like bankers,' said one insider. Within this context, it is hard to know where the moral high ground lies.

Greed and fear

Greed and fear are lethal bedfellows. They stoke the flames of paranoia, often fuelling toxic cultures in the process. Since the 2008 crash, the UK banking industry has received widespread criticism of its practices, in par-ticular its 'excessive' bonuses and its lack of customer care. Then, in Decem-ber 2013, banking practices came to light that severely shocked customers of Lloyds TSB and its Halifax and Bank of Scotland subsidiaries. It involved 43,000 staff who worked within the banking group. Together they managed to rack up huge bonuses in a scheme that was one of the most lucrative in high street banking. In the first three months of 2012, branch staff shared bonuses of £20 million. It was also, according to the Financial Conduct Authority (FCA) one of the riskiest schemes – creating incentives to sell products that customers may not have needed. As the regulator pointed out, staff at Lloyds and its subsidiaries were encouraged to sell items such as share ISAs and critical illness cover through a harsh carrot-and-stick system.

Lloyds TSB employees who hit certain targets were eligible for a 'champagne bonus' which amounted to 35 per cent of their monthly salary, while advisors at Bank of Scotland and Halifax could win a one-off £1,000 payment. This was known as 'a grand in your hand'. A branch manager in Cambridge had sold more mortgages, life assurances, products and paid-for current accounts than almost anyone else in the taxpayer-backed bank. Thanks to the lucrative bonus scheme, the manager was in line for a windfall of £28,000 for just three months' work. In Birmingham, another manager was also beating all sales targets that had been set. A £25,000 bonus was paid out for the first three months of the year. Then another £28,000 followed from sales made from April to June that year. One might respond, 'Good for them. Successful people should be well rewarded' – but there are several issues to be considered:

- After the 2008 financial crash, Lloyds TSB and its subsidiaries were bailed out by the UK government, so it was arguably UK taxpayers' money that was being used to reward bank staff.

- Perhaps more relevant to organizational fear was the way in which those who missed their high targets were treated by the bank. If they did not hit 90 per cent of their targets over a nine-month period they were demoted and their salaries slashed. For an average employee this could result in a vast pay drop of almost 50 per cent. Fear was the driver for these employees and they were strongly motivated to achieve their targets whatever it took.

- Fear undermines morale. Targets may be met in the short term, but there is generally a high cost in terms of drop in quality and production, employee burnout and the tarnishing of the company's image.

According to the FCA one Halifax employee was so desperate and fearful of a drastic pay cut that he sold protection policies to his wife and a colleague in order to hit his target. These types of high-pressure sales schemes had been common in the run-up to the banking crisis of 2008, but they had been widely condemned and most had been disbanded. It was a shock to discover that Lloyds had launched such a scheme in 2010 and that it was only disbanded in 2012. Even more shocking was the fact that the scheme was implemented *after* taxpayers had already had to bail out Lloyds following previous scandals. The bank was fined £28 million by the regulator, which was a fairly trifling sum in banking terms. The banks have now replaced these schemes. However, given that the practices continued in the wake of the financial misconduct scandal that had sunk the financial sector only a few years earlier, we might wonder how long this will last.[13]

Corporate psychopaths

Creating psychologically healthy workplaces is not just a matter of encouraging the positives within organizations. It is also about ensuring, as best we can, that we exclude those elements or individuals who are destructive, who undermine morale, who do not support the work of others or who deliberately sabotage good working relationships. I am not talking about disengaged, depressed or cynical staff who feel beaten down by an environment of fear and disillusionment. With a change of climate and supportive managers many of these staff could be encouraged to re-engage with the organization and become more productive. I am talking about employees or potential employees who could be classed as 'corporate psychopaths'.

This sounds quite extreme. What do we mean by corporate psychopaths? Professor Robert Hare is a criminal psychologist and the creator of the PCL-R, a psychological assessment used to determine whether someone is a psychopath.[14] For decades he has studied people with psychopathy and worked with them in prisons and elsewhere. 'It stuns me, as much as it did when I started 40 years ago, that it is possible to have people who are so emotionally disconnected that they can function as if other people are objects to be manipulated and destroyed without any concern,' he says.

Psychopaths differ in the degree of their condition but typically they may demonstrate characteristics including: glibness, superficial charm, a strong sense of self-worth, pathological lying, cunning, lack of remorse, emotional shallowness, callousness and lack of empathy, unwillingness to accept responsibility for their actions, tendency to boredom, a parasitic lifestyle, impulsiveness, promiscuous sexual behaviour and so on. They do not seem to be particularly pleasant characters, so why are we focusing on them here?

Psychopaths at work

There is substantial research on the effect of psychopaths within organizational life. Although they may be only 1 per cent of the population, the effect they have within an organization can be considerable because of the nature of their behaviours. One research study carried out by Clive T Boddy,[15] conducted among 346 corporate employees in Australia in 2008, described a highly significant and negative influence of corporate psychopaths on all of the measures of corporate social responsibility and organizational commitment to employees used in the research.

Psychopaths exhibit a cluster of characteristics, including a lack of conscience, insincerity, arrogance and manipulation. Although they are usually intelligent, they are self-serving, lack empathy or the ability to love and have a strong need for stimulation. Corporate psychopaths who are in a leadership role often create the illusion of being successful leaders: they are attracted to positions of leadership because these offer rewards and power. Because they are good at faking emotion and empathy, their true character is not initially obvious. However, over time their less savoury characteristics emerge.

Psychopaths on the loose

Indeed, Boddy suggests that:

> Corporate Psychopaths have no qualms about buying up companies, tearing them apart, firing all the employees and selling off parts of the companies to earn a nice profit. They are not concerned about employees or about their mental health. They often escape with impunity and receive huge payoffs, in spite of the chaos they have caused. Often they have no regrets or empathy for the millions of people whose financial lives were destroyed. Frequently they blame others for the causes and results that ensue. When Corporate Psychopaths are present in leadership positions within organizations, employees are significantly less likely to agree with the view that 'the corporation does business in a socially desirable or an environmentally friendly manner'.[16]

Employees are also less likely to agree that the corporation shows commitment to employees, that the employees receive due recognition for doing a good job, or feel that their work and efforts are appreciated and rewarded. It is in these ways that a small number of psychopaths within an organization can have a very significant and detrimental effect on the organization as a whole. In fact, Boddy suggests that, just as criminal psychopaths are responsible for a greater share of crimes than their number would suggest, so too corporate psychopaths may be responsible for more than their fair share of organizational misbehaviour including accounting fraud, stock manipulation, unnecessarily high job losses and corporately induced environmental damage.[17]

Boddy goes on to say that the existence of corporate psychopaths should be of interest to those involved in corporate management and corporate governance because their presence influences the way in which corporations are run and how they affect society and the environment. Indeed, the subject of poor corporate management and governance through bad leadership has become a topic of academic research and interest because it is increasingly recognized that inept, dysfunctional or immoral leaders can damage the welfare of employees as well as of corporate stakeholders. Management literature is also coming to understand that the personality issues that senior executives exhibit are a valid topic for research into organizational success, for example the role of emotional intelligence.[18]

In their book, *Snakes in Suits: When psychopaths go to work*,[19] Paul Babiak and Robert Hare argue while psychopaths may not be ideally suited to traditional work environments, due to a lack of desire to develop good interpersonal relationships, they have other abilities such as reading people and masterful influence and persuasion skills that can make them difficult to be seen as the psychopaths they are. Babiak and Hare argue that the number of psychopaths within organizations is much higher than we think, and considerably higher than that of the general population. They estimate that somewhere between 3 and 25 per cent of executives could be assessed as psychopaths. The vagueness of these estimates reflects the limited work that has been carried out on this area, as well as the difficulties of defining and treating psychopathology. For instance, Kevin Dutton in his book *The Wisdom of Psychopaths*[20] argues that 'traits that are common among psychopathic serial killers are also shared by politicians and world leaders'.

The growth of psychopaths in business schools

Gudmundsson and Southey,[21] writing in the *Journal of Social and Behavioural Research in Business*, contend that business schools may be compounding the problem of corporate psychopaths by their focus in business school curricula. A study of these students showed that, in comparison with the general population, business school students, as future leaders, value empathy least, are more self-interested, demonstrate more cheating behaviour, are less cooperative, more likely to conceal mistakes, less willing to yield and more likely to defect in negotiation.[22] They emphasize the need for a long-term view to change the stereotype of business leaders, which currently focuses excessively on the charismatic, extroverted, celebrity type of leader. Instead, they suggest that leaders need to cultivate individuals who have integrity, character, empathy, and are led by principles such as honesty and transparency. In fact, as we have seen, where there is a cooperative atmosphere at work and a shared purpose, productivity rises.

Leadership and megalomania

In 1988 Fred Goodwin was brought in as the deputy chief executive to the Royal Bank of Scotland (RBS), a bank that was chartered in 1727 and was profitable and well respected. He later rose to the role of CEO. Goodwin, together with his board, set about the aggrandizement of the Edinburgh-based bank. He had already acquired a reputation as someone not to be messed with. One former employee claimed that he 'manufactured fear'. In the early 2000s RBS succeeded in a hostile takeover of NatWest. In the process, RBS became Europe's largest bank and the fifth largest in the world by market capitalization. At 42, Goodwin was one of the most powerful men in the world. Five years earlier he had not even been a banker.

As Iain Martin describes in *Making It Happen: Fred Goodwin, RBS and the men who blew up the British economy*,[23] Goodwin launched into a spending spree. He ordered new headquarters to be built. He had a private jet. He was obsessed with the executive car fleet, and the colour of each car had to be a particular blue called Pantone 281. His behaviour was certainly strange and he was famous for terrorizing his senior executives. As a result he acquired the nickname 'Fred the Shred', coined by a manager who got on the wrong side of him and was publicly chastised. Goodwin was fixated on the cleanliness of the bank branches, and ordered mass tidy-ups and mounted patrols, springing surprise inspections on unsuspecting staff. He had a particular hatred of any public use of Sellotape. If he spotted a Sellotaped notice in a branch, he delivered a sharp rebuke. Nonetheless, under Goodwin's control the Royal Bank of Scotland briefly became the biggest bank in the world.

By all accounts, Goodwin had only a very limited grasp of the activities of investment banking. The only thing that mattered to him was growth and he was always on the prowl for the next takeover. The board waved through each plan, apparently with a lack of curiosity or knowledge of the complex issues. According to colleagues, this did not concern him. One of his colleagues said, 'We would spend hours in meetings discussing the wrong things.' On one occasion his mother rang in the middle of a meeting to let him know that someone had dropped a cigarette butt on the step outside the head office of RBS. Goodwin immediately stopped the meeting and phoned a senior executive to get the offending butt removed.

What is really intriguing is how Fred Goodwin managed to reach the heady heights of CEO. How was he recruited in the first place? Who selected him? In retrospect it seems baffling that he would have been chosen to run the Royal Bank of Scotland, a bank that was once profitable and highly respected. Was Goodwin aware that he was building a toxic organization? Did he believe that fear acted as a useful control on employee behaviour? Did he simply not care? Or was he – as I believe is true in many toxic organizations – unable to change the nature of the organization or indeed his own behaviour? A colleague at RBS explained:

> Some people say you have to be a psychopath or at least a sociopath to want to do some of these [senior management] jobs because they are nightmare jobs. People like Goodwin are clever, able, good at their jobs, until they reach their level of incompetence. The child within is controlled by him and by circumstances, but then it's liberated. You have to remember that, by that time, he is used to having power. Power corrupts and absolute power corrupts absolutely. He has come to believe in his own abilities. His own hype is reinforced. By the time he gets to the top, he won't be challenged and also he is very convincing. He tells a good story. Lots of people in Scotland believed that the bank would be the most important in the world. Alex Salmond was deeply supportive of Fred. This was part of the Scottish narrative. This was going to be part of the great Scottish story.

Sadly, the story of RBS was not to be the one that Scotland hoped for. The bank briefly became the biggest bank in the world; that is, before its disastrous and ill-timed takeover of the Dutch bank ABN AMRO, which set off a chain of events that led to the eventual collapse of RBS in 2008. Its failure was attributed to 'multiple poor decisions'. Goodwin has been pilloried. He lost his knighthood. Yet, as Martin points out, to fixate solely on Goodwin misses the point. Many others were involved and no one managed to stop it happening. Equally, nobody important was jailed. After a short period of purdah huge bank bonuses have returned and there have been minimal changes in banking culture and practice.

The paradox of recruiting leaders

Crises of management are by no means restricted to the banking sector. Adrian Furnham, a management expert and professor of psychology at University College, London, makes a very pertinent observation on the role of senior management within large organizations:

> Perhaps the greatest paradox in the literature on leadership is that the usual criteria for the appointment of leaders are entirely inappropriate. The road from supervisor through manager to director can mean that those who are promoted have little aptitude, knowledge or skill to do the job . . . the problem of upward mobility – the journey from tea boy to chief executive – is fundamental. Nearly always people are promoted into supervisory roles because they have demonstrated excellent technical skills, not leadership potential. Most accept promotion with the perks that it brings, but few enjoy it. They carry on doing what they like and are good at, and often neglect the fundamental tasks of leadership. The result is that the organization loses a good worker and gains a poor supervisor.
>
> Of course nowadays management trainees cannot spare the time to work their way up the greasy pole. The 'long and winding road' takes too long. Young and hungry, they want to rise quickly in the organization. How do they win the race against the others?
>
> The answer is understanding politics and power. You need to know whom to impress and how to charm them. Networking and guile, self-confidence and presentation skills are vital . . . so when the trainees arrive at the desired destination, the senior management job, they may be a little stymied. It's nice to have the corner office, the personal assistant, the first-class travel. But to what extent are they able to form and motivate a high-performance team? The fast-tracked wunderkind may be a genius but he or she is unlikely to be an inspirational leader.

As Furnham pithily sums up:

> This process of recruitment and training does not encourage the development of old-fashioned management skills. Organizations are likely to end up with technically focused supervisors, power-worshipping managers and shadowy consultants 'doing leadership'.

Creating healthy workplaces is always 'work in progress' and we can never afford to be complacent. However, employees who work in a psychologically healthy environment tend to be more resilient to the ups and downs of organizational life and less likely to be undermined by small misunder-standings or minor disputes. By contrast, those employees who described themselves as working in a constant state of alert or anxiety often expected the worst. Minor incidents can be misinterpreted or blown out of proportion because fear distorts reality. Banter can turn into picking on colleagues or ignoring them. Fear spreads easily and quickly contaminates a working environment. However, a positive, supportive environment can be equally contagious. Sometimes it just needs one manager or an influential member of staff to change the work environment in a department.

Promises of reform

Barclays claims to be the first of the big banks to take this message of transparency and ethical banking to heart. It claims to have instigated a cultural revolution that 'puts the customer ahead of everything'. This is a big promise and a familiar one. Bankers seem to have short memories. To my knowledge, since at least the early 1980s, the personal banking industry has adopted mission statements and straplines that promise 'the personal touch' phrased in myriad ways. Currently we have a cluster of promises from banks, assuring us of their care and attention, for instance:

Addison Avenue FCU – *We listen. You prosper.*

Aventa Credit Union – *We're already there.*

Allstate – *You're in good hands.*

American Eagle FCU – *The right way to go.*

Amica – *We keep our promises to you.*

Aviva – *Taking care of what's important.*

And that is just a few I selected from the As.

We can only hope that this time round, the lessons have been learned and the personal banking industry and the general public will somehow achieve a mutually acceptable accommodation.

It is apparent from many of the issues discussed in this chapter, and in earlier chapters, that organizations in many countries around the world are undergoing considerable upheavals; attempting to reconfigure their organizations to adapt to a new world order. This is a challenging process for those who are working within organizations, whether they are at the top or the bottom of the hierarchy. It is likely to involve considerable stress, insecurity and fear.

We will now move on to the second part of this book. In this part we will take a broader look at organizations and, in particular, the human beings that work within them. We will ask questions such as: What makes people happy at work? Why do some people thrive in stressful environments and others flounder? What promotes productivity? What does it mean to be human and how can we create a more healthy and human working environment?

Notes

1 www.knightsbridge.com/Develop/TeamEffectiveness.aspx

2 See Stacey, R (2003) *Complexity and Group Processes*, Routledge

3 Chris Welford, Sixth Sense Consulting, www.sixthsenseconsulting.co.uk

4 Kranz, J (1990) Lessons from the field: An essay on the crisis of leadership in contemporary organizations, *The Journal of Applied Behavioural Science*, 26 (1) pp 49–64

5 Engage for Success [online] www.engageforsuccess.org/

6 Starkey, K, Academic View: A new philosophy of leadership, *The Economist* [online] www.economist.com/whichmba/academic-view-new-philosophy-leadership

7 Griffin, D (2002) *The Emergence of Leadership: Linking self-organization and ethics*, Routledge

8 Quoted in Starkey, K, Academic View: A new philosophy of leadership, *The Economist* [online] www.economist.com/whichmba/academic-view-new-philosophy-leadership

9 Parnes, S J (1967) *Creative Behavior Guidebook*, Charles Scribner's Sons (out of print)

10 Xueming Luo, Vamsi K Kanuri, and Michelle Andrews (2013) Long CEO Tenure Can Hurt Performance, *Harvard Business Review*, March

11 Why Your CEO Could Be in Trouble, *Wall Street Journal,* 15 September 2011 [online] http://blogs.wsj.com/deals/2011/09/15/why-your-ceo-could-be-in-trouble/

12 CEOs must keep learning to avoid the five-year axe, *Daily Telegraph*, 18 May 2013 [online]www.telegraph.co.uk/finance/business club/management-advice/10064862/CEOs-must-keep-learning-to-avoid-the-five-year-axe.html

13 Shah, O and Dey, I (2013) When Will the Banks Ever Learn?, *Sunday Times* [online] www.thesundaytimes.co.uk/sto/business/Finance/article1352356.ece

14 Hare, R (1999) *Without Conscience: The disturbing world of the psychopaths among us,* Guilford Press

15 Boddy, C (2005), The Implications of Corporate Psychopaths for Business and Society, *AJBBS,* **1**, (2)

16 Why are there more psychopaths in the boardroom? *Psychology Today,* December 13, 2013

17 Boddy, C (2011), *Corporate Psychopaths, Organizational Destroyers*, Palgrave Macmillan

18 Goleman, D (1996) *Emotional Intelligence: Why it can matter more than IQ,* Bloomsbury

19 Babiak, P and Hare, R (2007) *Snakes in Suits: when psychopaths go to work,* HarperBusiness

20 Dutton, K (2013) *The Wisdom of Psychopaths,* Arrow

21 Gudmunsson, A and Southey, G (2011) Leadership and the Rise of the Corporate Psychopath, *e-journal of Social and Behavioural Research in Business* [online] www.ejsbrb.org/upload/e-JSBRB_Gudmundsson_Southey_2011_2.pdf

22 Why are there more psychopaths in the boardroom? *Psychology Today,* December 13, 2013

23 Martin, I (2014) *Making it happen: Fred Goodwin, RBS and the men who blew up the British economy*, Simon & Schuster

PART TWO
How we can harness fear to improve productivity and organizational health through promoting human values

Being human

08

"No former generation has had so much bad news as we face. The constant awareness of fear and tension should make any compassionate person question seriously the progress of our modern world ... Science and technology have worked wonders in many fields, but the basic human problems remain. There is no doubt about material progress and technology but somehow this is not sufficient as we have not yet succeeded in bringing about peace and happiness or in overcoming suffering ... THE DALAI LAMA

The halfway house

We are halfway through this book and it is time for a change of focus. In the first part of the book we explored fear at work in its various manifestations: mostly negative, occasionally positive. We examined how fear can limit us as employees and as human beings, how it can inhibit us from speaking out because we might be penalized. It can stunt our creativity and our abilities to look at situations from different perspectives. It inhibits risk-taking. It emphasizes power differences and allows individuals to frighten others through institutional hierarchies.

It is time to move on from this fear-ridden place and to restore fear to its rightful position, rather than allowing it to dominate in the workplace and seep into our outside world, to neither overestimate nor underestimate its importance but to keep it in proportion. In order to do this, we need to look at the bigger picture: to explore what it is to be human and, in particular, to appreciate the huge spectrum of abilities, skills and potential that we human beings possess. In doing so, we will temporarily stray over the boundaries of work and address human beings in all their complexity, before returning to more work-related issues in the next chapter.

In this second part of the book, we will concentrate on harnessing fear as a stimulus for change. Fear is a huge energy source. We can use fear to generate the confidence to experiment, to try new approaches to work tasks and to work differently with colleagues. If we can more easily accept failure as part of learning and growing – maybe even as a form of play – we can utilize the positive effects of fear to help us to achieve our personal and organizational goals.

Throughout the rest of this book we will work towards the development of a healthy work (and out-of-work) environment, greater creativity, enhanced productivity and a higher level of engagement within the workplace. And perhaps we can throw out that anachronistic model of work–life balance. Work and out-of-work are both *life*. We are the same person, just doing different things.

We may aspire to be rational beings, but rationality is not always what it's cracked up to be. Much of our behaviour is anything but rational – *and often this is a benefit*. Some of our human characteristics seem contradictory, illogical or overemotional. They may be surprising or even shock us. But that is what we are as human beings, with all our contradictions and foibles. Understanding some of the complexities of being human provides us with a huge armoury of knowledge to help us to deal with work situations and enable us to thrive within contemporary organizational life. This knowledge may enable us to improvise more effectively – a much undervalued skill. It may allow us to see different or wider perspectives, to gauge how to respond, to sense whom to form alliances with, to know when to speak out and when to stay silent. Such knowledge can help us to decide how to handle difficult situations and, ideally, how to succeed and enjoy working life.

Groucho Marx seemed to have cracked the knack of a good life when he explained his vision:

> Each morning when I open my eyes I say to myself, 'I, not events, have the power to make me happy or unhappy today. I can choose which it shall be. Yesterday is dead, tomorrow hasn't arrived yet. I have just one day, today, and I'm going to be happy in it.'

Not a bad philosophy. But, first of all, we need to go back to the beginning and ask the key question.

What does it mean to be human?

Is there a straight answer? Probably not, although we can circle around the issue of what it means to be human in our contemporary culture. I am curious about the ways in which our thinking, attitudes and practices in the workplace are developing. In my view, human-ness is becoming devalued by the dominance of an over-rational, linear and limited interpretation of human nature. As we observed in previous chapters, this mechanization of our thinking, which is particularly prevalent in large organizations, can limit our abilities to work cooperatively, to develop trust and to innovate. Ultimately it limits the profitability of the organizations that employ us.

It is easy to see ourselves as victims in this process, cogs in the wheel, but we do have some choice; we are not powerless. Each of us has the ability to push back a little, to assert the benefits of a more human approach in the workplace. And if we all pushed back in unison, we might gradually restore humanity in workplaces where being human has largely been forgotten.

We take being human for granted, as if we all know what we mean when we say: 'I'm only human', 'a human response', 'inhuman behaviour'. So what *does* being human mean? What are the elements of human-ness that are particularly useful, or even essential, for developing satisfying, healthy and innovative home and working lives? What makes some organizations productive, fun and uplifting places to work, whereas others are depressed and depressing? Is it possible to change a stagnant workplace into an environment that is energized, innovative and a psychologically healthy place to work? If so, how do we go about it?

Clearly these are not questions that have any easy answers, but they are questions that we need to think about as we explore how we can make workplaces more human, how this humanity is manifest and ways in which it can be developed, especially in the workplace. By now, it will be obvious where my interests lie. I am passionate about re-humanizing organizational life. I have, over several decades, worked as a researcher and change consultant within the private and public sectors. However, my roots lie in psychology and my interest is in helping people within organizations to work more effectively and with more engagement, joy and excitement. This is what drives me.

It is, of course, impossible to do justice to the topic of being human in a single chapter. Instead, we will meander though some of the themes of human-ness that I personally find interesting and which I hope will interest you too. My aim is to shake up some of the assumptions that have settled within organizational life, to question the usefulness of these ideas and maybe offer alternatives. Some of the themes that I touch upon may grab your interest. Others may leave you cold.

The beginnings of humanistic psychology

The post-war years of the late 1940s and the 1950s were a time of psychological exploration and reflection on what it meant to be human. World war, the Holocaust and the Korean War had created horrors, the nature and scale of which had not been experienced or observed in living history. People turned to the fledgling science of psychology in search of answers that might explain how these horrors could have come about and, more specifically, to understand if and how we could prevent them from happening in the future. Was it possible to create healthy, productive, peaceful societies? Was it possible to end all war?

Nowadays, it is unrealistic to address such huge questions. We know too much. We also know how little we know. We have abandoned the big questions in favour of those that will deliver an answer. We have become pragmatists. But in the post-war years, psychologists wanted to change the world and, fired with passion, they *did* change the world, or at least our understanding of what makes us human.

Four psychologists – Abraham Maslow (1908–70), Carl Rogers (1902–87), Harry Harlow (1905–81) and John Bowlby (1907–90) – created a climate for psychology and a humanistic tradition which became part of our culture. Rogers developed humanistic psychology and the concept of client-centred therapy, Maslow worked on his famous hierarchy of needs, Harlow explored the importance of love in healthy human development, and Bowlby developed attachment theory, the concept that we are biologically pre-programmed to form attachments with others.

The ways in which we bring up our children today, our education policies, psychiatry and various forms of psychological therapies, our views on social housing, how prisons are created and run, how we treat illegal immigrants and how we are as societies have all been coloured to some extent by the seminal work of these pioneering psychologists. In particular their thinking has contributed a great deal to organizational life. Their understanding of human motivation, the drive to achieve, self-esteem, trust and reciprocity are all just as pertinent in helping to shape organizational life today as they were at the turn of the last century. Arguably, they are even more pertinent, when it often seems that we have lost the sense of being human, particularly within organizational climates of fear and uncertainty.

Carl Rogers and self-actualizing

According to the renowned psychologist Carl Rogers, society and culture are natural by-products of a 'self-actualizing' tendency.[1] In other words, we are all hard-wired to do and be the best we are capable of doing and being, provided we have right opportunities and support, and provided we are not constrained – or constrain ourselves – by fear and anxiety. Rogers believed that we humans have an overriding drive to self-actualize: to fulfil our potential and achieve the highest level of human-being-ness we can achieve. Self-actualizing is the process of growing to fulfil our full potential, provided that the conditions are good enough. However, if we are constrained by our environment or our own nature, then we will be unable to flourish. Rogers passionately believed that every individual had unique potential, although we develop in different ways according to our personality. He also believed in the inherent goodness and creativity of people and that destructiveness only arose when poor self-concept or external constraints overrode our sense of self-worth. Essentially he regarded self-actualization as a lifelong ambition – always work in progress.

Some of the core themes of Rogers's philosophy were: being open to experience, being able to live and fully appreciate the present, being in touch with different experiences, avoiding prejudging and preconceptions, living for the moment, trusting our feelings, creativity and fulfilment as well as looking for new challenges. Would we disagree with many of these? Probably not. Would we like these principles to pervade our working environments? Almost certainly yes. These characteristics are broad enough for almost everyone to relate to, and they have stood the test of time, probably because they reflect basic human needs – as Maslow understood only too well. Bringing these human values back into the workplace through fostering employee interaction, trust, taking initiative, cooperative working and collaboration, experimentation and so on can reap remarkable rewards, as we will discuss in Chapter 11.

Maslow's hierarchy of needs

The humanist psychologist Abraham Maslow has continued, over decades, to be a household name. Maslow first introduced his concept of a hierarchy of needs in his 1943 paper, 'A Theory of Human Motivation', and his subsequent book, *Motivation and Personality*.[2] In these titles, he suggests that people are motivated to fulfil basic needs before moving on to other, more complex, needs. Maslow enshrined his hierarchy of needs in a pyramid, which has imparted its wisdom to generation after generation of students. The lowest levels of the pyramid constitute the most basic needs (food, sleep, warmth etc). Once these needs are met, we move up the pyramid to the next level (safety and security) and so on up. The more complex needs are located at the top of the pyramid.

As people progress up the pyramid, needs become increasingly psychological and social. Soon, the need for love, friendship, and intimacy becomes prioritized. Further up the pyramid, the need for personal esteem and feelings of accomplishment is added to the mix. Like Carl Rogers, Maslow emphasized the importance of self-actualization, which is a process of growing and developing as a person in order to achieve individual potential.

Over the years there have been criticisms of Maslow's hierarchy and numerous adaptations and additions. Nonetheless, it has maintained its basic appeal largely, I believe, because it makes sense to most people irrespective of their interest in psychology. In its simplest form it offers a 'rough and ready template for our stages of psychological development and allows us to examine our priorities. We have a lot to thank Maslow for. He was one of the first psychologists to bring psychology into the workplace and, over subsequent decades, the general public has come to accept psychology as an integral part of life in an organizational context.

What would Maslow, Harlow, Bowlby and Rogers make of contemporary organizational cultures? Their pioneering research was driven, in part, by a desire to expunge the recent, savage memories of two world wars. They sought to restore a sense of human values and to build a world that would eradicate such horrors in the future. It was a noble dream and I suspect they would be disappointed with our progress in promoting and practising the human values they espoused. Nonetheless, decades on, we are still individuals seeking a sense of purpose in our lives and in the ideal world we achieve a good deal of that purpose through our work. Retaining and developing human values such as sensing, problem solving, creativity, cooperation, teamwork, reciprocity, empathy, intuition, curiosity, taking the initiative, pride in our work, experimentation, achievement, trust, humour, passing on skills to the next generation, and so much more, need to be a high priority, not only for the good of the workforce but also as an economic imperative.

There is still a long way to go before these human values permeate all workplaces and much of the progress that was achieved in the post-war years has, arguably, been lost. The world is now a very different place. Psychology has blossomed, fragmented and become more specialized; it is impossible to incorporate it all in a single discipline. Nowadays, researchers narrow down their field of interest and, as a result, the big questions go unanswered – but they have not gone away. What does it mean to be human? It is the perennial question. We will attempt, however inadequately, to address some of the issues that are subsumed within this question.

Using all our brain power

Broadly, there are three different parts to our human brain, each with very different functions. There is the old reptilian brain, the part of the brain stem at the top of the spinal column that we have in common with all other vertebrates, including lizards. The old brain is only interested in survival. It is the part that senses fear and danger and reacts instinctively. It does not know the difference between past and present, but it constantly scans to check whether or not the environment is safe or dangerous *right now*.

The second part of the brain, the mammalian brain – also called the limbic system – is where our feelings are stored. We can supress our feelings, but not destroy them, because they still exist in our brain. If your reptilian brain senses danger, it alerts the mammalian brain which will then feel afraid – and probably take steps to reduce the fear. Equally, when the danger has passed, the mammalian brain stands down.

The 'new' brain, or cerebral cortex, is vital for sensing and interpreting input from various parts of the body and also for maintaining cognitive function. Sensory functions of the cerebral cortex include hearing, touch and vision. Cognitive functions include thinking, perceiving, understanding language and also the capacity for creativity and intuition. In this way, the cerebral cortex can be said to shape intelligence. It is also responsible for planning and organization.

It is easy to dismiss our old brain in favour of the new one, the brain that we are more comfortable with and can more easily understand. However, our reptilian brain is vital to our well-being. Our old brain is instinctive and intuitive. It is good at sensing mood, different emotions, ambiguity, potential conflict and much more. It may not be so good at expressing itself but, when combined with new brain skills it can provide vital and potentially life-saving information. Our tendency in organizations – as in life in general – is to prioritize the rational over the arational and the new brain over the old. However, by over-concentration on the new brain, we risk ignoring some of our most useful faculties. To make the most of our human abilities, it is important that we have access to *all* of our brain's capacities. This means that we need to practise different types of brain awareness, in order that we have the broadest spectrum of information available to us.

For example, intuition or a sixth sense is common but often we ignore these cues as irrational. Next time you are aware of a feeling or sense that is odd or unfamiliar, try letting it sit in your mind, rather than instantly discarding it. Just see what happens. Perhaps nothing will, but instincts are often low-level bodily cues that emanate from the reptilian brain. They can be useful indicators of information that is too weak for your conscious mind to register. In an organizational context, it can be very useful to be alert to these weak, bodily cues. Developing a practice of active listening and observation, in which we simply *receive* information, attempting not to judge, interpret or categorize, can provide a great deal of unfiltered information which to some extent bypasses our normal cognitive processes. This can enable us to develop a broader perspective on organizational issues.

Our evolutionary heritage

There is a tendency to take for granted or ignore the remarkable skills we have developed in our evolutionary journey. Typically we present our rational face, at least within a work context, and suppress our emotions. However, behaviour is never devoid of emotion, as we all know from our own experience. The ways in which we – and others around us – behave affects how we feel, just as the way we feel affects our behaviour. We convey huge amounts of information without even speaking. By acting in a rational and unemotional way, by ignoring our feelings, intuitions and other bodily responses, we screen out important information. As humans, we have self-awareness, yet often we act on impulses that remain hidden, even from ourselves. As a result, our behaviour and thinking can become more *distanced* from our bodies. Why does this matter?

Well, imagine you are given a brief by your boss. He or she asks you to absorb the data and put together a short summary, with strategic recommendations, to deliver to the board that afternoon. You read the first half of the document. You've got the gist of it, no sweat. Unfortunately, it is the last three paragraphs that contain the key points, and somehow you overlook them. You deliver your presentation, but it is incomplete. The board members are puzzled, then angry. Why have you not done a thorough job? Clearly the recommendations are inadequate. It is not your finest hour. In the situation above, it will be clear to you on reflection where you went wrong. You were sloppy. You did not consider all the data. There is no one to blame but yourself.

However, if the information you were considering was non-verbal, that is, body language, would it be so obvious? In almost all situations, personal or professional, integrating *all* the data that is available, both verbal and non-verbal, is important for understanding the issues and providing a response. However, too often we focus on the words, the language used, and prioritize these aspects over the non-verbal communication, which is often just as important as the verbal. Arguably the non-verbal is more important because we often try to conceal our emotional responses in a work context and we fail to pick up the body language of other people. Too often we miss so much vital non-verbal communication; facial expressions, tone of voice, bodily posture, eye movements, as well as the instinctive responses of our colleagues, because we focus mainly on verbal communication and ignore all else. In addition, when we are agitated, distracted or over-focused, we are less able to tune in and take on board the subtleties of body language – and yet it is often the most important and accurate element of the communication. This is a topic that we will come back to in Chapter 11.

The effects of 'mechanized' language

Sometimes it seems that, in our attempt to remove emotion from organizational language, we have almost forgotten that we are human at all. Consider the sort of language we use in organizations today. Here are just a few examples I dug out from organizational literature:

Teams represent the new machines of business in the knowledge economy.

Virtual teams are the simple unit of production.

Organizations are complex systems.

Complex responsive processes of relating.

HR as Change Architecture.

Rewiring your organization.

The New Organizational Currency: Designing Effective Teams.

These ways of describing human interaction elevate the rational and diminish the emotional and physical. They sidestep the fact that when we are face to face with another human being, when we see their expression, their smile, hear their tone of voice, see how they are responding to us, we make assumptions (right or wrong) based on this information. These assumptions, in turn, colour whether or not we like that person, whether we feel we can trust them, maybe even employ them. Much of this sizing up is done on the basis of human instinct, although in formal work situations we often deny this and we back up our decisions with an assessment, to prove that we are impartial. There is often something disingenuous about this process.

Human judgement is by no means perfect, but intuitive and non-verbal skills are an invaluable component of judgement and decision-making and are well worth honing.

Survival of the fittest vs cooperative behaviour

'Survival of the fittest' is one of those assumed truisms of evolution. It has become adopted within many work organizations as an explanation or justification for management policy. The strong survive and thrive and the weak are discarded or culled, as it is now sometimes called – only partly ironically. However, survival of the fittest is only half the story. In Western culture we have an ingrained tendency to think in terms of either/or. If A is true, then B must be false. So, if survival of the fittest is true, then cooperation between animals – or between human beings – must, by definition, be false. But this is not what actually happens. Both survival of the fittest *and* cooperation strategies are part and parcel of human existence. The strategy adopted depends on the circumstances. According to Martin A Nowak, writing in *Scientific American*, far from being a nagging exception to the rule of evolution, cooperation has been one of its primary architects. Indeed, without cooperation, human beings would never have got off the ground as a species. And, of course, it is patently obvious from our own experience in day-to-day life that human beings are genetically and socially primed to cooperate with others – with complete strangers as well as family and friends – even where the individual him/herself may be harmed in the process.

In April 2011, as reactors at the Fukushima Daiichi nuclear power plant in Japan were melting down following a lethal earthquake and tsunami, a maintenance worker in his 20s was one of those who volunteered to re-enter the plant to try to help bring things back under control. He knew the air was poisoned and expected the choice would keep him from ever marrying or having children for fear of burdening them with health consequences. Yet he still walked back through Fukushima's gates into the plant's radiation-infused air and got to work – for no more compensation than his usual modest wages.

'There are only some of us who can do this job,' the worker (who wished to remain anonymous) explained. 'I'm single and young and I feel it's my duty to help settle this problem.'[3]

Selfless behaviour abounds in nature. Cells within an organism coordinate to keep their division in check and avoid causing cancer; female lions within a pride will suckle one another's young. And humans help other humans to do everything from obtaining food to finding mates to defending territory. Retaining these cooperative instincts in the workplace is a natural drive within employees. It boosts employee satisfaction, just as it boosts productivity and profits. So, too, in the workplace, cooperation is usually the norm and, provided the work climate and relationships with colleagues and managers are not undermined or corrupted in some way, most employees are generally happier when working productively and cooperatively. Indeed cooperation is a crucial aspect of most employees' sense of engagement and satisfaction within their workplace. We disrupt these mutually supportive working patterns at our peril.

The relentless drive to mechanize brains

In some quarters, a mechanistic brain is already seen as the ideal. In 2007 Larry Page, co-founder of Google, described his vision of the future at the American Association for the Advancement of Science. He said:

> My theory is that, if you look at your [human] programming, your DNA, it's about 600 megabytes compressed, so smaller than any modern operating system . . . and that includes booting up your brain, by definition. So your program algorithms probably aren't that complicated. [Intelligence] is probably more about overall computation.[4]

While some of us might use a mechanical metaphor as shorthand, because it conveys an approximation of the brain, most of us probably don't view our brains as machines. In Page's case, he appears to use mechanical analogies because he does view the brain as a machine and because he believes that a mechanical brain would be superior to a human one. Not surprisingly, Page's business partner, Sergey Brin, also favours a mechanical brain, as he described to a *Newsweek* reporter in 2004 when he said, 'Certainly if you had all the world's information directly attached to your brain, or an artificial brain that was smarter than your brain, you'd be better off.'

This thinking is seductive – and it's spreading. Recently, a client described to me, without apparent irony, that once we are able to download data directly into our brains, we would become superhuman. 'Overflowing with information' is how he described it. However, without the ability to prioritize, analyse and contextualize Big Data it has no value. It is white noise. We still need human skills – at least for the moment – to select, prioritize and interpret data and turn it into knowledge that we can use.

The ways in which the human body operates are very different from the ways in which machines currently function; it is equivalent to the difference between quantum and Newtonian science. We humans are animals, in the best sense of the word. We are not automated machines led purely by rational thought. We have hugely complex patterns of instincts, genetic programming, behaviours, thoughts and culture, which have been honed over millions of years. There is still much to be understood about the brain. It is only very recently, with the development of sophisticated technologies and neuroscience, that we are really beginning to appreciate just how amazing we human beings are.

It is not just the technologically sceptical who are questioning the benefits and unintended consequences of viewing human beings as machines. Jaron Lanier, a philosopher, author and notable computer scientist at the forefront of technological innovation, is now surveying the world he has helped to create, with some dismay. In his book *You Are Not a Gadget: A manifesto*, he says, 'Online culture is filled to the brim with rhetoric about what the true path to a better world ought to be, and these days it's strongly biased towards an antihuman way of thinking.'[5] Or, as Idries Shah, the Sufi scholar, expressed it pithily way back in 1968, 'People used to play with toys. Now the toys play with them.'[6]

This model of man as machine is rife within many organizational contexts. Target culture, compliance, rules and regulations, whether used consciously or not, often act as tools for dividing, controlling, diminishing and dehumanizing the workforce. At this stage in our knowledge, it is impossible to predict the long-term effects of a web-based world. It is a complex picture. However, we appear to be moving away from the rather hostile notion of *man vs machine*, and towards the model of *man and machine as symbiotic*. The antidote to over-mechanization of our working practices may lie in greater blending of the human and technological and there is a strong and growing move towards technologies that complement human abilities, such as thought-controlled motor functions for people with limited mobility, mechanized 'soldiers' who help save human comrades' lives, even the invisible cycle helmet[7] – to mention just a few.

Why does all this matter for organizations and the people who work within them? Innovation is a result of seeing things differently, of recognizing possibilities and opportunities. It is fuelled by curiosity, and fanned by enthusiasm and a quirky way of understanding the world. We need diversity in our thinking if we are to see things differently and create new ways of understanding. As the blogger Avi Schneider puts it, 'We need automated technologies to help human beings become better human beings, not help machines to become better human beings.'[8]

Developing attitudes, beliefs and habits

Have you ever wondered how we can each develop very different views on life? Much of this is due to *priming* and *framing*. Priming involves an enhanced sensitivity to particular stimuli as a result of previous experiences. For example, if you have been bitten by a dog you may be *primed* to avoid dogs in future, or if you have had an unpleasant experience when flying, you may be reluctant to go on a plane again.

Similarly, *framing* provides a situational context which influences what you might or might not do. For instance, if you are going out for a meal with a group of college friends, you are likely to go to a different venue and behave in a very different very different manner than you would if you were meeting your Great Aunt Maud for tea. Framing within conversations is also common; for example, asking, 'Do you *really* want another cake?' is clearly worded in such a way as to shape a particular response, for instance, 'Oh no, thanks. I couldn't eat another thing.'

However, unlike the situations above, shaping and framing are often unconscious processes; we are not aware that we are being influenced to behave in these ways. They can impose rules on our behaviour which then become so habitual that we are no longer aware of them. They prepare us to interpret the external world in certain predefined ways. For example, if we expect people not to like us we may unconsciously give off the message that we do not want to be approached – and so we inadvertently create the exact situation that we seek to avoid.

Priming and framing are crucial and ongoing influences on our perceptions. Our behaviours shape and are shaped, in large part, by other people, often without us having any idea that it is happening, because such influences operate below our conscious awareness, in our adaptive unconscious.[9] Fear can easily reinforce priming and framing behaviours which can, effectively, become habits within a work context. For instance, we may become *primed* by past experience to avoid speaking up or offering our ideas at work. We may avoid contact with a particular manager because of an historical conflict. Alternatively our expectations of being overlooked for promotion may be *framed* by our previous experiences of rejection. We expect to be passed over again and so we may unconsciously avoid situations where rejection is anticipated or even, perversely, court rejection to prove our theory: 'I knew they wouldn't choose me.' In order to change these patterns, we need to constantly observe our own behaviours and question our interpretations on an ongoing basis, attempting to make the unconscious more conscious and assessing whether or not our behaviours are useful. And if they are not, we need to try to change them.

What implications does this have for organizational life? If we accept that an organization is not just a 'thing', but is also a network of ongoing relationships, then it follows that organizations are susceptible to the same processes of priming, framing and emotional contagion as individuals. While we cling to the view that change results from our conscious choices, as we have seen, the reality is that we are often unaware of our motivations and what triggers our actions. Beliefs and values that we consider to be individual and deep-seated can turn out to be adaptable and our emotions may be so contagious that they can spread like wildfire, drawing individuals in their thrall. Developing greater awareness of our behaviours, attitudes and habits is the route to changing them. When we notice how we behave, we can choose how to be in a work context and out of it.

The importance of emotion in a work environment

We tend to regard emotion as rather woolly, indulgent and somewhat suspect, at least within a work context. However, the research evidence would suggest otherwise. According to the renowned neuroscientist, Antonio Damasio:

> The neurological evidence simply suggests that selective absence of emotion is a problem. Well-targeted and well-deployed emotion seems to be a support system without which the edifice of reason cannot operate properly. These results and their interpretation call into question the idea of dismissing emotion as a luxury or a nuisance or a mere evolutionary vestige. They also make it possible to view emotion as an embodiment of the logic of survival.[10]

So we return once again to question our tendency to make a god of rationality, to elevate reason above other human faculties. However, to understand the bigger picture, we also need to consider complementary forms of knowledge that are acquired through context and practical experience: emotion, intuition and the knowing that is held within our bodies, and that we access without even being aware of it. In Western culture these ways of knowing are often downplayed, if not ignored altogether. We have a wide range of ways in which we can learn and know. Using all our capacities gives us greater knowledge and more flexibility.

In particular, the *belief* that our decisions are purely rational is deeply flawed. Consciousness is simply the tip of the iceberg and all sorts of activities that crucially affect our decision-making go on beneath conscious awareness. Whether or not we are aware of it, emotion, intuition, bodily knowledge and context are key ingredients of decision-making. We rarely appreciate their importance; we often act as if our emotions do not exist while unavoidably employing them in every decision we make. We need to acknowledge the breadth and depth of our personal and emotional input and accept that our experiences are valid inputs to our decision-making. Our feelings are not random or irrelevant. They arise in response to our diverse experiences, our interaction with the world. As such, they are vitally important and, indeed, are the basis for good decision-making, which is as much experiential and emotional as cerebral. What we experience, what we feel – and what others experience and feel – are valid. If we attempt to cut this out, then we revert to literal interpretation, to taking what people say at face value, to missing the nuances. By openly acknowledging the importance of emotion, we broaden the scope of the discussion; it becomes more true to real life and in this way it enables us to gather more relevant knowledge.

However, Damasio is at pains to point out that emotion is not a substitute for reason and emotions should not be allowed to reign unchecked. We tend to dismiss emotion as somehow lowerorder. We talk about *controlling emotion,* having a *rational* conversation, and we criticize those who are overemotional or cannot control themselves. We distrust our emotions because we fear they are unmanageable and we cannot always understand where they come from. Uncontrolled emotion is seen as childlike and unpredictable and we have been taught to distrust what we cannot logically understand or control.

On the other hand, we think of rational, considered thought as being higher-order brain activity, the most effective way of communicating and an aid to effective decision-making. It is regarded as the evolutionary peak of our communication abilities. However, this is simply not true. Damasio's research suggests that too little or too much emotion interferes with rational choice. Too much we can accept, but too little? This seems counter-intuitive in our individualistic, fact-focused culture. It is the balance of conscious reason and emotion that provides balanced decision-making.

According to Damasio, 'emotion assists reason, especially when it comes to personal and social matters involving risk and conflict'. He suggests that emotion helps with the judgement aspects of decision-making. It provides emotional intelligence which helps our reason to operate most effectively. It may seem paradoxical in our society that, in truth, we cannot make rational decisions without emotional input. Nonetheless, being aware of the balance between emotion and reason within organizational contexts provides us with a broader canvas on which to work and it is useful to hone our awareness of these complementary abilities.

Groupthink

The well-documented riots that took place in London in the summer of 2011 sent shockwaves around the world, not least because the disturbances were broadcast in real time on national television. Viewers watched large swathes of London being ransacked and set on fire. Many of the participants in the riots were interviewed, both during the course of the rioting itself and in subsequent days. There were striking similarities in some of the explanations that rioters gave for their behaviour. Many looked puzzled when asked why they did it. They did not seem to know. They just 'got caught up in it'. The microclimate of rioting and the scores of people doing it encouraged them to join in, they claimed. Of course this is not a justification, but it is an interesting phenomenon, perhaps reflecting the need to belong, to be part of something, or to succumb to the emotional pull of acting as one, the primitive lure of the pack. If nothing else, it illustrates the power of contagion, how we can act in ways that undermine our normal values when caught up in an overwhelmingly emotive situation.

In Western culture we generally believe that we are free, independent individuals. We make our own choices. Individual choice is part of the cultural script. However, as we have seen repeatedly, this is largely an illusion. In practice we are herd creatures and much more likely to conform to those around us than to single ourselves out as rebels – unless everybody is a rebel. Most of us, at either a conscious or unconscious level, are fearful of standing out from the crowd. Belief in our individuality is credible – in spite of evidence to the contrary – only because individuality is so written into our sense of who we are that we cannot conceive of it being otherwise.

Back in the early 1970s, the psychologist Irving L Janis wrote *Groupthink*, in which he documented how groups of people make decisions. He used landmark political and social events, such as the attack on Pearl

Harbor, the Cuban Missile Crisis and the escalation of the Vietnam War to illustrate how decision-making processes can be distorted and corrupted by the strong human need to conform. It is quite disconcerting to realize that, for all of us, our beliefs, emotions, attitudes and behaviours are more whimsical and context-driven than we would like to believe.

In essence, groupthink is a phenomenon that may occur within groups of people who have a strong need for harmony or conformity. Alternatively, or in addition, groupthink may arise when groups are cut off from ideas that challenge their existing world view. The pressure to conform within the group can become very strong and result in decisions that, in the cold light of day, prove to be faulty or even catastrophic.

A classic scenario in which groupthink can occur is a jury. Twelve individuals are locked away from outside influence and have to make a joint decision. Extreme religious sects who are not exposed to alternative ways of seeing the world may also succumb to groupthink. One particularly disastrous example where groupthink allegedly played a part occurred on 28 January 1986, when the American Challenger space shuttle was launched and exploded shortly after take-off, killing all the crew on board. The intensive investigation that was carried out in the wake of the disaster revealed that workers were concerned about safety aspects but they were too scared to speak out. They never voiced their concerns for fear that they would be penalized. Challenger took off and within seconds it exploded. Groupthink was not the only reason for the disaster – the Rogers Commission Report attributed failure of the O-rings owing to poor engineering as a main cause – but it was believed to have contributed. Even today there are debates about whether or not this disaster can be attributed, fully or partially, to groupthink.

In organizations today, the same processes of groupthink go on all the time, though generally without such a disastrous consequence. Habits, expectations, comfort zones, not wanting to rock the boat, fear of ridicule, lack of confidence, laziness, boredom, resentment, fear of job loss and so on, all discourage us from stepping out of line and offering a challenging and potentially new perspective on a problem, or a possible solution. As ever, underpinning our reluctance to speak out is fear: fear of being wrong, of standing out, of being ridiculed. It is easier, safer, to huddle together and not step out of line.

Recent research in neuroscience is helping us to understand contagion, which appears to be brought about by mirror neurons in the brain. Apparently, mirror neurons may be part of the processes that enable us to understand the actions of others and also prime us to imitate what we see. It could turn out that mirror neurons are a part of what makes us social beings and, possibly, part of what encourages us to conform to the group, rather than to walk alone.

Psychologists Hatfield, Cacioppo and Rapson have extensively researched emotional contagion and describe contagion as possibly a 'primitive, automatic and unconscious behaviour'. This may be true from a purely rational perspective, but if we consider the breadth, subtlety and influence of this non-verbal behaviour, we can appreciate its invaluable contribution to human communication. For instance, recognizing emotions and acknowledging their origin can be one way to avoid emotional contagion.

A form of groupthink inevitably happens by default, through the ongoing activities of contact, conversation and copying that are part and parcel of all organizational life. Of course agreement is healthy, but it is too easy to agree. Agreement may not bring new thinking. We need to encourage healthy challenge and dissent in organizations and this will only happen when employees feel sufficiently confident to disagree. Instead of conformity, passivity and neutrality, we need divergence. We need people who have had a variety of different experiences, who can look at problems in different ways. Employing people who are mavericks may be uncomfortable, but it helps to reduce complacency. The acceptance of mavericks also encourages other staff to question and reappraise the supposedly self-evident.

In an organizational climate where groupthink and complacency are entrenched, there may need to be activities introduced that are specifically designed to disrupt habitual behaviours, for example short placements in different departments or locations, shadowing other employees, weekly peer group departmental meetings to instigate changes – whatever might work in specific contexts. Ideally these activities would be initiated by employees themselves and they would either be self-reinforcing or involve some benefit to employees. However, these initiatives will not succeed in a climate of fear, in which people are too afraid to challenge or offer a different perspective. It may take time, practice and a genuine desire on the part of all employees to create a more open culture that fosters shared learning.

To think differently, to challenge the obvious, to experiment and take risks, to bring in speakers who introduce different ideas are just some of the ways in which we can undermine the power of groupthink and this is most likely to happen within work cultures that foster new thinking.

In conclusion

In this chapter I have attempted to explore some of the diverse ways in which we are human. Of course there are very many aspects of humanity that we have not even touched upon. However, my primary aim in this whirlwind trip was to remind ourselves of how complex, paradoxical, ingenious, ever-changing, creative and fascinating human beings are. It is all too easy in an increasingly technological world to take for granted or discard human abilities, senses, ways of thinking and values. They are so familiar that we no longer see them. Equally, technology is providing us with untold possibilities and I am not in any sense disparaging the huge current and future benefits it offers. Our biggest challenge in years to come may well lie in working out how we can maximize and integrate the benefits of technology alongside human skills, without destroying the uniqueness of each. Humans are blessed with a huge spectrum of abilities that we have not yet fully understood or fully utilized. Rather than diminishing these abilities, as we have too often done within organizations that prioritize a mechanistic approach, we need to work out how best to optimize human skills within a technological world.

Notes

1 Rogers, C (1961) *On Becoming a Person*, Houghton Mifflin

2 Maslow, A (1954) *Motivation and Personality*, Pearson

3 Nowak, M A, Why We Help, What makes us human, *Scientific American, Special Collector's Edition*, **22** (1), Winter 2013

4 Talk given by Larry Page at the 2007 American Association for the Advancement of Science Conference

5 Lanier, J (2011) *You Are Not a Gadget: A manifesto*, Penguin

6 Idries Shah (1943) *Fables in the Sufi Tradition*, Penguin Books

7 Phil McKinney blog, November 25 2013 [online] http://philmckinney.com/archives/2013/11/creative-concepts-the-invisible-bicycle-helmet-blends-science-and-human-nature.html

8 Schneider, A (June 27 2013), Technology vs humanity – still no contest, *Geektime* [online] www.geektime.com/2013/06/27/technology-vs-humanity-till-no-contest/

9 Wilson, T (2002) *Strangers to Ourselves: Discovering the adaptive unconscious*, Harvard University Press

10 Damasio, A (2000) *The Feeling of What Happens: Body, emotion and the making of consciousness*, Vintage

Creating psychologically healthy workplaces

09

> *I am not what happens to me. I am what I choose to become.* **CARL JUNG**

Creating healthier futures

In this chapter we move on to explore how we might harness our energies in constructive ways in order to create working environments that are uplifting and energizing; that make us want to get up and go to work in the morning because it is such a great place to be and is full of people that we enjoy working with. I know this may be an ideal for some people, but until we can begin to imagine work as a place where we are engaged and challenged, where we can grow and enjoy working with colleagues, we have no road map. If we know what we want from our working life, we can try to create it. Or maybe we can decide that it is time to find work – or perhaps a working environment – that is more satisfying.

Leadership consultant Margie Warrell in her book *Stop Playing Safe*[1] stresses the importance of creating a 'culture of courage' as an antidote to fear and as a means of emboldening employees to rise above their fears. This, she believes, will create and sustain a competitive advantage. Given the consistent messages of workforce disengagement from a range of different employee studies, organizations clearly need leaders who not only engage employees but move them to think more daringly, to take smarter risks and to challenge the very assumptions that may have underpinned their success to date.

Why organizational health matters

I am using the term 'organizational health' rather loosely to mean a workplace environment in which people in the main and most of the time feel at ease; a place where they are engaged in their work and where they feel appropriately challenged. By this I mean that they might have a tough job to do but they generally approach it with relish, determination and feel a sense of real satisfaction when they achieve their goals. They feel supported by their peers and managers and they are able speak out without sanction. In this type of environment, people typically feel they can grow and flourish, that they are achieving something worthwhile and can be proud of their achievements. While fear may be an element in this environment, it ebbs and flows, sometimes acting as a positive stimulant, sometimes unpleasant but transient. Most importantly, fear does not dominate the workplace.

Why does organizational health matter? Well, having read through this book so far – and possibly having experienced a workplace that is unhealthy – you may be aware of the effects of toxic workplaces. At the most basic level, organizational health is a human right. How can it be acceptable to deliberately create fear in the workplace, or not try to prevent or reduce it where it does occur? By fear I do not necessarily mean intimidation, harassment or the threat of violence. This can happen, but more likely fear is the result of a low-level, persistent culture of implied sanctions and veiled threats. Somehow, behaviour that would never be tolerated in the outside world has become, if not acceptable, then tolerated within many organizational contexts. It is as if, in an era in which jobs are hard to get and redundancy a real possibility for many employees, the gloves come off and some staff feel that bullying is an acceptable way to behave. This is the backdrop to many contemporary organizations. What hope have we of creating a psychologically healthy workplace within this context? We will not achieve healthy and productive workplaces simply by upping controls, by driving employees to work harder or by imposing mechanistic targets that beat employees down and encourage them to find ways to ingeniously circumnavigate those targets. We are more likely to succeed by cooperation and mutual support across the organization.

We are talking here about re-humanizing the workplace; treating employees as human beings rather than just resources to be milked; thinking about and talking with groups of employees within different departments or groups to establish how best they can contribute, rather than defaulting to off-the-peg solutions. It is about building a shared purpose in which employees can feel confident to challenge their own and each other's assumptions, and where constructive feedback is accepted as part of learning.

Engagement and return on investment

Work engagement represents the extent to which an individual, a team or indeed an organization as a whole is committed to their work; that is, the extent to which they display a range of characteristics including: being energetic, mental resilience, dedication, proactivity, taking initiative, persistence in the face of difficulties, pride, rising to challenges and being happily engrossed in their work. This cluster of attributes is often summed up in the colloquial phrase 'being willing to go the extra mile'. In an ideal world we would feel engaged in our work all of the time, but life is not so obliging. Nonetheless, most of us would consider engagement at work to be a high priority.

It is easy to dismiss the concept of engagement as idealistic: an attempt to create a happier workforce. However, there is overwhelming research evidence to support the view that having employees who feel *engaged* and *involved* is likely to result in more successful organizations.[2] So what makes employees more engaged at work? Well, it isn't necessarily rocket science. If employees are provided with adequate resources to do their job, then engagement increases. No surprise there, you might think, but in a longitudinal study among 2,555 Finnish dentists, researchers found that job resources lead to greater work engagement, which in turn influences levels of personal initiative and work-unit innovation. Jari Hakanen and his colleagues suggest that organizations arrange working conditions with sufficiently motivating and energizing resources, on the basis that 'positive strengths in work life may cluster together, resulting in resource gains and upward spirals in individual employees as well as in their work communities'.[3]

We can obtain good estimates of employee engagement over time and there is evidence that engaged workers are characterized by low levels of burnout and neuroticism, and high levels of extroversion.[4] This isn't surprising. We only have to consider our own behaviour. A task that we enjoy doing is more likely to be achieved successfully than one which we take on reluctantly, resentfully and with no joy. This is simply a fact of human nature.

However, feel-good factors are not enough. If employee engagement is to be taken seriously in the boardroom, we need to be able to demonstrate its value through return on investment. No one would seriously argue against the notion of greater engagement of employees in the daily running of the organization – or indeed reinforcing its long-term goals. Nowadays, more than ever, employee engagement is assumed to be part of any company's key performance indicators and is likely to be tied in to decisions that affect return on investment. A well-aligned workforce results in a better bottom line on virtually all performance indicators. It also means comparatively better share performance. Clearly employee engagement matters and it is increasingly valued as a performance indicator.[5]

How return on investment can be measured and optimized

The science of measuring and following up on employee engagement has evolved over three decades, but it is still treated with some scepticism. In part this is due to insecurity about what the data will reveal and, indeed, what to do with it, particularly if it reveals a negative picture. When in doubt, it is often easier simply to sit on the data. However, according to the Hay group, a global management consultancy, the benefits of real engagement are increasingly being recognized, with even minor improvements bringing measurable, often significant, improvements in business outcomes. A highly engaged and resilient workforce can more easily weather the inevitable storms of organizational life. Indeed, the share performance curve of organizations with highly engaged employees is, according to Hay, generally smoother and moves in an upward direction compared to that of organizations with poor engagement.[6]

'I am not a human resource; I am a human being'

At the launch of a UK government-backed movement, Engage for Success in November 2012, a powerful video was shown. In it, a young man rails to the camera about how organizations in the UK should 'give employees a voice' and create a place where people want to shine. 'I am not a human resource; I am a human being,' he insists. The expression has caught on, says David MacLeod, co-founder of the Engage for Success movement. 'It all comes back to "four pillars"; strategic narrative, engaging managers, employee voice and organizational integrity.' These pillars (or enablers) were first identified by MacLeod and his co-founder at 'Engage for Success', Nita Clarke, some five years ago, when they were asked to produce a research paper on the importance of engagement to the UK economy. The paper subsequently evolved into a book, *Engaging for Success*[7] and the original report led to the creation of the Engage for Success taskforce. This was backed by the Department for Business, Innovation and Skills, which spearheaded a movement to bring together the experience of leading practitioners, the ideas and research of leading academics and the findings of think tanks to share learning, ideas and practical guidance on employee engagement.

Since its launch, the movement has taken on a life of its own, with more than a thousand people from hundreds of organizations becoming involved. 'We are not trying to write another book on engagement,' says MacLeod. 'We are trying to get insights from people to help others address things in simple, easy-to-harness ways.' However, Engage for Success has still much to do, especially within the corridors of power. 'The Treasury, for instance, needs to understand that engagement is a vital component of growth. If only a third of people in the UK workforce are engaged, then two-thirds are not giving their best . . . this is a vital topic for the country,' says MacLeod. 'Organizations are either going to emerge from the recession on their knees or in their running shoes. When things get better, people are either going to think, "I'm out of here," or they are going to think, "I'm looking forward to getting this organization back up and growing again."'

Improving engagement seems a no-brainer, so what stops organizations from embracing its principles, especially, as MacLeod puts it, 'If you are not trying to improve engagement, you might as well be standing on top of a building chucking money away'? Partly it's inertia, partly it is because, as MacLeod says, 'It isn't easy to do in a transformational way . . . when organizations start thinking about engagement, it can open up a Pandora's box and it throws up other internal challenges, such as silo working. Developing engagement needs to be expertly handled.' MacLeod claims that 70 per cent of employees are neutral or do not trust their bosses, which makes the task challenging, to say the least. He sums up four ways of improving business: great customer service, innovating, finding cheaper ways to do things and entering new markets. That, he says, 'needs trust, lack of hierarchies and less deference'. MacLeod has thrown down the gauntlet.[8]

Psychological health, happiness and productivity

Creating a psychologically healthy workplace is not just an altruistic exercise. If we are happy in our work, we work more effectively. This is pretty self-evident. It is also backed up by a considerable body of research that points to the importance of work as a factor influencing our state of happiness. The economist and happiness guru Richard Layard has isolated the 'Big seven factors affecting happiness'.[9]

> ## Big seven factors affecting happiness
>
> (The first five are given in order of importance)
>
> - Family relationships
> - Financial situation
> - Work
> - Community and friends
> - Health
> - Personal freedom
> - Personal values

Work comes third in the rankings of factors that affect happiness. We need family relations and a reasonably secure financial situation, but after that we need *work* (however we define this) to make us happy. Indeed, work is rated as more important than community and friends and even health, so it is clear that for most of us work is a hugely important factor in making us feel happy and fulfilled. Way back in Ancient Greece, Galen wrote that 'employment is nature's physician' and, when Freud was asked what a normal person should be able to do well, he is reputed to have said, 'Love and work',[10] so this is not a new phenomenon.

Just think about the implications. It is clear that, for most of us, work is an essential component of our sense of well-being. However, at the same time, study after study in recent years has delivered a similar picture: employees are unhappier at work than they have ever been since we started to record such data. As a society, this is a dangerous position in which to find ourselves. It is also dangerous in terms of organizational life, the mental health of employees as well as the level of productivity within organizations. Unhappy employees underperform, as we saw in Chapters 4 and 5 and, as a consequence, productivity falls. How can we stem unhappiness at work and start to reverse this situation?

We are intrinsically social beings and most of us need to feel that we are contributing to society in some way. Going to work– or working from home – is part and parcel of our sense of who we are, what we contribute and what we achieve. Being out of work or unemployed reduces not only our income but also our sense of self. As Richard Layard puts it:

> ... unemployment is such a disaster: it reduces income but it also reduces happiness directly by destroying self-respect and social relationships created by work. When people become unemployed, their happiness falls much less because of the loss of income than because of the loss of work itself. Economists almost always ignore this reality, and some even allege that the extra leisure must be a benefit to the unemployed ... unemployment is a very special problem. Moreover it hurts as much after one or two years as it does at the beginning.[11]

In this sense, you do not habituate to being out of work, and even when you are back at work, you still feel the effects as a psychological scar.

Even when in work, people fear unemployment and when unemployment levels rise it has a major impact on the happiness of everybody, including those in work. Consequently, with a rise in unemployment, not only are a greater number of people unemployed but there is greater anxiety among the employed. Layard concludes:

> Work is vital, if that is what you want. But it is also important that the work be fulfilling. Perhaps the most important issue is the extent to which you have control over what you do. There is a creative spark in each of us, and if it finds no outlet, we feel half dead. This can be literally true: among British civil servants of any given grade, those who do the most routine work experience the most rapid clogging of the arteries.[12]

Nonetheless, human beings can also have quite miraculous powers of recovery and, with a bit of love and attention, we too can bloom. As the psychologist Jonathan Haidt points out in *The Happiness Hypothesis*, there are a number of parallels between humans and plants in terms of our abilities to rejuvenate:

> I was not a very good gardener and I travelled a lot in the summers, so sometimes my plants withered and nearly died. But the amazing thing I learnt about plants is that, as long as they are not completely dead, they will spring back to full and glorious life if you just get the conditions right. You can't fix a plant; you can only give it the right ingredients – water, sun, soil – and then wait. It will do the rest.[13]

In this way, humans are similar to plants. There is an inbuilt drive to restore and grow. When the psychologist Harry Harlow took his students to the zoo, they were surprised to find that apes and monkeys would solve problems just for the fun of it. Harlow had noticed that animals, as well as people, have a basic drive to *make things happen*. We are hard-wired to make, do and create. Having and pursuing goals are part of being human and, for most of us, work is one of the most important arenas in which, at best, we find fulfilment. Even in organizations where cynicism and despair are rife, the human spirit can often be rejuvenated if employees believe that genuine and ongoing change is possible.

A Western perspective on a Japanese workplace

We have mainly focused on a Western perspective of the workplace; to cover different cultures in any depth is outside the scope of this book. However, as we saw from the extensive workplace studies covered in Chapter 4, there is a high degree of similarity in attitudes and behaviours across many different cultures. Even where the cultural differences are quite extreme, there are particular learnings which can be migrated to our own workplaces.

My name is Simon. I am British and I have been working for a large Japanese company for the last five years. I spend about six months a year in Japan. The company has 190,000 employees distributed around the world, although wherever the offices are located, the company does business there with other JOCs (Japanese Originated Companies). Even now I am still absorbing the culture and I find myself phoning a Japanese friend, asking her to give me some meaning for some of the things that are happening. Here are some of the things that have surprised or fascinated me.

All of the big companies have massive intakes all at the same time of year (spring). So you see loads of identically dressed young men and women moving around a bit like starlings at dawn. At this point in their career they are likely also to have the same work bag, shoes, everything. Anything the 'boss' says seems to be met with great humour. This tradition goes up right through the schools when the New Year seems to take on even more meaning than it does in our culture. Remember also that they could be joining the company for life. So I sit here now looking across an open-plan floor of about 100 people who would all know and respect where each other sits in the hierarchy. As a 'year 3' person you know exactly what you should be doing and the likely chance of movement up (or not) to become a manager.

The office day starts here at 08.20 – that's when you must be in, and if I (as an outsider) want to create a good impression I should be in before then. Lunch for this floor is from 11.30–12.30 and that's when we all go. The floor is deserted and lights go out. It is a very deep ritual that virtually never gets interrupted and you would not dream of setting up a meeting during that time.

Meetings are an interesting thing. It is very much 'line of sight' working and if you are not in or at your desk you are probably not working! In the 'West', if there were 10 things you needed to talk with someone about at an internal business meeting you'd store them up and have an agenda. Here you might well have 10 meetings about those 10 things – fascinating.

Lifts are a good illustration of how protocol and respect operate, with people standing in identical clothes, adopting identical postures.

Salarymen are a real phenomenon. Busy by day and working late, not wanting to leave before the boss, sometimes sleeping in the office, and then raucous in the evening where you might literally step over one of your colleagues on the pavement, a bit worse for wear. But it's the time that you are allowed to let your hair down; smoke, sing and drink sake.

I see no sign of anyone cutting across convention or hierarchy in the workplace. You know your lot and 'put up or shut up' – but this is not a phrase the Japanese would use.

I have spoken with some of my colleagues in confidence; some of them are happy to talk. I am interested in finding out their aspirations and how they view their role in the organization, especially in the long term. My understanding is superficial, I know, but it seems that they are quite accepting, as if they feel they cannot change their path. They hope that the next reorganization will take them to where they want to, or feel they should, be. Expectations here are very different from those I have experienced in my own culture. There is less individuality expressed, more acceptance. The recent reorganization here ran to over 60 pages and was the source of massive interest as, not surprisingly, everyone wanted to know where they'd go. Some things are universal. Are Japanese workers happy with their lot? I can't say – I think much of it is bottled up! I am sure only a very small percentage ever leave jobs without somewhere to go. It amazes me how different working cultures can be.

In terms of working practices, Japan and Western Europe are extremes, and it is illuminating to consider the differences between them. In Japan a job for life, knowing your place in the hierarchy, clearly defined expectations and responsibilities are the norm. In much of Western Europe, the norm is increasingly self-sufficiency, risk of redundancy, autonomous working and a precarious future. Human beings are very adaptable; it is why we are so successful as a species. However, at least in the West, we may be reaching the limits of our adaptability: a place where uncertainty becomes unbearable.

Bhutan, work and well-being

Those of us who have been reared in Western-influenced societies – and many who have not – are familiar with the consumerist model: the lure of acquisition and how status is often judged in terms of wealth. We take it for granted. However, there are some societies that prioritize happiness or well-being over acquisition, and there is much to be learnt from them. Bhutan is one such example. It is a tiny Himalayan kingdom of about 600,000 people, sandwiched between two giants, China to the north and India to the south, and virtually isolated from the rest of the world until the 1960s. For many years it was ruled by King Jigme Wangchuck, a greatly loved monarch, who came to the throne as a teenager in 1972 and abdicated in favour of his son in 2006. Over time, the king moved Bhutan from a medieval backwater towards the 21st century, although it is still ranked as one of the poorest countries in the world.

Most countries measure their success in terms of gross national product (GNP). Bhutan is different. It has a philosophy of gross national happiness (GNH), developed by His Majesty the King, since he came to the throne. This philosophy has directed government policy, including educational, economic and ecological development, for more than 30 years. Bhutan's philosophy celebrates happiness as the goal of every sentient being and starts from the principle that GNH is more important than GNP. Although it is acknowledged that economic growth is important, this is always tempered by the development principles of gross national happiness.

In 2006 I visited Bhutan as part of a research project on happiness and well-being. It is a stunning, quixotic country that leaves you breathless and disorientated. The men wear smart tartan tunics and the young monks are dressed in burgundy robes and sandals although, like teenagers the world over, many of them are glued to their mobile phones. It came as a surprise to discover that the national sport in Bhutan is archery. The Bhutanese are excellent archers and, as you travel through the country, you come across the most wonderful sight of archery competitions. Bhutanese men, their tartan skirts flowing, aim with frightening precision at the bull's eye, and all of it couched in the dramatic scenery of sheer cliffs, gold-layered temples and elaborate monasteries perched on impossibly steep mountaintops.

My first interview was with the then prime minister, His Excellency Jigme Thinley. He is a delightful, interesting, pragmatic and worldly man, who is both very well informed about the outside world and also totally committed to ensuring that Bhutan will develop in ways that maintain and strengthen its cultural values. In his view, the global economic crisis of 2008–9 was based on insatiable human greed. As His Excellency explained:

> There is a glimmer of hope that we will pursue happiness collectively as a human race and in so doing, we will enjoy greater stability and peace. A country, a people, a community that is pursuing happiness cannot be belligerent, cannot want to possess what their neighbours have. Happiness is to do with sharing and the wonderful thing about happiness is, you know, sharing gives joy. It's amazing. Happiness is infectious. And it is compassionate. Its base is founded on compassion. You feel care for others and it grows with sharing.
>
> (His Excellency, Minister Jigme Thinley, 12 September 2006)

Bhutan is such an intriguing country. On the one hand, it is about as far as you can get from Western lifestyles and values. On the other hand, its leaders are thinking about and addressing issues such as creating healthy societies, life–work balance and sustainable development in ways that the West is only beginning to grasp or, more accurately, that the West is only recently willing to think about. In Bhutan, decisions on development and growth are examined in the wider context of human values, and decisions are made in the context of the Bhutanese 'four pillars': equitable and sustainable development, preservation and promotion of cultural values, conservation of the natural environment and the establishment of good governance.

It is interesting that both His Excellency Jigme Thinley and David McLeod have come up with the notion of four pillars of success within organizations and indeed society in general. Although each camp approaches the issues from a different perspective, they each emphasize the importance of cultural values, good governance, engagement and productivity.

Constancy and change

To the Western eye there are many paradoxes within Bhutan. For example, I found it difficult to grasp how Bhutan has a very strong attachment to tradition and an equally strong attachment to change. In the West there would be two camps; the traditionalists and the radicals (by whatever names) and they would probably be fighting one another. But in Bhutan there is no obvious 'taking sides' or conflict. Chime Paden, the secretary general of the Tarayana Foundation, explained this apparent lack of conflict to me:

> We are taught from toddlers about the impermanence of everything. We are taught that change is the only thing that is permanent. You have to constantly change. Everything is changing. Who you are now is different from who you were 24 hours ago, because you have accumulated information, your total processes have moved on. It is a guiding philosophy.

I found this explanation intriguing. In the West we easily become locked into our opinions and beliefs, as if letting go of them may fracture our very sense of self. Either/or mentality prevails and we treat the world as a collection of disjointed and fixed things; objects, thoughts, beliefs and so on. The late Alan Watts, an expert on Zen Buddhism and a prolific writer, challenged this staccato way of viewing the world. In his wonderfully named *The Book on the Taboo of Knowing Who You Are*,[14] he states:

> A scanning process that observes the world bit by bit soon persuades its user that the world is a great collection of bits and these he calls separate things or events. We often say that you can only look at one thing at a time. The truth is that in looking at the world bit by bit, we convince ourselves that it consists of separate things . . . we also speak of attention as noticing. To notice is to select, to regard some bits of perception or some feature of the world as more noteworthy, more significant than others. To these we attend and others we ignore.

For Chime Paden, it was quite natural to hold two or more seemingly conflicting views simultaneously and for these views to be constantly evolving. In the West we prefer our thoughts to be more regimented. In fact, we even have a specific psychological theory – cognitive dissonance theory – which explains such conflict as the excessive mental stress and discomfort experienced when an individual holds two or more contradictory beliefs, ideas or values at the same time.

In a Western workplace, this notion of ideas and beliefs as transient truths could offer a very liberating perspective and, indeed, it glides rather nicely into some contemporary Western approaches to organizational change as processes of emergence.[15]

Social cohesion

In Bhutan, individuals are more interdependent; family and community bonds are very strong, with established, reciprocal and shared responsibilities within communities. This interdependence builds strong psychological resilience within communities, in sharp contrast to the West where we tend to emphasize individuality more strongly; as a result, we appear to be afflicted, to a greater degree, with loneliness and isolation.

As Chime Paden explained:

> Family ties are binding. Social controls are strong but so is social support. You *do* feel that the child is not just raised by you but is raised by everyone around you – because if you think you are the only one they [children] are answerable to, then God help you! Here, children know they are accountable to the whole community.

This sense of mutual support and responsibility has, to a large extent, been lost in Western cultures and organizations. Arguably, in Western thinking we tend to overestimate the importance of the individual and underestimate the importance of the community or organization. Within many organizations there is a need to rebuild mutual reciprocity and strengthen the bonds between individuals and between individuals and groups in organizations. In doing so, we strengthen the power of the group.

The Happiness agenda

His Excellency, Prime Minister Jigme Thinley, described the GNH agenda which was translated into four pillars; sustainable development, preservation and promotion of cultural values, conservation of the natural environment and, as an overriding aim, good governance. Essentially, the prime minister and his team viewed economic growth as one strand in the development of a happy and fulfilled society; a means to an end, not an end in itself. The policy is not just a vision. Bhutan has achieved remarkable results across the board in terms of its cultural, ecological, educational and development aims, including social infrastructure, roads, supplying electricity, telecoms across treacherous terrains and life expectancy. The prime minister is modest about Bhutan's achievements and stresses the work still to be done. However, it is an impressive journey so far.

Measuring happiness

In the West, we tend to the view that what cannot be measured has little value. Why else would we spend so much of our time attempting to measure such ephemeral concepts as happiness? Jigme Thinley was sceptical about the possibility or necessity of measuring levels of happiness through quantitative measures:

> There are those who feel that this is something that is best left without any attempts to measure, and when one does so one could make the mistake of measuring aspects that may not represent happiness in its entirety and therefore be pursuing wrong goals and objectives. We have done this with respect to GNH for all these years. What can't be measured and what is ignored may turn out to be the most important, but nevertheless, internationally, globally, there is a very strong feeling that anything that cannot be measured cannot be pursued or is not worth pursuing, and particularly if resources are going to be spent on pursuing it, then how does one justify presenting any sort of achievement against these measures?
>
> (His Excellency, Prime Minister Jigme Thinley, 12 September 2006)

It is interesting that the different perspectives between East and West (put very crudely), in terms of how each understands happiness or psychological health, may not be so much about culture or country or even philosophy. Perhaps it is more specific than this. It may boil down to the age-old qualitative–quantitative debate; the clash between a quantitative way of seeing the world (numbers, percentages, units) and a qualitative way of seeing it (meaning, emotion, context, fluidity).[16]

This is one of the most long-running and intransigent hurdles that organizations in the Western world have to address. Pitting qualitative and quantitative understanding, the one against the other, is futile. They are chalk and cheese. Both are useful. But they are different. More importantly, using quantitative data when qualitative is needed is more than futile and can be lethal, as we discussed in Chapter 6. Chime Paden sums up the essence of GNH as follows:

> At the end of the day, GNH is another name for enlightened governance, keeping in mind the needs of individuals and communities to lead healthy, productive and harmonious lives. It is the constant awareness that win–win situations are preferable to the win–lose equation that is the norm in a GDP society. It is the sincere commitment to ensure that future generations are not compromised by the greedy lifestyles of today, where consuming for the sake of consumption is

leading to unsustainable utilization of our resources. Bhutan's collective merit brought us visionary kings, who have gifted us this precious concept of GNH, an enlightened developmental path to proudly call our own.[17]

Bhutan, in spite of its modest standing on the world stage, is developing interesting approaches to psychological health and sustainable development. These approaches may also provide us with very useful steers in terms of our own understanding of the elements that contribute to psychological health in general and particularly within the workplace.

The qualitative–quantitative divide

What do we mean by 'qualitative' and 'quantitative'? Essentially these are different ways of understanding the world, although nowadays they are most commonly associated with different approaches to market research.

In essence, a *qualitative* perspective is about exploring how people make sense of the world. We start with an attempt to understand the world as the person or people involved experience it, gaining some knowledge of what is important to them and the context within which they are operating. We might well ask questions such as 'How do you feel about . . .' and 'What does this mean to you?' Essentially the approach is open-ended and fluid. A qualitative conversation is likely to meander, with the participants moving back and forth across topics in an improvisational manner. Ultimately qualitative perspectives seek connection, interpretation and understanding. Individuals with a qualitative bias will typically gauge information they receive in terms of what 'feels right' in light of their past experiences.

A *quantitative* perspective will be more structured and analytical and is likely to include numerical data, as this is believed to be more reliable than qualitative data. It is likely to be focused, and will seek to define, count and capture. Quantitative perspectives on the world tend to seek certainty or at least tangible replicable truths. Questions are more likely to try to tap into rational, more surface beliefs, attitudes and behaviours and to favour statistical and numerical data over opinion or judgement. An individual who has a quantitative bias will tend to distance themselves from the data, as a way of objectifying and evaluating it as a fixed entity.

The differences between the two modes may seem theoretical or even irrelevant to our understanding of organizations and psychological health. However, in practice, the qualitative–quantitative divide permeates all aspects of organizational life. It may be so taken for granted that it is invisible, but it shapes almost every decision and every practice we engage upon.[18] In the ideal world, qualitative and quantitative understandings would be used according to what mode is more appropriate for the task. For instance, when measuring the dimensions of a room, a quantitative approach is probably more useful. When planning the layout and colour scheme for the room, a qualitative approach makes more sense. Most important, if the qualitative and quantitative weightings get out of balance, then we can have a distorted view of the world.

In Chapter 6 we talked about the strong emphasis on measurement, control, compliance and other targets within organizational life. These constraints bias organizational practices, decision-making and initiatives towards the quantitative end of the spectrum. As a result, they encourage a mindset that is linear, literal and mechanistic and we move into territory in which meeting the target is the aim, rather than the targets simply acting as a signpost. We have seen, not least in the Mid Staffordshire NHS Trust, how destructive this can be. This mindset is in sharp contrast to the way in which His Excellency Jigme Thinley spoke implicitly about measurement:

> There are those who feel that this is something that is best left without any attempts to measure . . . one could make the mistake of measuring aspects that may not represent happiness . . . and therefore be pursuing wrong goals and objectives . . .

In essence, keeping qualitative and quantitative perspectives roughly in balance is critically important if we want to sustain a healthy organizational life; we need that breadth of experience. In particular, the qualitative perspective ensures that we maintain creativity, improvisation, imagination, experimentation and the sheer joy of doing a job well. Whilst both qualitative and quantitative perspectives are important, organizational life has veered too much towards the quantitative. We need to shift the balance more towards the qualitative. Quantitative diehards will argue that these soft values are insubstantial. I wouldn't call them soft. I'd call them subtle.

Fresh approaches to organizational life

A minority of large organizations have developed alternative ways of working in order to foster a psychologically healthy workplace. Famously, Google developed its organization in line with its strapline 'Don't be evil,' and the company is often lauded for the way it treats its employees. For instance, the staff are encouraged to spend 20 per cent of their time on exploratory research. Google Maps and gmail emerged from this initiative. *Fortune* magazine ranked Google at the top of its list of the best companies to work for in 2013, for the fourth time. Perhaps in part this is because Google's corporate vision includes such axioms as 'You can be serious without a suit.'

As the then CEO, Eric Schmidt, put it:

> The goal is to strip away everything that gets in our employees' way. We provide a standard package of fringe benefits, but on top of that are first-class dining facilities, gyms, laundry rooms, massage rooms, haircuts, carwashes, dry cleaning, commuting buses – just about anything a hardworking employee might want. Let's face it, programmers want to program, they don't want to do their laundry. So we make it easy for them to do both.

Employee perks are the envy of many a non-Google employee. In the office employees get around on Segway and Razor scooters and, more recently, custom bicycles. But for the longer morning commute from home they are offered free bus rides to the main Mountain View office. 'We are basically running a small municipal transit agency,' said Google's director of security and safety. The buses feature bike racks and leather seats, internet access, and allow pets on board. For nearly a quarter of Google's home office staff, this transportation keeps them from having to spend hours in the Silicon Valley traffic.

An organization will not develop towards psychological health without intent; it needs thought, effort and investment, especially by the leaders, who create the culture through their actions, although inevitably this culture spreads and evolves over time. Google was a vision made real. Regardless of the size or nature of the organization, leaders can choose to create a psychologically healthy workplace – or not.

Developing employee engagement and well-being

The FTSE 100 public report 'Employee engagement and well-being',[19] which is jointly funded by Business in the Community, BUPA and Towers Watson, summarizes some of the initiatives in employee health and well-being within large organizations over the last year. The findings illustrate that 'what gets measured gets managed'. The authors stress the importance of highlighting need, raising awareness and embedding best practice through public reporting. However, this feedback highlights the lack of reporting on psychological health and sporadic reporting on mental health support, although this is changing and there is growing awareness of employee health as an investment.

For example, Cavill Associates and the University of Salford recently released a report highlighting best practice in promoting employee health and well-being in the City of London.[20] The research looked at the range of workplace health and well-being interventions that organizations are using to retain their competitive advantage in a challenging economic environment, and it provides recommendations for the future.

GSK initiative

Similarly, GSK had set up an initiative with the aim of enabling employees to be healthy and high-performing at work and home. A combination of consultations, workshops and cultural support on energy and resilience was initiated, with significant results. Ninety per cent of employees who completed the Energy for Performance programme reported increases in energy and well-being 12 months afterwards. Eighty per cent said that their performance at work had improved up to three years after completing the training and participants were more likely to make improvements in their lifestyle, especially diet, and to report that they were in excellent health.

BT well-being initiative

Similarly BT initiated a project with the aim of creating an interdependence mindset among employees in which they take personal responsibility for their well-being and for that of those around them. Specialist employee support services were implemented. This included faster access to appropriate services for employees, enabling them to remain in work or return to work, and developing a culture of self-help among the company's workforce and managers, with support available from experts. To shift mindsets, BT has instigated a number of forums and a community of health, safety and well-being champions and business leads, working in association with the group advisor, a clinical psychologist.

The total cost associated with workplace injuries and ill health in Great Britain in 2010–11 was some £13.8 billion, so this makes it good financial as well as good health sense for employers to give more attention to employee health.

A time to think differently about organizations

Many of us have experienced organizational initiatives that have attempted to rejuvenate organizations through large-scale change management programmes. Typically they are implemented by outside consultants, and change is imposed through top-down initiatives. These programmes have had variable degrees of success in creating long-term or ongoing changes in organizational culture, and they have sometimes provoked resistance and cynicism from within the workforce. This is especially true when employees have lived through several earlier change programmes and believe that these initiatives have caused upheaval, were expensive and did not live up to their promises. One employee described it as 'Here we go again. Upheaval, hassle, lots of pep talks and six months later we are back where we started.'

The assumption that behaviour patterns within organizations can be changed quickly and efficiently through logical intervention without the active participation of employees is, at best, naive, as many organizations have discovered to their cost. Indeed, change programmes of this type can seem increasingly out of step with contemporary organizational life and the ways in which many large organizations now operate, with faster, multimedia communications, multiple sources of data, dispersed locations, mobile staff and so on. Indeed, contemporary organizations can more accurately be viewed as complex, fluid interconnected systems rather than the traditional 'buildings where we work'.

In hierarchical organizations, there is the implicit model of superiority at the top of the organization and inferiority at the bottom. Historically this differential was clearly reinforced, for example with special canteens or parking bays for managers. Status is now more subtle, although in many organizations hierarchy is still very much alive and well, even as it is concealed. Of course hierarchies are not the only structures that exist within organizations. There are teams made up of individuals with complementary skills, departmental specialisms, marketing, finance, HR and so on; all the visible, acknowledged aspects of the organization.

The shadows

At the same time, we have the shadows, which exist within all organizations. The shadows are where employees share rumours, gossip, anger, joy, fears and anxieties. Conversations are at least partially illicit, involving contentious or emotionally charged content. We catch other people's behaviours and feelings in the shadows, as they catch ours, and we share our ideas with people we trust. Managers and those who cannot be trusted are generally excluded. This sort of talk is sometimes subversive but it can also be constructive and fertile, especially where employees feel frustrated because they believe that work practices can be improved but they feel that they have no forum to discuss their ideas or put them into practice. Harnessing or tapping into the power of the shadow organization can enable employees to develop, capture or seed new ideas, in particularly where these are relevant to their particular work area.

Meanwhile, managers are often nervous of the shadows; they are beyond their sphere of control and the assumption is that they house subversive elements. To a degree, the managers are probably right. The shadows can be subversive, but they can also be constructive. Where staff can shed their suspicions and share ideas across departments or hierarchies, the shadows can lead to constructive change. They may enable employees to do something useful with their ideas and to offer the opportunity for grass-roots development, feeding in to a psychologically healthy workplace.

Hive connections

By bringing the shadows into the light we can consider the hive, the parallel network that exists alongside traditional communications, although we don't usually view it in this way. In practice we are all familiar with the hive, the informal network of communications that links employees so that directly or indirectly every individual both influences and is being influenced by others within the organization *at the same time and all the time.* Sometimes this influence occurs in a conscious way, as when we discuss a work brief with a colleague, but it can also happen without our conscious awareness, through influence, contagion and by mirroring the behaviour of our workmates. The hive embodies the network of shared values, practices and norms that we call organizational culture. Culture is not 'out there', separate from us. We, and the ways in which we interact, work and create things together with others *are* the organization. Take the people out of the organization and what do you have? You have a building, not an organization.

Every employee, regardless of job, seniority or tenure, has an influence – for better or worse – on other employees they have contact with. It is how human being *are* together, mutually influencing their co-workers is an ongoing process. Viewed in this way, all employees are not only co-contributors to the health, productivity and prosperity of the whole organization. They *are* the organization.

Richard Seel, an organizational change consultant, summarizes the differences between a traditional command-and-control approach in organizations and a *hive* or emergent approach. While it is never a situation of either/or, some organizations tend to emphasize the command-and-control model and others tend to emphasize the hive model. Both models are outlined in Table 9.1.

At best, the hive model encourages greater flexibility in working relationships because employees have more freedom to consult with other employees without being overburdened by hierarchy. This encourages greater initiative. When we are able to vary the worlds in which we live, we can transform the ways in which we behave. A hive approach encourages employees to learn from each other, to take initiatives, to experiment. Doing so helps to foster more initiative in a workforce and greater innovation. It also helps to reduce fear and anxiety, because groups of like-minded individuals are self-supporting.

We tend to view an organization as a thing, something separate from the individuals who work within it. We talk about organizational rules

TABLE 9.1 Command and control vs emergent paradigms

Command-and-control paradigm	Emergent or hive paradigm
Keep people in silos	Build connectivity
Ensure everyone salutes the flag	Encourage diversity
Manage communication initiatives	Have conversations in corridors
Blame people for failures	Learn from events
Make it clear who's in charge	Give everyone leadership opportunities
Tell people what to do	Tell people what not to do
Set objectives	Agree clear goals
Keep busy	Wait expectantly

SOURCE Seel, 2003, www.new-paradigm.co.uk/articles.htm

and protocols, as if the organization has a mind of its own. In reality, the organization is not out there, separate from the employees. The employees *are* the organization and the way in which they interact, work and create together with others *is* the organization at work, a living, changing, interactive organism.

My hope is that the post-recession era will trigger a reassessment of the way in which organizations, in particular large organizations, function. Ideally, greater importance will be given to happy and healthy relationship networks that are acknowledged and fostered to the same degree as organizational structures. I say this not so much because it is a good thing for employees – although undoubtedly it would be – but because there is clear evidence that healthy organizations with happy employees enhance profitability.

More than 20 years ago the organizational guru Peter Senge described his vision of learning organizations as:

> organizations where people continually expand their capacity to create the results they truly desire, where new and expansive patterns of thinking are nurtured, where collective aspirations are set free, and where people are continually learning to see the whole together.[21]

Senge, who described himself as an idealistic pragmatist, focused on introducing systems theory into organizations and bringing human values into the workplace. Systems thinking views organizations as a mesh of dynamic connections. In our hard-nosed age, it is easy to dismiss these sentiments as over-idealistic. However, we have only to glance at the state of some large organizations today to understand the need to explore alternatives to target-driven and high-anxiety cultures. There is considerable empirical evidence that a psychologically healthy workplace increases productivity, employee satisfaction and innovation. We need to heed this research and act on it.

From the broad to the focused

This chapter has ranged widely across working practices as well as life in general, but that reflects what we are as human beings: we have a tremendous spectrum of skills and abilities, but we have a tendency to silo our abilities rather than developing them in different arenas. For instance, negotiating skills at work can stand us in good stead in social situations or our hobbies or interests can sometimes be usefully fed into the workplace. This cross-fertilization benefits both arenas and is likely to increase our value and sense of satisfaction. It makes us more rounded as individuals.

Having talked very broadly about psychological health at work and the range of factors that influence this, we will now focus down. It is self-evident that when we feel physically and emotionally strong, able, motivated and enthusiastic about engaging in our work, we can contribute much more – and we get a greater sense of satisfaction in our work. In the next chapters we will explore specific aspects of building our practical and creative abilities and strengths in the workplace, so that we are both more productive and get more satisfaction in what we do.

Notes

1 Warrell, M (2013) *Stop playing safe,* John Wiley & Sons

2 Attridge, M (2009) Measuring and managing employee work engagement, *Journal of Workplace Behavioural Health,* **24** (4)

3 Hakanen J, Perhoniemi, R and Topinnen-Tanner, S (2008) Positive gain spirals at work: From job resources to work engagement, personal initiative and work-unit innovativeness, *Journal of Vocational Behaviour,* **73,** pp 78–91

4 Schaufeli, W B, Taris, T W and Van Rhenen, W (2008) Workaholism, burnout and engagement: Three of a kind or three different kinds of employee well-being, *Applied Psychology: An International Review* 57, 173–203

5 Driving performance and retention through employee engagement, Corporate Leadership Council executive summary [online] www.usc.edu/programs/cwfl/assets/pdf/Employee%20engagement.pdf

6 Employee Engagement, *Hay Group* [online] www.haygroup.com/ww/challenges/index.aspx?id=98

7 Macleod, D *Engaging for Success* [online] www.engageforsuccess.org/ideas-tools/employee-engagement-the-macleod-report/#.VDQRzPldU3s

8 Engagement Special: David Macleod and Nita Clarke on Engage for Success, *HR Magazine* [online] www.hrmagazine.co.uk/hr/features/1076832/engagement-special-david-macleod-nita-clarke-engage-success

9 The World Values Survey has been carried out four times since 1981. It has been analysed by John Helliwell of the University of British Columbia and his results cover 90,000 people in 46 countries.

10 Haidt J (2009) *The Happiness Hypothesis*, William Heinemann

11 Layard, R (2005) *Happiness: Lessons from a new science*

12 Hunter D J, Popay J, Tannahill C, Whitehead, M and Elson, T (2009) The Marmot Review Working Committee, Institute of Health Equity

13 Haidt, J (2009), *The Happiness Hypothesis*, William Heinemann

14 Watts, A (1993) *The Book on the Taboo Against Knowing Who You Are*, Abacus

15 For example, Professor Ralph Stacey (2003) *Complexity and Group Processes: A radically social understanding of individuals*, Routledge

16 Keegan, S (2009) *Qualitative Research*, Kogan Page

17 Chime Paden, One Village at a Time, *India Seminar* [online] www.india-seminar.com/2010/614/614_chime_paden_wangdi.htm

18 Keegan, S (2009) *Qualitative Research*, Kogan Page

19 www.bitc.org.uk/our-resources/report/ftse-100-public-reporting-well-being-and-engagement

20 www.cityoflondon.gov.uk/business/economic-research-and-information/research-publications/Documents/Research-2014/employee-health-and-well-being-in-the-city-of-London-final.pdf

21 Senge, P M (2006) *The Fifth Discipline: The art and practice of the learning organization*, Random House Business

Leadership and appreciative inquiry

10

Find the good and praise it. **ALEX HALEY**

The emergence of positive psychology

In the last half century, psychology has been largely concerned with abnormal behaviour and mental illness, with the exception of a few luminaries such as Abraham Maslow and Carl Rogers who were exploring self-actualization and humanistic psychology way back in the 1950s. It is only quite recently that the boundaries of psychology have become more relaxed so that the discipline can embrace more than simply the scientific method. For instance, exploring *positive* aspects of human experience has become of great interest. It is generally agreed that the modern positive psychology movement began with psychologist Martin Seligman's presidential address to the American Psychological Association (APA) in California in 1998: 'Building Human Strength: Psychology's forgotten mission'.[1] Since then, Seligman has become known as the 'father of positive psychology' and he has called upon psychologists to build up a large body of knowledge on 'what is good and right about people and to explore how these qualities can be nurtured'. In Seligman's view, it is important to explore how building on human strengths can make normal people stronger and more productive. As a result, in the last 15 years, many psychologists have been trying to address the historical imbalances within psychology. Seligman has summarized this endeavour as follows:

> [Researchers have] discovered that there is a set of human strengths that are the most likely buffers against mental illness: courage, optimism, interpersonal skills, work ethic, hope, honesty and perseverance. Much of the task of prevention will be to create a science of human strength whose mission will be to foster these virtues in young people. (Seligman 1998)

Positive psychology in the workplace

Positive psychology has not only highlighted the benefits of a positive frame of mind, in a personal as well as a work context, but it also puts at least part of the responsibility for creating a positive work environment on us as individuals. In this sense, we jointly create the organization we work within, even if we do it by acquiescing, staying silent, being obstructive – or indeed challenging, offering suggestions and trying something different.

Equally, we are all responsible, in different ways, for leadership within our organizations. The notion of leadership as being solely a top-down control process is fast becoming obsolete. Senior management cannot possibly keep track of multiple fast emergent scenarios. Employees across all levels of an organization need to be trained as leaders and to have the authority, confidence and self-trust to make decisions in the moment. This increases organizational efficiency as well as job satisfaction and overall productivity.

Common sense tells us that when people are happy, they are more productive at work, and a recent study at Warwick University, carried out by economists and led by Professor Andrew Oswald, appears to confirm this popular belief.[2] The researchers at Warwick found that, in a laboratory setting, happiness made people around 12 per cent more productive. The study, to be published in the *Journal of Labor Economics*, included four experiments with more than 700 participants. Professor Oswald commented:

> Companies like Google have invested more in employee support, and employee satisfaction has risen as a result. For Google it rose 37 per cent. They know what they are talking about. Under scientifically controlled conditions, making workers happy really pays off.

Dr Sgroi, one of the research team, summed up:

> We have shown that happier subjects are more productive. The same pattern appears in four different experiments. This research will provide some guidance for management in all kinds of organizations. They should strive to make their workplaces emotionally healthy for their workforce.

It is clear that, in the current work climate, in which many employees feel oppressed, frightened and insecure, there is considerable scope for positive psychology in order to help counterbalance the predominance of fear within organizations and, equally important, to motivate staff to work effectively, productively and with enthusiasm. In essence, positive psychology in the workplace is about identifying strengths and amplifying these strengths in order to promote positive affect among employees, while simultaneously minimizing and shifting attention away from the negative aspects of work: stress, job insecurity, burnout and so on.

Although most of us would agree with this aspiration, it is often difficult to implement. Ingrained fear and unhappiness within organizations cannot easily be eradicated. So what are the practical implications of this study in real-life work situations? How can we utilize this, and similar studies, within workplaces in which we may have a limited ability to change our working environments and where we are nonetheless required to work and manage? What help can positive psychology provide in order to support employees in high-risk, unpredictable working environments?

This is an emergent area and researchers are experimenting to establish the factors that support the aims of positive psychology. Hope, altruism, optimism, resilience, job satisfaction, work happiness, positive mood, helping behaviour, collaborative working and many more characteristics have been suggested as factors that help foster positive affect within the workplace but, to my mind, these abstract notions have little meaning unless we explore them within the environment we are trying to understand. We need to adopt a systemic approach which recognizes that contexts, relationships and power dynamics are fluid and evolving. No situation stays the same and although it is useful to define what is happening on the ground, it is important for us to remember that we are describing an approximation, a point in time, which will rapidly move on and become something else. This notion of emergence is a theme that has attracted growing interest within management theory[3] and, in a world in which change has become something of a cliché, we need to remind ourselves that life flows, integrating the known with the unknown – and we cannot always predict where it will take us.

Appreciative inquiry (AI): a route towards improving positive affect within organizations

We have talked a good deal about the negative aspects of work and the culture of fear that pervades many organizations, but how can we, as individuals, managers and leaders, improve this situation? One route, which has attracted attention and a growing body of practitioners over the last decade or so, is appreciative inquiry (AI), which consciously focuses on the positives within organizations, rather than the all too familiar problems.

Sue Annis Hammond,[4] an AI practitioner, sums up the essence of appreciative inquiry as follows:

> Appreciative Inquiry is an exciting philosophy for change. The major assumption of Appreciative Inquiry is that in every organization *something works* and change can be managed through the identification of what works, and the analysis of how to do more of what works.

The principles of appreciative inquiry

What does this mean in practice? It can seem a very radical approach within organizations that are infused with the notion that 'we look for the problems and then we try to solve them'. Indeed it is so radical that initially it may be quite difficult for us take on board. It may even feel *wrong* because we are so familiar with the 'look for problems and solve them' model. Setting out the differences, if rather crudely, between problem solving and appreciative inquiry, as in Table 10.1, can help us differentiate the two approaches.

So, if we decide to explore appreciative inquiry, how do we get to grips with the processes of understanding and selection that underpin AI and how can we incorporate this approach within our working lives? Can it benefit us personally or help employees who are working within fear-ridden organizations?

TABLE 10.1   The distinctions between problem solving and appreciative inquiry

Problem solving	Appreciative inquiry
Identify a problem to be solved	Identify what works well / what gives value
Determine the cause of the problem	Imagining what might be
Decide on possible solutions	Engaging in dialogue about what should be
Implement the solution	Innovating what will be

Sue Hammond, in her *Thin Book of Appreciative Inquiry*, summarizes the different approaches of appreciative inquiry and problem solving as: *'What problems are you having?'* versus *'What is working around here?'* These two questions, she says, underline the difference between traditional change management theory and appreciative inquiry. The former focuses on the negative and the latter addresses the positive. Appreciative inquiry turns the practice of change management around by starting from the assumption that organizations are not, in essence, problems to be solved. Instead, as Cooperrider and Whitney[5] describe it:

> Every organization was created as a solution designed in its own time to meet a challenge or satisfy a need of society and further the world around them. [AI] involves the art and practice of asking questions that strengthen a system's capacity to apprehend, anticipate and heighten positive potential. It is the cooperative co-evolutionary search for the best in people, their organizations, and the world around them.

Cantore and Passmore[6] define the five core principles of appreciative inquiry as:

1 The Constructionist Principle. Reality as we know it is a subjective state rather than an objective one.

2 The Principle of Simultaneity. Inquiry is intervention and creates change. They happen at the same time, not in stages. The moment we begin to ask a question we begin to create change.

3 The Poetic Principle. Human organizations are an open book and their stories are constantly being co-authored. Pasts, presents and futures are endless sources of learning, inspiration or interpretation. We have a choice about what we study, and what we study changes organizations.

4 The Anticipatory Principle. Human systems move in the direction of their images for the future. The more positive and hopeful the image of the future, the more positive the present-day action.

5 The Positive Principle. Momentum for large-scale change requires large amounts of positive affect and social bonding. This momentum is best generated through positive questions that amplify the positive core of the organization.

(Adapted by Cantore and Passmore from Cooperrider and Whitney 2005)

Appreciative inquiry in action

This discussion may seem quite theoretical and removed from everyday work life. You may be asking yourself, 'How can I use appreciative inquiry in my own work context and how can it help me?' Essentially appreciative inquiry is a consultancy tool, used to bring about strategic change within organizations through focusing on positive aspects of the environment and amplifying these positive changes to impact on other areas of the organization. As a tool and way of thinking, it can be used in a wide variety of ways, just as qualitative research can be adapted and utilized to help develop understanding, strategy, creative input and so on.

Appreciative inquiry can take many forms. It can be a major top-down initiative which involves the whole organization. It may be focused on particular departments or staff groups. It may be rolled out over time. The common denominator, however, is the use of appreciative inquiry as an engagement technique with the potential to change the way people within organizations *talk and interact* with each other. It puts employees in the driving seat of cultural transformation. Appreciative inquiry uses structured dialogue to generate a collective image of a new and better future for the organization and its employees. It does this by exploring and retaining the best aspects of the organization while at the same time being forward looking. In essence, by encouraging people to talk about what is *good* in their organization and how it can become better, belief and hope can *become* reality, in the sense that we become what we think about. The act of focusing on the positive influences the outcome and, in doing so, AI can break the cycle of negativity, unlock experience and knowledge and release the creativity and development potential of the organization. We have more confidence in the future when we rediscover and carry forward the achievements of the past. It helps us to repeat and build on success.

Perhaps one of the greatest potential strengths of appreciative inquiry is its potential to spread leadership across the organization. Different departments, work teams, levels of seniority, different sites might work together. Possibly even suppliers, competitors and academic and research institutions could be involved in a joint venture.

How to initiate an appreciative inquiry process

Simple appreciative inquiry questions to initiate discussion could, for example be as follows:

1 Think back to a time in your career; locate a moment that was a high point, where you felt engaged and effective. Describe how you felt. What aspects were most important to you?

2 Describe a person or incident when you felt that someone was being fair. What were the circumstances? What were the consequences?

3 Remember a time when you worked well as a work group. What was it that made it work and what are the factors that you would like to carry forward to a similar situation?

These simple questions can open up quite profound discussions. At best AI accelerates changes of all kinds. It can create motivation and energy among work groups and organizations. It can improve communication, trust, understanding and relationships and it can give people the confidence to take risks. It can even re-motivate employees who are feeling threatened and oppressed in their current work environment. Essentially the thrust of these conversations is quite simple: to identify what currently works well within the organization and how we can get more of the things that work well.

Of course we have to be cautious about the claims for appreciative inquiry; it is not a panacea. Each organization is different. Cultures vary. However, in some organizations, it has acted as an important step towards revitalizing the workforce, as solicitor and consultant Claer Lloyd-Jones describes below.

I'm Claer Lloyd-Jones. I am a qualified solicitor and work as a consultant now. The first time I used appreciative inquiry was in 1997 during the creation of a new unitary local authority, what became Brighton and Hove City Council. There were quite a few new unitaries set up then. The one that I was involved in had been the old Hove District Council, the old Brighton District Council and a third of East Sussex County Council, so all the functions came together in the city and I was supposed to be setting up the legal department. And I guess, for me, I was looking at trying to create something new and positive. The whole point about AI is that you accept that things have gone wrong in the past but you can leave them to one side. What we were able to do was to take the three cohorts and get them to address the same questions. We needed a single management framework to run the department and so we used the three cohorts to address a variety of questions. In the case of dealing with correspondence, for example, we asked 'What were the good things about what you did before?' And we concentrated on those good things – on what each organization could bring to the table – and then we decided on what was the best of the three ideas. The process had to be rigid and time limited. I ran it in a very tight way because I knew we didn't have much time. I think if you don't do it very quickly it can get chaotic. What I was trying to achieve was three into one without there being three different organizations inside one organization. Whenever you bring organizations together you see the cultures retained, so I felt it was important to create something new. We called it 'the fourth way'.

Every Friday morning we had a staff meeting where we went back to the discussion of the previous week. We started off with, say, 'handling correspondence', and talked about the good things and some sort of agreement emerged as a result of that discussion. And then the agreement was immediately turned into a document for consultation. So we then spent the rest of the meeting talking about the next stage, for example, 'This is what you said last week (about a new procedure) – we have now published it.' Then we got someone from each of the three groups to say, 'What was good about what you did with eg file management?' And so everyone got into this, looking into the future but bringing with them stuff that they thought was useful.

Once you get people into the mindset, it becomes easier. I see it like making vinaigrette. You have got to keep it moving. If you put it down it will separate rapidly into its constituent parts. What was good about it was that I decided to put in for ISO accreditation and we got it. Also the Law Society had set up a kite mark called LEXCEL and we were the first authority to be awarded it. Then I put us in for the Legal Team of the Year award and we won. It was fantastic.

AI is a way of acknowledging that people have come from somewhere, that some of what everyone has done in the past was good. It's quite easy, I think, when a new organization is created, to assume that everything that has happened before was wrong and that you don't talk about it. 'Let's not do any of that. We'll start with a clean sheet.' That really upsets people and undermines them.

I try to use AI in terms of how we can think differently. It's a way of getting everyone involved. It means that anyone can say, 'I thought that what we did before was quite good, but I always wanted it to be changed or improved by saying A, B or C.' When AI is working well, the atmosphere is such that people can say what they want to say – nobody can say anything wrong. It is going to be a lot of ideas. You have to just tell people that is how it is. And keep telling them that this is how it is. You have to behave consistently with that.

We did have several people who were sticklers, who didn't want to do anything different, so I had to work hard with them. And I had to make sure the management team was all signed up to this because they were going to have to manage people between meetings. Some of them needed support to do that. The key thing is to create a group mentality. You are going in a different direction, but it's a direction that everyone can influence.

Not everyone is sympathetic to AI, though. I have experienced some resistance. For most people it's not a normal thing to do. It's not obviously helping you to meet your targets or the corporate objectives. Sometimes my feeling was that people were living in such a battened-down way for so long that it was very difficult to open them up to an optimistic mindset – and the cultural fear had become second nature for everybody. People are hardening themselves to the possibility that redundancy is going to happen.

Overall, my feeling is that AI is a very useful tool. In my experience, where it works well, it's magic. It works by giving us a common purpose.

Appreciative inquiry, by its very nature, is likely to attract scepticism. Sue Hammond describes a sceptical senior manager who, on being introduced to AI, responded, 'I am not advocating mindless happy talk. When you get a survey that says 94 per cent of your customers are happy, what do you automatically do? You probably interview the unhappy 6 per cent rather than asking the 94 per cent what we did to make them happy.' This is not an unreasonable response.

Does appreciative inquiry work?

For me, the key question is: Could appreciative inquiry help us to work in ways that are proactive, constructive, creative, collaborative and so on? Any such organizational initiative has to be questioned: Might this help us achieve our goals? Can we trial it? How can we best evaluate it? As with all organizational interventions it needs to be assessed on an ongoing basis.

Appreciative inquiry is often seen as a rather off-the-wall technique, but if we look at the detail of it, much of it is actually quite familiar from established management theory and cognitive psychology. A fundamental tenet of appreciative inquiry is the belief that language creates our reality. Words have definitions but some words carry emotional meanings as well. Steven Pinker[7] and others have been talking in these terms for many years and a social constructionist approach that views language as creating reality is well established. Framing or 'what we focus on becomes our reality' is another established psychological concept which has been incorporated within appreciative inquiry. Then we can also learn a great deal from sports psychology. Visualization has been around for a long time, but sports psychology has made significant progress in the last 30 years by incorporating it within training. Many academic studies have been conducted on techniques such as mental rehearsal and self-monitoring. These studies have illustrated how a positive approach leads to better performance. Sue Hammond sums up the benefits of AI as follows:

> The tangible result of AI is a series of positive images phrased as if they were already happening. Because they are amplifications of what has already happened, they are easily visualized. Organizational members use those images as guides to do more of what they have already done well (positive self-monitoring). People have more confidence and comfort to journey to the future (the unknown) when they carry forward parts of the past (the known) and if we carry parts of the past forward, they should be what is best about the past.

The scope of appreciative inquiry

A wide variety of organizations have employed appreciative inquiry either as a top-down initiative or in specific pockets of the organization. For instance, Cooperrider and Whitney describe the British Airways experience of appreciative inquiry. After two years of ongoing organizational changes, including new alliances, technology upgrades, leadership transitions and refurbishing, British Airways North America introduced a programme of AI in order to help address flagging employee survey scores and to revitalize the British Airways culture of passion for service. A whole-system process, using appreciative inquiry, was instigated to transform the organization's culture. The working group agreed on two factors for success; management commitment and the involvement of the whole workforce. During the initial stages of the process one member of staff raised an issue that was critical: *baggage*.

There was widespread agreement that this was the highest priority. Among many innovative ideas, it was agreed that *exceptional arrival experience* was the absolute priority for future development.

In a very different sphere, Cooperrider and Whitney describe in *Appreciative Inquiry* how the management of Roadway Express decided to launch an initiative to drive costs down by creating an organization with leadership at every level. They held AI sessions throughout their North American operation. All staff within the organization, including dock workers and truck drivers, were involved in AI sessions. When the initiative started, Roadway stock was around $14 per share. In two years, the stock rose to more than $40 per share. Jim Staley, Roadway's CEO, described tremendous employee involvement and engagement. He summed up as follows: 'It's not that we don't deal with the negative any more, but the value of appreciative inquiry is that, in anything we do, there's a positive foundation of strength to build on in addressing those problems.'

The Appreciative Inquiry Commons website includes a wide variety of AI initiatives, such as 'A case study of leadership development within the United States Navy', 'Revitalizing schools through AI', 'Appreciative Inquiry in diversity work' and many more.[8]

Appreciative inquiry feeds leadership

I have touched on the critical importance of leadership skills throughout this chapter and make no apologies for ending the chapter on the same note. In my view, leadership, as a skill to be actively developed throughout all members of the workforce, is perhaps the most important organizational asset. A traditional view of leadership involves a delineated hierarchy: a structured matrix and clearly defined responsibilities cascading down the organization. This structure is still important as the backbone of the organization, and senior managers are a prime influence on the culture of an organization. Nonetheless, in today's fast-moving world, in which decisions often have to be taken on the hoof, sometimes without consultation with senior staff, all employees are required to be leaders within their particular sphere of influence. Appreciative inquiry can help employees at all levels to develop leadership skills.

Appreciative inquiry has the potential to challenge the negative state of many of our contemporary organizations by giving employees a greater degree of autonomy and engagement, but it requires a leap of faith on the part of both senior managers and the body of the workplace. There is a lot at stake. Instigating a programme of appreciative inquiry from top to bottom of the organization is a high-risk strategy, but it is perhaps even more risky to continue in a state of inertia, with a workforce that is passive, disengaged, fearful and possibly hostile. If we are serious about creating a culture of risk-taking, experimentation, innovation and productivity, we have to change the nature of our organizations and that means changing the nature of relationships within them.

Leadership is essential in all levels of an organization, not just at the top. It is a shared responsibility across all functions and levels, a way of working collaboratively with others. Where appreciative inquiry is embraced and actively developed, it can enable employees to work, grow and create a healthy and profitable organization together. If the organization can progressively be transformed through appreciative inquiry into a culture of positivity, curiosity, collaboration and experimentation, this can set the scene for the development of a range of skills that we will examine in the upcoming chapters.

Notes

1 www.positivedisintegration.com/positivepsychology.htm

2 Oswald, A (2014) Happiness and Productivity, University of Warwick [online] http://www2.warwick.ac.uk/fac/soc/economics/staff/academic/proto/workingpapers/happinessproductivity.pdf

3 Wheatley, Margaret J (1999) *Leadership and the New Science,* Berrett-Koehler, provides a very accessible introduction to complexity theory and emergence

4 Annis Hammond, S (2013) *The Thin Book of Appreciative Inquiry,* 3rd Edition, Thin Book Publishing

5 Cooperrider, D and Whitney, D (2005) *Appreciative Enquiry: A positive revolution in change,* Berrett-Koehler

6 Cantore and Passmore (2012) *Top Business Psychology Models: 50 transforming ideas for leaders, consultants and coaches,* Kogan Page. The five core principles of appreciative inquiry are adapted from Cooperrider and Whitney (2005)

7 Pinker, S (2002) *The Blank Slate,* Penguin

8 www. http://appreciativeinquiry.case.edu/

Developing resilience

11

I have not failed. I've just found 10,000 ways that won't work. **THOMAS EDISON**

Some are born with super-resilience

Thomas Edison, the inventor of the electric light bulb, supposedly said the words above before he went on to invent a functioning bulb. According to legend, Edison made thousands of prototypes before he finally hit upon the bulb that worked. Indeed, he worked tirelessly on a wide range of inventions, made thousands of prototypes which showed him how *not* to do things, and was awarded more than 1,000 patents. Most of us would have given up long before, but Edison was made of sterner stuff. His resilience gave the world some of the most useful and ingenious inventions of the 20th century, including the movie camera, the carbon microphone, the quadrupled telegraph and the mimeograph. However, his most modest and yet most life-changing invention remains the humble light bulb. Where would we be without it? The Edison website quite rightly extols his genius:

> He led no armies into battle, he conquered no countries, and he enslaved no peoples . . .
>
>   Nonetheless he exerted a degree of power, the magnitude of which no warrior ever dreamed. His name still commands a respect as sweeping in scope and as world-wide as that of any other mortal – a devotion rooted in deep gratitude and untainted by the bias that is often associated with race, color, politics and religion.[1]

Above all, Edison had resilience, but he is not alone in this. Modern-day inventors can be just as tenacious. In 1978, James Dyson became frustrated with his vacuum cleaner's diminishing performance. Taking it apart, he discovered that its bag was clogging with dust, causing suction to drop. He'd recently built an industrial cyclone tower for his factory that separated paint particles from the air using centrifugal force. Could the same principle work in a vacuum cleaner? He set to work, determined to find out. Five years and 5,127 prototypes later, he had invented the world's first bagless vacuum cleaner. Edison and Dyson clearly possessed a level of resilience that was way beyond the normal, but what is resilience and is it possible for those of us who are naturally less tenacious to develop this skill?

Resilience – the drive to keep going

The idea of being stretched and challenged to breaking point and still being able to bounce back is intriguing. It appeals to individuals who would like to cope more easily with life's daily problems and the bigger knocks that we all inevitably have to endure from time to time. It also appeals to many employers who would like their workforce to be better able to adapt and cope with organizational changes and difficulties. 'Resilience' is the term commonly used for this desirable trait, although there is some disagreement as to the nature of resilience or indeed the extent to which it can be developed.

Luthans and Youssef[2] claim there is a general misconception that resilience is an extraordinary gift, a rare capacity that results only from genetic variables. They point out that positive psychological resources such as hope or resilience, once thought to be reserved for the 'gifted', now have empirical support to show that they can be developed. Therefore, instead of viewing resilience as a gift from God, they see it as a common adaptive human process and one that we can all develop. Probably both perspectives are true: that is, we all possess different degrees of resilience and some of us are better than others at developing it. What *is* agreed is that resilience is the ability to recover quickly from adversity, especially after a stressful event or process. The business psychologist Professor Ivan Robertson[3] provides a succinct definition of personal resilience as 'the capacity to maintain well-being and work performance under pressure, including being able to bounce back from setbacks effectively'. Our natural resilience is therefore a combination of personal characteristics and learned skills – although it seems that the quality of our resilience can be developed whatever an individual's starting point. In the current work climate of change and uncertainty, resilience has become an increasingly important attribute for individuals, groups and in terms of business performance as a whole.

Resilience is a relatively new area within psychology. It was first written about in the 1970s and 1980s in relation to the experience of children as they developed into young adults. However, it is only with the emergence in recent years of *positive psychology*, which focuses on developing healthy individuals (as opposed to focusing solely on individuals with specific psychological problems) that the adult experience of resilience has come to the forefront.

There are numerous factors that cumulatively contribute to a person's resilience, including the ability to feel positive emotionality and also to effectively balance negative emotions with positive ones. Indeed, some researchers consider resilience to be a process rather than a trait, one that is demonstrated within individuals who can effectively and relatively easily navigate their way around crises and utilize effective ways of coping.

Characteristics of resilient individuals

Resilient individuals are usually characterized as those who are action-oriented and pride themselves on being able to handle whatever life throws at them. Typically they are flexible, adaptive, optimistic and learn from experience. They have a clear mission and a sense of purpose – or at least this is the stereotype. Significantly, the resilient individual is likely to recognize what support they may need to bounce back after a knock. For instance, in the work context this may include increased support from colleagues.

According to psychologists Cooper *et al*,[4] raising the levels of resilience within organizations provides a range of benefits including:

- increased self-awareness and personal empowerment: employees learn to self-manage their physical, psychological and emotional health;
- reduced absenteeism and increased workplace engagement;
- enhanced productivity through increased vitality, motivation and concentration skills;
- team-building through interactive, group-based learning and a unified approach to managing stress, challenge and change;
- minimization of risks associated with work-related stress and organizational transformation;
- accelerating team development;
- enabling the transformation of an underperforming organization;

- increases in core capabilities in an organization that routinely faces demanding and stressful conditions;
- providing an essential component of leadership development, especially in difficult and challenging times.

If building greater resilience within the workforce can contribute, even in small part, to the skills and benefits listed above, then there is an overwhelmingly strong argument for resilience training at work. This is both an economic and a well-being argument. Put simply, employees who are happy and engaged perform more effectively and are more productive. There is a strong economic argument for training all staff to become more resilient.

Building up resilience

To be truly effective within an organizational context, resilience needs to be consciously rooted within working practices, developed over time and reinforced through different structures and practices within the organization itself. Ideally this will happen on an individual, team, *and* organizational level – all at the same time – so that layers of resilience building will be developed. The effects of this become cumulative, with individual resilience feeding into teams which in turn feed into the organization as a whole, which feeds into individuals, and so on in a virtuous circle. This is both hive culture and contagion in action. On a personal level, developing resilience is an ongoing process that involves a mixture of practical and cognitive adjustments, including:

- developing a positive image of the future;
- having supportive work networks and healthy relationships;
- focusing time and energy on things that we have some control over rather than expending energy on aspects of life that are outside our control;
- trying to avoid seeing crises or stressful events as unbearable problems;
- having clear goals and a desire to achieve them;
- taking decisive actions in adverse situations;
- actively looking for opportunities for self-discovery and broadening our perspectives;

- practising cognitive restructuring: changing the way in which we think about negative situations and unhappy events;
- paying attention to our body as well as our mind: getting enough sleep, exercising regularly and learning to manage stress, paying attention to one's own needs and feelings;
- building self-confidence, empathy and strong relationships with colleagues;
- keeping a long-term perspective and considering the stressful event in the broader context;
- maintaining a hopeful outlook, expecting good things and visualizing what you want to happen.

I always feel rather squeamish about these to-do lists in relation to changing human behaviour. The lists are easy but making the changes rarely is – none of us can be perfect all the time and our capacity for resilience varies, depending on what is happening in our lives, both at work and at home. Often personal resilience is best achieved through a succession of small choices and changes, rather than by big change decisions, which are usually difficult to put into practice and near-impossible to sustain. Too often we set goals that are unrealistic and which we do not achieve, with the result that we beat ourselves up and feed the cycle of failure. Deciding on a few simple goals, achieving them, then moving on to other achievable goals builds up resilience over time, and in a relatively painless way. In general, changing our habits requires time and application and we need to tailor the changes to our own needs. If we can do this, the rewards of increased resilience, particularly when working under stressful conditions, can be considerable.

A study of resilience in the nursing profession

Debra Jackson and her colleagues[5] explored the concept of personal resilience as a strategy for responding to workplace adversity, and to identify strategies to enhance personal resilience in nurses. Workplace adversity in nursing is associated with excessive workloads, lack of autonomy, bullying, violence and organizational issues such as restructuring. It has also been associated with the problems of retaining nurses in the workforce. However, despite these difficulties, many nurses choose to remain in the profession, to survive and even thrive despite a climate of workplace adversity. Why do these nurses stay when they have to face these difficulties, sometimes on a daily basis?

The difference between those who stayed and those who left appeared to be, at least in part, to do with resilience: the ability of the individual to positively adjust to adversity. Jackson and her colleagues found that resilience can be applied to building personal strengths in nurses through strategies such as fostering positive and nurturing professional relationships, maintaining positivity, developing emotional insight, achieving life balance and spirituality, and becoming more reflective.

Jackson's study suggests that nurses can actively participate in the development and strengthening of their own personal resilience to reduce their vulnerability to workplace adversity and, in doing so, improve the overall healthcare setting. Her study recommends that resilience-building be incorporated into nursing education and that professional support should be encouraged through mentorship programmes outside nurses' immediate working environments.

Since Jackson conducted this study, the need for resilience within the nursing profession, in the UK at least, has become considerably more prominent in the wake of hospital scandals related to poor patient care as a consequence of overworked staff, lack of resources and target culture.

Resilience at individual, team and organizational levels

Of course, it is not only nurses who can benefit from resilience training. Many of us might wish to have greater resilience. And, as we have seen, with training and practice, almost all of us can learn to be more resilient. Although it seems that Edison was fortunate enough to be endowed with an abundance of it, we mere mortals also have considerable stores of untapped resilience and, with some effort and determination, it is possible to boost our abilities. Psychological resilience is a topical issue in a climate in which employees feel increasingly anxious and disengaged at work. Teaching resilience is one route towards building stronger and more resourceful workforces and, equally, it is a way in which individual employees can feel better resourced and able to cope in challenging workplaces.

Building resilience within teams is a particularly important part of creating a healthy and productive workplace environment. Resilient teams are based on a range of factors including mutual trust, social norms, participation and social networks – and resilient teams are more likely to be productive and high-performing. Resilience provides a protection factor for individuals, teams and the organization as a whole. It helps us to work more effectively, especially in times of change, high pressure and stress. At the most basic level, good job design will go a long way to promoting a healthy workplace and building resilience.

In essence, building resilient teams is about effective leadership, team cohesion, mutual support and open, honest communication. Equally, a resilient team is one in which people have a shared sense of purpose and connectedness. Interaction and reinforcement of team efforts are important.[6] Both individuals and teams need to be nurtured and acknowledged, not only through team cohesion, but also through role clarity, so that employees understand the links between their work and the wider objectives of the organization. Recognizing progress, effective communication, mutual support, promoting personal skills and, indeed, utilizing our considerable human skills are all part of building and reinforcing resilience.

However, resilience on its own is not enough in situations in which employees are constantly drawing on their resilience alone to cope with poor managers, highly stressful situations, work overload, poor systems of work and difficult interpersonal relationships with managers and peers.

The economic benefits of resilience

Of course we cannot ignore the economic implications of resilience or lack of it. Resilience in the workplace matters. Resilient employees are less likely to have time off, or to come to work when they are unwell. By contrast, employees who are less resilient may have more sick leave or be disengaged at work. This not only affects the individual involved, but also the staff who have to cover for absentees. The knock-on effects of staff absence include heavier workloads for other staff members, disruption of work plans and staff resentment because they are 'carrying' staff who are regularly absent. There can also be significant financial consequences for organizations: employing additional staff, more training, rescheduling etc.

Poor health in the workplace is estimated to cost the British economy over £100 billion annually through sickness, absence and worklessness.[7] The latest figures from the Office for National Statistics show that in 2011,

131 million workdays were lost due to sickness absence in the UK. An estimate for 2012 by the Confederation of British Industry is higher at 160 million working days lost. There are some discrepancies on numbers, but taking a broad view, it is clear that the high cost of sickness absence means that employee health is an important issue for businesses and economies around the world, as well as on an individual level. Employers have a duty of care in terms of their employees. Preventative care in terms of resilience building is therefore both a benefit to employees and a potential financial saving in terms of employee costs.[8]

When resilience is thrust upon us

When organizations fail for whatever reason, the fallout can be catastrophic. It is not only a financial disaster for all employees, but there is also a sense of insecurity, responsibility, perhaps bitterness and rage. Managing a failed organization back to health is tough, but sometimes possible given the right circumstances. This may be achieved not only by funding and other support but also by human determination and endeavour. Getting the right motivated staff on board and working ridiculously hard, you may achieve the near-impossible, as Claer Lloyd-Jones discovered.

Until recently I was the CEO of a national regulator, the social housing regulator, and before that I was a director in three different local authorities. Sequentially! I'll talk about Hackney. That was the most difficult local authority I worked in. It had been in a pretty bad state for a long time before I joined in 2001. Nothing was going right and there was a lot of political infighting. Two councillors were in prison for election fraud when I arrived. The finances had got into a really bad state, and the Secretary of State had to step in. Part of the deal was that the local authority got £23 million from the government.

When organizations have such a poor reputation, people don't want to work there. You can't easily attract high-calibre staff. But in fact the corner had already been turned when I arrived and the new Labour leader was strong and knew what he was doing. They recruited a new chief executive. He picked the people he wanted and so it was a completely new team, including me. That was the framework for change. It was more than a full-time job. After I arrived there was an election and Labour got in as a majority. There was one single party and they were very clear about the improvements they wanted.

What was the mood like when I arrived? Mmm. I'll talk about my own department, the legal department. People were very confused. There was no communication from top to bottom, so people found out what was going on by reading the *Evening Standard*. People need communication. They need to feel that they belong. But they were put in a building miles away. It was like being sent off to Siberia. Seventy-five per cent of them were temps. Mind you, no one used the legal department anyway – they rang up solicitors and ordered legal advice like pizzas. The legal budget was massively overspent as a result.

The Labour members really wanted it to be good. They wanted to turn Hackney into a borough they could be proud of. I suspect it had been bad for some time but if you don't have stable leadership, it's difficult to do much. It shows you how important leadership is. You have to train up people on the front line or they don't do it right. I needed to bring stability to all the teams that I was responsible for, so I made sure I had a good team and tight, visible management.

A climate of fear? I think we had gone far beyond that. It was a form of anarchy. People did what they thought was the right thing because there was no one to tell them anything else. It was a steep learning curve for all of us. There was a huge amount of change, and we had to make sure we didn't rush it. You have to understand the principles of change. I learnt a lot about that. And motivating people. If you want people to work 100 per cent you have to help them to understand what it means for them, acquiring new skills, promotion, opportunities to do different things – so you are growing people as well as getting from A to B – which means that when you get to B you have bright people already trained. In all the studies I've looked at, the reward is not just about money. It's about all the recognition and appreciation you get for doing the job. You need to be appreciated for the effort you put in and that is what gets people up in the morning.

I think the reason we were successful is that we built optimism. It couldn't get worse. We could only go in one direction. Some people left. It was inevitable. We wanted happy volunteers and that's what we got. It was a very hard seven-days-a-week job. There were some bad times, but I have to say that the politicians were a solid bunch. They motored solidly in the right direction. People now think that Hackney is a good place to live and work, a good place for transport, a good place to raise children. It's got the train, and the streets are clean. The mayor concentrated on the basics. People started to see things change and it became a rolling process. But there is always drag – a perception drag which took about two years to fade.

Actually, after that I was employed by the Tenant Services Authority originally as the director of corporate services. There was always an issue of whether or not the TSA would survive the election of the coalition government – and it didn't. When you are in a national organization, there is always a slight frisson in terms of what government is going to do next, regardless of what the government is. Policy imperatives change very regularly. You are quite happily heading off in one direction and you are suddenly told that the agenda has changed. And so there is a sort of fear factor – what do we do now? People on the ground don't feel this as intensely as management.

I felt that it was part of my job to absorb a lot of that and not pass it on. I have always felt that, in my position, it is part of the deal. The message that you deliver should not be one of terror. You have got to be realistic in what you are going to do but also you have to show people where the path is. The day our abolition was announced – it was done without notice – it struck terror into everybody's heart. The then chief executive was uncontactable on holiday, I think. I was his deputy by then and I decided that what we needed was to get everyone together. All people had was this thing on the news wires. So we rounded up everyone and I managed to get someone from the board, who also didn't know much about it: the board was going to meet later in terms of the future. It was actually very good. The technology worked, so one of the projects I had managed was a success. It meant that we could get everyone, either virtually or physically, in the same room. We were juggling laptops and had people on mobiles dialling in, trying to simply explain to everyone what we knew, which wasn't very much, but it was an opportunity for people to ask questions. And I had a member of the board who had managed to turn up very quickly, and people could see that I was the deputy chief executive – we still couldn't contact the chief executive – and we were able to show that we were committed to making sensible decisions, and if the organization was going to be closed, that we were going to follow but also leave a brilliant legacy. One of the things I committed to do because, of course, you cannot close an organization like this without legislation – that is why it took two years – was that we would be committed to ensuring that there would be an orderly transfer of regulators into the receiving organization. I committed myself to ensuring that TUPE (Transfer of Undertakings (Protection of Employment) regulations) applied. It is on the face of the legislation. I did it. Perhaps, ensuring that protection for staff is one of my greatest achievements.

I had started a Friday afternoon letter and every week, without fail, it was in everyone's inbox. It became a chief executive's letter which was drafted on Wednesday and Thursday and sent out on Friday afternoon. My commitment was that people knew what was happening and everyone had choices and options. Amazingly enough, because we did staff surveys, levels of staff satisfaction went up. It's an attitude. If you are constantly thinking about it – I have this bit of information, who else needs to know about it? It is up to the other person to decide whether it is useful to them, not me.

Of course building resilience within organizations is not easy. It is a step-by-step process of trial and error and our capacity for resilience varies, depending on what is happening in different areas of our lives. It is not a constant trait. Nonetheless the basic sentiment holds true. Often personal resilience is best developed by a succession of small choices and changes, rather than by big decisions. Deciding on a few simple goals, achieving them and moving on to other achievable goals builds up resilience over time – and in a relatively painless way.

In organizational terms, resilience is reinforced by a supportive atmosphere that encourages the building of positive relationships across the organization. Research carried out by Warner and April of Ashridge Business School[9] suggests that initiatives focused on emotional intelligence can play a key role in helping people to build their personal resilience, as will a culture of honesty, self-belief and helping people to cope with change. Organizations that develop a broad range of strategies to help their employees to cope in difficult times will be best placed to build a more resilient workforce that can thrive amid adversity. The key is to learn how to apply the resources flexibly and appropriately.

Indeed, as the psychologist and specialist in 'happiness' Richard Layard[10] points out, a whole cluster of characteristics can be linked to increased resilience, for example, optimism, persistence, a positive view of the future, achieving goals and empathy, in addition to factors such as genes and upbringing, over which we have little control.

Given the levels of anxiety, suspicion, lack of trust and caution that exist within many contemporary organizations, there is a strong argument for considering resilience training as an element of all staff training, from senior to junior. Resilience, like fear, is catching but, unlike fear, it is a useful thing to catch, in that it may help restore organizations to a healthier state. It is worth emphasizing that we may be missing a trick if we limit our focus on resilience to *individuals*. To be effective, developing resilience needs to be an individual, a team *and* an organizational concern for all employees.

Notes

1 www.thomasedison.com

2 Luthens, F and Youssef, M (2004) Experimental Analysis of a Web-based Training Intervention to Develop Positive Psychological Capital, *Academy of Management Learning & Education* 7, (2), pp 209–21.

3 www.robertsoncooper.com

4 https://www.cipd.co.uk/binaries/5490%20Developing%20Resilience%20 RI%20(WEB).pdf

5 Jackson, D, Firtko, A and Edenborough, M (2007) Personal resilience as a strategy for surviving and thriving in the face of workplace adversity: a literature review. *Journal of Advanced Nursing* 60 pp 1–9

6 Working Well: An organizatioinal approach to preventing psychological injury [online] www.comcare.gov.au/forms_and_publications/publications/%20 safety_and_prevention/?a=41369

7 Barnes, H, Garratt, E, McLennan, D and Noble, M (2011) Department for Work and Pensions, Research Report No 779, Understanding the worklessness dynamics and characteristics of deprived areas

8 Cavill Associates and University of Salford (2014), Best Practice in promoting employee health and well-being in the City of London[online] www. cityoflondon.gov.uk/business/economic-research-and-information/research-publications/Documents/Research-2014/employee-health-and-well-being-in-the-city-of-London-final.pdf

9 Warner, R and April, K, Building Resilience at Work, *Ashridge Faculty Publications* [online] www.ashridge.org.uk/Website/IC.nsf/wFARPUB/ Building%20personal%20resilience%20at%20work?opendocument

10 Layard, R (2005) *Happiness: Lessons from a new science*, Penguin

Building trust within organizations

12

Trust in God, but tie up your camel. IDRIES SHAH

The foundation of trust

Maintaining effective relationships within organizations, between management and employees, within work groups and with suppliers and customers involves credibility, respect and fairness. Trust can make the difference between success and failure in an organization. Without mutual trust, organizations and their employees will struggle. Equally, to work collaboratively with people we need a degree of trust and cooperation; an organization that is full of fear, distrust, suspicion and anger will never thrive. It may survive for a while as contracts, greed or power tie employees in, but it is a battle against human nature.

Trust and resilience are not just soft skills. They are the social glue that holds teams together and boosts their effectiveness. Organizations that have built resilience and trust within their workforces are likely to be rewarded by increased staff loyalty and productivity. Professor Paul Zak, a neuro-economist at Claremont Graduate University, claims that countries with a higher proportion of trustworthy people are more prosperous and he has conducted research to determine the biochemical effect that trustworthiness might have on our brains.[1] 'What is behind the human instinct to trust and put each other's well-being first?' he asks. Why do people cooperate? Zak researches oxytocin, a neuropeptide that affects our everyday social interactions and our ability to behave altruistically and cooperatively, and he applies his findings to the way we make decisions. He has demonstrated that oxytocin is responsible for a variety of virtuous behaviours in humans such as empathy, generosity and trust. Interestingly, he has also discovered that social networking triggers the same release of oxytocin in the brain – meaning that e-connections are interpreted by the brain in the same way as in-person connections.

According to Zak, most humans are biologically wired to cooperate but business and economics ignore the biological foundations of human reciprocity. When oxytocin levels in individuals are high, their generosity to strangers increases by up to 80 per cent, and in countries with higher levels of trust, there is less crime, better education and the country fares better economically.

Trust and vulnerability

Communication and trust go hand in hand. A study carried out by Towers Watson found that high-communicating companies had 47 per cent higher total returns to shareholders.[2] This raises the question: If trust and good communications are so important to success, and technologies have made global communications easier than ever before, why are we not better at communicating?'

'Companies that communicate with courage, innovation and discipline, especially during times of economic challenge and change, are more effective at engaging employees and achieving desired business results,' says Towers Watson. These firms were also the best financial performers. But what is trust and how might you define it? How would you explain it to someone who had never experienced trust? Explaining trust is not easy because, although we know very well what it means in an intuitive, emotional way, it is hard to put into words. It is one of those concepts that we accept without analysis or challenge, as a good thing. We know instinctively, in our bones and from lifelong experience, that trust is the bedrock of relationships. Indeed, it is the bedrock of life itself. It is the first and essential response we have when we emerge screaming and bloodied into the world. The psychologist Erick H Erickson described this as 'original trust'.[3] At birth, we trust our parents or carers. We are hard-wired to bond with them and, with few exceptions, they are hard-wired to bond with us. Trust is a two-way street which is reinforced by positive contact: our child's first smile, the glimmer of recognition, their palpable neediness. As we grow up, we trust that our carers will look after us. There is no other way that we can survive. Most of us – if we have had good enough parenting – come to take this trust for granted. We intuitively understand the importance of trust in all our relationships, even if we don't verbalize it.

Why is trust such an important element in human interaction? It is a primeval instinct that grew out of necessity, a way of protecting the group or clan from danger, and it is an instinct that has stood us in good stead over the millennia. Books have been written on the meaning of trust, how to recognize it and the role it plays in our lives. But it is not always necessary to precisely define something in order to understand it. After all, we throw 'love' around fairly liberally and we allow its meaning to adapt effortlessly to fit the needs of the situation. A colloquial understanding of trust is 'a belief and hope that the other person or persons will honour our intentions and wishes, and that they will reciprocate in like manner insofar as they are able'. Trust involves each party making themselves vulnerable, putting their faith in the hands of the other and hoping that he or she will respect the often unspoken agreement. This notion of trust is based on shared understanding and respect. Trust and love are close allies. It is hard to have love without trust and equally it is hard to have trust without a degree of affection, or at least respect. In essence, trust reflects people's perception of others' reliability. I particularly like Pritchard and Littlewood's definition of trust: 'Trust exists most notably where the individuals concerned are using their natural energies, where they can add and create more value, and where they feel less threatened by others.'[4] The implication is that curiosity, relating with colleagues, safety and experimentation combine to raise levels of trust within organizations.

Do we still trust trust?

However, there are some signs that our attitudes to trust are changing, although the evidence is complex and sometimes contradictory. Lying behind the statistics on higher crime and family break-up in many Western societies is a profound change in attitudes to the self and society.[5] In various studies people have been asked, 'Would you say that most people can be trusted – or would you say that you can't be too careful in dealing with people?' In 1959, 56 per cent of Britons said yes, most people can be trusted. By 1998 that figure had fallen to 30 per cent, although recently there are signs of a reversed trend and a small increase in levels of trust, according to OECD indicators.[6] In the United States, trust appears to have fallen from 56 per cent in the mid 1960s to 33 per cent today.

Clearly this is a complex area and we cannot easily generalize across countries and cultures. Statistics need to be treated with caution, not least because the use of language and social norms change over the decades, which means that we cannot easily compare like with like in these studies. Nonetheless there are signs that, overall, trust in Western societies is falling. If this is the case, then we might expect that this will impact on working life and undermine trust in the workplace.

Trust in the workplace

If our early experiences with trust were positive, we may assume that we will experience the same degree of trust in the workplace, but we do not always find it. This can be confusing, even frightening. Faced with lack of trust we may withdraw, become cautious and hold back. We feel that our trust – which is arguably the most important ingredient in the workplace mix – has been betrayed. The management consultant Reinhard Sprenger sums this up rather nicely:

> In business, nothing is more important than trust. No company can prosper without trust between management and employees, among colleagues and partners, and between the organization and the outside world. Trust is the strongest foundation for customer loyalty, staff motivation and market confidence.[7]

Of course, nothing exists without a context. Trust should not become yet another organizational tool, devoid of judgement. Neither should we trust our line manager implicitly. However, all things being equal, I am suggesting that we err on the side of trusting, rather than not trusting, especially in a context which we believe to be relatively safe, such as with our workmates or possibly our line manager.

Paradoxically, trust is one of the most talked-about concepts in business, but not necessarily in a positive sense. It is often accused of being nebulous and woolly. Many believe that trust has to be earned rather than assumed. Alternatively, it is seen as simply a feel-good factor, lacking in substance or efficacy. But this is missing the point. In our hard-nosed rational world, we tend to dismiss what we cannot measure. Do you love your spouse less because you cannot easily put into words what you feel about him or her? Trust is like this. You can feel it, know it, then use it, without having to analyse and measure it. You may say that there are different rules in the workplace and that we are naive to assume that the patterns of trust that exist within families or groups of friends can be replicated at work. Of course there are differences, but we are not different people at home and at work. We just play different roles. We still need to trust and be trusted. What is an organization if not a network of relationships? In case we have any doubts about this, there is considerable academic research that reinforces the view that trust is vital within successful organizations.[8,9] But here's the rub. At the same time as these studies point out that trust is crucial for successful organizations, they also confirm findings from research within the general public: that is, trust within organizations is at an all-time low.[10] How can this be? We know, from our own experience and from a wealth of studies, just how important trust is within organizations. We know that lack of trust impacts on job satisfaction, productivity, staff turnover and innovation.[11] Yet, at the same time, the chasm between employees' need to feel a sense of trust in the organizations in which they work and their perception that trust, particularly between management and staff, is low has, perhaps, never been greater. This suggests that their commitment and willingness to engage with their work is also low – and this is borne out by the Towers Watson study we examined in Chapter 4.

Redundancy or risk of redundancy, reduced job security and lower wages all contribute towards undermining trust in organizations. At the same time management trends over the last couple of decades have moved towards increased performance monitoring and target-setting for individuals, departments and boards, who in turn are increasingly beholden to shareholders. The combined effect of these factors has amplified fear and insecurity in many workplaces.

Lack of trust inhibits risk-taking and innovation

Lack of trust is one of the biggest barriers to innovation, and indeed to a happy and productive workforce. Numerous academic studies conclude that trust lies at the root of effective organizations. It is not just a nicety; it is an economic necessity, especially within current fast-moving and often turbulent markets. This makes it all the more difficult to explain the growing tendency among many senior managers to attempt to control the workforce through crude performance targets that are often interpreted by employees as symptomatic of a lack of trust.

Reinhard Sprenger describes the mesh of history, regulations and protocols that often stultify performance and innovation within organizations as follows:

> Many companies are held in an invisible prison. Red tape, rigid administration procedures and mushrooming regulations prevent any emergence of business dynamism. The walls and bars of this prison are the basic assumptions about the economy and human behaviour.

Ten years on, nothing much has changed. Indeed, the evidence is that lack of trust has increased. Fear of losing control lies at the root of this. Senior management is fearful that, in such a rapidly changing world, they will lose control of the organization's direction, its activities and its performance. They are right to feel this, but it is unrealistic to expect that it is possible to turn back time and recreate a controllable organization. Technology; social media, internet, Twitter and the plethora of other communication devices, along with peripatetic working lives, have changed and fragmented the work world for ever. It is no longer possible for senior managers to know what is happening throughout their organization. Perhaps they never could, but in a slower pace of organizational life, it mattered less. Managers can no longer micro-manage employees, although there is still an expectation that they should take the blame for mistakes and misdemeanours – that they are the ones who must fall on their sword because, well, someone has to do it and after all, they get paid to do that sort of thing, don't they?

The future of trust?

Inevitably, managers will lose more control as globalization and technology speed up information delivery while communication processes and knowledge become more copious and more dispersed. With Big Data huge amounts of information can be acquired and processed through mega-computers. This means that many business analysts will inevitably become redundant. We will no longer require human intervention in the process as humans cannot possibly compete in terms of speed and data retention. The only viable option is not to attempt more stringent and widespread control over employees, but to trust them to do the jobs that still remain for humans.

Trust is essential for successful businesses

Although there are many different meanings and interpretations of the word 'trust', we all know what it means and the evidence suggests that employees who have high trust in the organizations in which they work stay longer, put in more effort and work more cooperatively, while those with low or no trust often work less effectively, engage in counterproductive behaviour such as obstruction or seeking revenge[12] or simply decide to leave.[13] It therefore makes absolute sense in terms of company growth and productivity to cultivate a climate of trust, as far as possible, not least because building trust is much easier than trying to restore it. As occupational psychologist Professor Rosalind Searle puts it: 'Despite growing attention towards trust, our understanding about how it can be repaired has been slower.'[14] In other words, people can easily lose trust in their managers but it is a hell of a job and an uphill struggle trying to restore it.

Conversely, in organizations where there is high trust in management and a sense of solidarity, honesty and collaboration, employees feel better able to weather the storms of organizational upheaval. For instance, in 2012, the John Lewis Partnership, a long-standing and very well respected company, implemented a restructuring scheme that resulted in redundancies on a scale never experienced in its 80-year history. The company involved and informed staff of the difficult decisions, which, in spite of the trauma of redundancies, actually enhanced trust[15] because staff were involved in the decision-making and understood the necessity for it.

Equally, when redundancies were inevitable, the CEO of Sunderland City Council involved the local community in an effort to minimize job cuts and maintain public services. Difficult decisions could not be avoided, but the community tackled the issues together. As with the restructuring within John Lewis, trust was enhanced.[16] Trust in the organization and/or senior managers reduces fear in times of upheaval. In turn, reducing fear increases the ability of most employees to continue working and to work more effectively, even in the midst of organizational uncertainty.

Trust as an organizational goal

In one sense, organizational trust is a big and complex area. However, it is also a simple human need. Without trust we are rudderless. We know from personal experience that trust forms the basis of most of our personal and business relationships. We talk about the importance of negotiations, of making deals, of winning and presenting, of what we are doing, all in a way that sounds cautious and rational. But it is not only this. Having an instinctive sense of trust in the group of people we work with – and particularly in our managers – allows us to go the extra mile, even when times are tough. We dismiss the importance of organizational trust at our peril. Retaining and building trust need to be an important and ongoing priority throughout the organization, especially for senior management. This has never been truer than it is at the present time. Any significant organizational change needs to be assessed, among other factors, in terms of its effect on levels of trust within the organization. This is not just an idealistic goal. It is a business necessity. Innovation, in particular, is a risky endeavour, especially for the individuals who are actively involved in it. To experiment, fail and persevere with no guarantee of success, individuals need to feel the confidence of a trusting organization to back them up. As Sprenger puts it:

> Creative work is fragile and uncertain: ideas have to be developed, proposed, tested and justified or abandoned. People engage in such a process only when

they feel secure, in an atmosphere of trust, respect and goodwill. Trust makes it easier to cope with deviations from routines and rules, especially when innovations and experiments end in error or failure.

The human face of trust

We like to talk about the huge changes that technology has wielded in our lives. We live faster, we fly halfway round the world at the drop of a hat, our communication devices are diverse and never off, in the blink of an eye we can gather more data than we know what to do with. But too often we fail to mention the opposite, which is equally true. Not that much has changed in terms of human drives, emotions and dreams in the last thousand years. In spite of the veneer of automated living, we are still individuals seeking love, acceptance and a sense of purpose at home and at work. And our need to give and receive trust has not eroded. Millions of years of evolution have not dented these basic needs. Arguably they have grown stronger rather than becoming more diluted as we fight to maintain human values in the face of relentless mechanization of our societies.

In an organizational context, we need to be consciously building trust as a route to re-humanizing the workplace; treating people as human beings, rather than simply resources or fragmented work functions. We need to be thinking about, and talking with, groups of people within particular departments and groups to establish how best they can contribute, rather than defaulting to off-the-peg performance targets as the automatic solution. This is about building a shared purpose, in which employees can feel confident to challenge their own – and each other's – assumptions and where constructive feedback is accepted as part of ongoing learning.

It is easy in our current cynical work climate to dismiss this approach as idealistic. However, there is overwhelming research evidence to support the view that happy, involved employees lead to more successful organizations.[17] Commitment, flexibility and trust tend to go hand in hand. If we want to get the innovation engine going, we have to gear our organization to flexibility, not efficiency.

Building trust in the workplace: the Continental story

At Continental Airlines, employees in the baggage reclamation department were faced with the possibilities of layoffs. When this news reached them, the staff responded in an interesting way. Before talking to management, they all met up and jointly worked out a plan for all full-timers to move to part-time status so that no one would need to be laid off. They took the proposal to their managers, discussed the issues, and waited to see what would happen. What was unusual was that the employees took positive action to propose a solution to a dilemma facing them and, indeed, the company as a whole. They were confident that management would listen to them, which they did, and together they worked out how they would go forward. Positive relationships between management and employees continued, helping to sustain a great working relationship and ensuring that employees and managers will want to stay with the organization in the long term – and resolve difficulties when necessary.

In many other companies the events would have panned out very differently. For example, unhappy staff would have resulted in increased absenteeism, high levels of turnover and growing resistance to any changes proposed by management. So what was going on at Continental that supported the development of positive relationships between employees and management? The simple answer was trust. This was the critical factor that supported effective communications, an ability to collaborate across departments and hierarchies and the willingness to seek fair resolutions to difficult situations. Trust gave employees the confidence and overall ability to support the management's vision for the future.

Trust also provides a degree of consistency within organizations. Although we talk a good deal about innovation, risk, experimentation and so on, in practice employees also need consistency. As employees, we need to understand – more or less – what is expected of us. Trust provides this stability. Where trust is felt and where there is a reciprocal understanding between employees and management, within work groups or across departments, resolution is possible. In an ideal world, both employees and management would start with a position of mutual trust. How they resolve a difficult incident reflects this level of trust. If it is successful, trust is reinforced and grows. Where there is no existing trust, resolution is much more difficult or even impossible. Developing and maintaining high levels of trust should therefore be a priority within all organizations.

Trust is not just a nebulous ideal to be plastered on the wall as this year's mission statement. It needs to be practised, reinvented, on a day-by-day basis. It means being straightforward, admitting mistakes, keeping promises, showing vulnerability, letting go of grievances. In fact, it is the same sort of stuff that many of us try to practise day by day outside our workplaces. Equally, employees who are themselves committed to doing their best work will not tolerate other employees who are slack or dishonest. In this sense the workforce can become self-regulating. Perhaps most importantly, trust acts as a short-circuit to action in organizations. As Steven Covey puts it: 'Strong trust in organizations can improve speed of decision-making and reduce costs, whereas low trust can result in reduced speed and increased costs.'[18] Trust can really improve the bottom line.

Trust in action

Timpson, a UK family business set up 1865 as a shoe retailer and still going strong today, is a good example of self-monitoring employee behaviour. The business, which is 100 per cent family owned, provides a range of high street and business services from key cutting, shoe repairs, photo labs and house signs to jewellery engraving and watch repairs. James Timpson represents the fifth generation and runs the business, which has a £175 million annual turnover, alongside his father, group chairman John Timpson. The founder was the innovator, while the second generation provided the real entrepreneurial muscle to get the business going. The leader in the third generation was more of a 'steady Eddie' who needed to deal with a lot of family politics. Then came John and James, who were both very entrepreneurial.

Regardless of the different skills each generation has brought to the business, there is consensus that there is no option but to be entrepreneurial, otherwise the family risks being swallowed up by change. In 1987 John took the hardest decision of his life when he sold the group's shoe shops, but this represented the sort of reinvention that is sometimes needed to revitalize a family firm and make it sustainable. 'When my father took over, Timpson's was basically a shoe retailing business,' explains James, 'and now we take £500,000 a week on watch repairs.'

This ability to innovate is backed up by management focus on nurturing home-grown talent, developing their workforce and spreading the entrepreneurial culture across the group. Their business model is known as 'upside-down management', and it promotes the idea that it's the people who serve Timpson customers who should run the business. These colleagues, as they are called, have complete authority to operate their shops however they wish. A particularly interesting aspect is that the staff monitor themselves. The success of each store is dependent on every employee pulling his or her weight. If one employee falls short, it is the responsibility of the rest of the employee group to resolve the problem in whatever way they see fit.

It appears to be a winning formula and the company has many plans for staying agile and seeking out new expansion opportunities. On family involvement and ownership, James sums up the policy very clearly: 'The management is determined to keep all the company shares together and this means finding an entrepreneurial owner/manager in each successive generation.' The whole multi-million-pound organization is based on trust, with staff themselves ensuring that trust is not broken. Can this model really work? you wonder. Well, as Ernest Hemingway put it, 'The best way to find out if you can trust somebody is to monitor their behaviour when you trust them.'

Trust assumes vulnerability and in trust there are no guarantees. When we choose to trust someone, there is risk. We can never be sure that our trust will not be misused. Equally, trust can be used as a camouflage or decoy. Many years ago, I worked for a client who had a mission statement – they were very fashionable at the time. The statement was emblazoned over the door of their corporate offices. It said, 'You are now entering a total quality zone.' It made my day every time I entered their offices. It was a classic attempt at top-down indoctrination. Of course it was counterproductive, as all transparent propaganda is. Visitors found it amusing. Employees found it embarrassing. It was a crude attempt at instilling groupthink in employees and visitors alike. It failed because it acted as a label stuck on to the organization rather than reflecting the values that had grown out of a long-standing and authentic corporate culture. Trust needs to be genuine. We humans are very good at recognizing and reacting to fake emotions.

How can we practise trust?

If trust is such a critical element in organizational life, how can we practise trust in ways that are low risk to ourselves, our job function and our relationships with colleagues? Most employees who are working in organizations where there are high levels of fear are reluctant to make themselves vulnerable. Our natural instinct is to withdraw, to cut off, to suppress emotion. However, with enlightened management and receptive staff, a strong climate of trust can be built over time. It is not an easy process, especially within organizations that have become cynical of ongoing management change programmes. However, if handled with trust and honesty, the outcomes can be both surprising and robust. In order to trust we have to overcome fear, and in this sense trust is a choice we must consciously make, based on what we know of the context, the people we choose to trust and the possible outcomes. It is risk based, but not foolish or naive.

Trust that grows and trust that just is

We can make a distinction between two different understandings of trust which we can call assumed trust and earned trust. Earned trust is the more common interpretation of trust. It is thought to grow slowly and tentatively as we gradually come to know and develop a stronger relationship with the other person or persons. All being well, we eventually reap the reward of mutual trust. When this happens, we talk about 'this person never having let me down'. There is a bond, a mutual respect. We have found a soulmate. But in our fragmented, fast-moving work lives, there is often little time for building trust in this way.

The alternative approach to trust is more pragmatic and might be more relevant in situations where we are constantly working with new colleagues. In a world in which employees are expected to pitch up and contribute, there is little time for the niceties of *built* trust. Instead, we *start* from the position of trust as assumed, unless proved otherwise. In this interpretation, trust is a choice and people do not need to *earn* trust; they can only lose it by their actions.

However, trust in a person or an organization is rarely absolute. In every situation where trust is involved, we need to make judgements based on the current situation, the level of perceived risk and the consequences if that trust turns out to have been misplaced. Nonetheless, trust is always an integral and evolving part of organizational life.

Can we teach trust?

Trust lies at the core of most, if not all, successful organizations. When we find employees who work constructively together; where there is a sense of camaraderie, where there is healthy communication between different levels of the organization, where people feel free to offer suggestions or improvements and so forth, then we are very likely to find high levels of trust between employees.

Then we might ask: How does trust develop and can it be taught?

In an organizational context trust can be addressed through a well-thought-out process of building reciprocal relationships between individuals and groups within an organization, such as the one described within the Mental Health Trust, below. Change can be achieved by gradually increasing awareness of the importance of trust and the benefits that can accrue both for organizational productivity and for employees themselves. Building trust, as we have seen, can be tough going, especially where attitudes are entrenched and the staff are reluctant or over-stressed.

Introducing a trust-building programme within a mental health organization

Working within a climate of conflicting demands

Campbell Keegan was invited to be part of an organizational team working with an NHS Mental Health Trust in the East End of London. Like most NHS organizations, the Trust was heavily target-bound and the staff were under considerable pressure. Managers described how they felt torn between the dual and – as they saw it – conflicting demands of client care and meeting externally enforced targets. Senior managers acknowledged that targets were useful, but nonetheless believed that meeting these targets distracted them from what they considered to be their real job, which was looking after their clients. They felt judged and pressured by targets, whereas they felt a sense of personal satisfaction when they had time to fully support their clients. Consequently, staff felt that there was ongoing tension between these two objectives: client care and meeting their targets. As one manager put it, 'I have two full-time jobs.' In addition, senior managers and clinical staff felt the pressure of silo working, which was exacerbated by the geographical dispersal of different Trust units across the borough. This dispersion often led to duplication of effort and to limited and confused communications. Different units were sometimes wary of one another and so avoided non-essential contact. This, in turn, led to inefficiencies and limited the opportunities for shared learning.

Addressing the problems through shared learning

However, the Trust was fortunate in that it had a very enlightened CEO who was keen to implement a leadership programme for senior managers which would address some of these issues. The team was led by a senior manager within the Trust, who specialized in organizational change. In addition there were a number of facilitators, specialists in organizational change work – and me. I had a dual role as a researcher/facilitator. I monitored and assessed the efficacy of the programme on an ongoing basis in order to provide a full report for the NHS, which was funding the programme. In addition, as an organizational change specialist, I participated in the change process itself.

After much discussion between the CEO, the leadership training team and the researcher (me), the exact aims of the programme were hammered out. The leadership programme would focus on increasing networking and shared learning, on providing support for managers who felt isolated and unsupported, and on helping them to deal more effectively with the pressure of externally imposed targets.

The Trust then embarked upon the leadership development programme which included all senior managerial and clinical staff who were accountable through a director and who had substantial management and leadership responsibilities within the Trust. The programme, which ran for nine months, was designed as a collaborative venture, with participants developing their own work areas and learning objectives. It drew on recent developments in complexity theory to inform the approach, emphasizing the importance of relationship, conversation and interaction in bringing about change.[19] The anticipated outcomes of the programme were to develop reflective, collaborative networks between senior skilled staff, out of which new ideas, initiatives and changes could occur.

Getting staff on board

Senior managers were keen to reduce work pressure and work more productively. However, many balked at the anticipated time commitments of the leadership programme. They had all been on various leadership and training courses over the years, with varying degrees of perceived value, and the prospect of being involved in a programme for almost a year, with two- to three-day stints every month, was simply overwhelming. How would they make time to meet their targets? However, the CEO was adamant. He argued that, if the work culture and patterns of interaction within the Trust were to change, then every senior manager, without exception, needed to attend the programme. With some reluctance, all the managers eventually came on board.

The evolution of the programme

Over the course of the programme, we engaged in a wide range of activities which were designed to build up familiarity and trust between managers. A crucial aspect of this was managers establishing networks with other colleagues across the Trust. This allowed managers who were developing similar initiatives to build working relationships, share experiences and act as co-workers, where possible. This increased their sense of autonomy and made their working practices more efficient. Over time, the managers developed and shared strategies. They learnt from one another how and what to prioritize. They developed strategies that enabled them to satisfactorily deal with external targets. They learnt who to go to for help, when needed. They learnt to trust their colleagues and work with them in an honest and collaborative way.

Outside speakers introduced new ways of conceptualizing organizations, in particular feeding in thinking from the complexity sciences and the role of emergence in organizations. Participants, working in diverse groups, explored how these ideas might be implemented in their particular situation or in specific contexts. Action Learning sets were encouraged. This involved groups of four to five participants who met regularly outside the programme days. They jointly worked on real challenges, sharing the knowledge and expertise of the small group of people, combined with skilled questioning, to reinterpret old and familiar concepts and produce fresh ideas.

At one stage, all the members of the Trust board were invited to join the programme for the day and to talk with the senior managers. The board members were visibly anxious as they entered the room. As with almost all hierarchical organizations, there was some ongoing friction between layers of management. The senior managers were forthright and keen to discuss a number of provocative issues. This created a slightly tense atmosphere to start with, but the board members were open and receptive, in spite of their apprehensions. They acknowledged the issues that the senior managers raised and took on board the grievances expressed. Gradually both sides relaxed and by the end of the day most of the staff claimed that they had gained a better insight into the position of other managers and departments. The exchange of views and experiences was deemed to have been a success by all of the participants.

The long-term outcomes of the initiative

The initiative sowed the seeds for further networking, extending to and from the board. Each level became more engaged with levels above and below them; they had a better understanding of the concerns of others and could work jointly with a wider range of staff, when necessary.

The outcomes of the initiative were broad and partly unexpected. To summarize, the large majority of participants believed that they gained a great deal from the programme, even many who had been very sceptical of 'more management training' before the programme started. However, we were particularly convinced by their actions. In the large majority of cases, the networks and working groups that were formed during the programme were still operating six months after the programme had finished, *even though there was no obligation on employees to continue with the groups*. Many managers described these as invaluable supports. Although their workloads had not reduced, managers reported feeling more relaxed and more productive. They felt supported and they had colleagues they could call on if need be. Perhaps the most interesting feedback was that they felt better able to meet all their targets *as well as* serving their clients. Participants reported that targets, both qualitative and quantitative, provided useful feedback. In contrast to their irritation with targets before the programme, managers had time to absorb and use the data they received.

Overall, senior managers and board members felt that the organization had become 'healthier' as a result of the programme, and levels of self-defined trust rose dramatically. They felt that they knew and could rely on their colleagues to a greater extent and their own feelings of confidence, being in control and being supported had filtered down to other staff in the organization. As a result, the CEO planned a similar programme within the next layer of management. One participant summed up the experience as follows:

> I really didn't want to go on this course. I didn't have time. I didn't think it would be useful. I went kicking and screaming. But it has changed me. I feel re-energized. God help me, I even enjoy going to work. I now know the people who can help me, that I can work with, and that makes such a difference; we can build things together. It's exciting.

How else can we build trust in organizations?

Trust has that ephemeral quality of 'being there until it has gone'. Ironically we are more likely to notice trust by its absence than its presence. Trust needs to be nurtured and consciously attended to, if it is to stay strong. Advertising and marketing are littered with earnest pleas that we should trust particular companies and their products and often these seem transparently false. We have good antennae for rooting out disingenuous and implausible advertising. Misguided approaches to building trust highlight the inadequacies of superficial slogans. To be effective, trust needs to be at the core of the brand's values, as a living embodiment of what it stands for.

There is no magic solution to building trust, and we have seen that it is better to try not to lose it in the first place. We can start by examining our own behaviour and by trying as best we can to be open, cooperative and respectful with our colleagues, as we would in situations outside work. If we ask people to list the qualities that generate good working relationships and build trust in their working lives, they have no difficulty in listing them: respect, helpfulness, humour, being willing to work through conflict, cooperative working, shared commitment, being supportive of colleagues, honesty, straightforwardness, humour, openness, and so on. However, the problem often lies in the doing.

Companies have attempted to rebuild trust through a variety of routes, for example organizational surveys as aids to help them understand and then address trust issues by profiling of individuals and teams, by high-impact team workshops and by converting this learning into action. But too often these initiatives involve measuring or doing things *to* people. Alternatively they may be big one-off initiatives, managed by external consultants. Sustained cultural change rarely happens like this in the real world. The culture may change in the short term, but the underlying dynamics of the organization often remain untouched. The consultants come and go and gradually the organization returns to 'normal'. Real change is messier, unpredictable and emergent. However, if there is a sufficient movement for change within workforces at all levels, and if it is clear that an engaged workforce is more productive, and if trust builds bridges, then these human values are likely to eventually win out.

We need to regularly remind ourselves of what sort of working environment we want and then individually and collaboratively try to create it. I believe that most of us want to feel useful, productive and cooperative. We are genetically programmed to work and achieve satisfaction through working together. As we have seen, far from being a nagging exception to the rule of evolution, cooperation has been one of its primary architects. In essence, trust forms the foundation for effective communication, employee retention, and motivation. It can be regarded as the extra effort that people voluntarily invest in the workplace. When trust exists in an organization or in a relationship, almost everything else is easier and more comfortable to achieve. This surely must place it near the top of organizational goals.

Notes

1 http://ted.com/speakers/paul_zak

2 Capitalizing on Effective Communication: How courage, innovation and discipline drive business results in challenging times, *Towers Watson* [online] www.towerswatson.com/en-GB/Insights/IC-Types/Survey-Research-Results/2009/12/20092010-Communication-ROI-Study-Report-Capitalizing-on-Effective-Communication

3 Erickson, E (1994) *Identity and Life Cycle*, Norton

4 The Journey of Trust: What can we do to reverse the decline? Talk given by Neville Pritchard and David Littlewood at an Association of Business Psychology event, September 2013

5 Layard, R (2011) *Happiness: Lessons from a new science*, Penguin

6 Society at a glance 2011, *OECD Social indicators*

7 Sprenger, R (2004) *Trust: The best way to manage*, Cyan Books

8 Child, J and Mollering, G (2003) Contextual confidence and active trust development in the Chinese business environment, *Organization Science*, **14** (1) pp 69–80

9 Searle R, Hope-Hailey, V and Dietz, G (2012) Where has all the trust gone? *Trust in Organizations* [online] www.trustinorganizations.com/Resources/Documents/WhereHasAllTheTrustGone.pdf.pdf

10 Edelman (2012) Trust Barometer [online] http://trust.edelman.com

11 Moorman, C, Zaltman, G and Deshpane, R (1992) The relationship between providers and users of market research: The dynamics of trust between organizations,, *Journal of Market Research* **xxix**

12 Tripp, T M and Bies, R J (1996) Beyond Distrust: 'Getting even' and the need for revenge, in Kramer, R and Tyler, T (eds) *Trust in Organizations: Frontiers of theory and research*, Sage

13 Dirks, K T and Ferrin, D L (2001) The role of trust in organizational settings, *Organization Science*, **12** (4) pp 450–67

14 www.coventry.ac.uk/research/excellence-with-impact/urc-trust-peace-and-social-relations/rosalind-searle/

15 Engaging for Success: Enhancing performance through employee engagement, *People Management*, March 2012 p 93

16 Work in Progress: Meeting the local needs with lower workforce costs. Good practice case studies, *Audit Commission* [online] http://archive.audit-commission.gov.uk/auditcommission/sitecollectiondocuments/Downloads/WIP-Case-Studies.pdf

17 Engage employees and boost performance (2001) *Hay Group* [online] www.haygroup.com/downloads/us/engaged_performance_120401.pdf

18 Covey, S (2008) *The Speed of Trust: The one thing that changes everything*, Simon & Schuster

19 Shaw, P (2002) *Changing Conversations in Organizations: A complexity approach to change*, Routledge

The power of language

13

Even though we face the difficulties of today and tomorrow, I still have a dream. It is a dream deeply rooted in the American dream.

I have a dream that my four little children will one day live in a nation where they will not be judged by the colour of their skin but by the content of their character.

I have a dream today.

I have a dream that one day, down in Alabama, with its vicious racists, with its governor having his lips dripping with the words of interposition and nullification; one day right there in Alabama, little black boys and black girls will be able to join hands with little white boys and little white girls as sisters and brothers.

I have a dream today. MARTIN LUTHER KING

How can we read these life-changing words, feel the passion and longing that lie within them and not marvel at the potency of language? Words can move mountains. We know the power of language in poetry and novels, in film and on the stage, and we can be brought to tears by these performances. We leave the theatre feeling excited by the ease with which the actors can change our perspective on life.

The power of everyday conversation

Most day-to-day conversations are not like this. Generally they are functional, casual and initiated with little thought. So where do day-to-day conversations fit in, and are they, too, capable of changing our lives? Everyday conversation may not have the widespread impact of Martin Luther King, but in a personal or work sphere it can be hugely powerful. We can all remember times when something that was said to us, something good or bad, had such resonance that we have never forgotten it. It is etched into our memory and, in some cases, it can even shape our future lives. When I was 13, my mother's friend casually mentioned that I had 'legs like tree trunks'. I wore trousers for years and I still haven't forgiven her, even though she is long dead. The old adage 'Sticks and stones may break my bones, but words will never hurt me' is a complete lie. Of course words can hurt.

In the routine of everyday working life it is easy to take conversation for granted, to drift into sloppy habits and downgrade its importance. We half-listen. We fail to fully engage with colleagues, we do not make eye contact, our body language implies a lack of interest, a passing-through. This mode of communication can easily become habitual. We may not even be aware that we are doing it, but lack of engagement with those around us can insidiously and dramatically undermine the strength of our work relationships. Perversely, we immediately recognize when *we* are not being acknowledged, when the person we are speaking with is 'not there', when they are distracted, irritated or bored. And we feel insulted. We remember the incident and it may colour future interactions with that individual. It has established a pattern which can be difficult to change.

Conversely, when we speak with someone who is interested and focused on us, we feel acknowledged and valued and we leave that person with a warm sense of having bonded. The world seems a better place. Think back to a time when a senior manager greeted you by name or specifically came by to thank you for your input into a project. How did you feel? These gestures are simple, easy to do and yet they can have huge significance.

More than 20 years ago, I travelled with a client down to Brighton to carry out some focus groups; he was to sit in on the sessions. We arrived at the venue and I opened my art pack to dig out the advertising concepts that I was to research. To my horror, I realized that I had brought the wrong concepts. With huge embarrassment, I confessed my mistake. There was a short pause and then . . . the client laughed and said, 'Well, you had better buy me supper!' I did and we went back the following week to try again – with the right boards. After all these years I still feel grateful to him.

Active listening

How often in a conversation do you find yourself impatiently waiting to have your say? You are not listening, you are waiting for a gap so you can leap in. You are only half there. *Active listening* is a simple method to help improve listening skills. The goal is to attend entirely to the speaker, not to oneself or one's own inner dialogue. It is to *hear* and *interpret* the speaker's verbal and non-verbal communication. This may include focusing on the face and orienting your body towards the speaker. It also involves a neutral, open attitude so that even remarks that are shocking or distressing are understood – not judged – by the listener. The aim is to receive information, not to give it; to be a witness, not a critic.[1]

Everyday language can be hugely powerful. What we say, what we fail to say, the tone of voice in which we say it, the level of attention we give to the person we are talking to, the words we choose, our facial expression, the type of body language we adopt – and much more – deliver complex and detailed information to the person or group we are addressing. Most of the time we are completely oblivious to this communication, as is the recipient. Nonetheless, it impacts on our behaviour. Our interpreting skills can be as subtle as a feather and as incisive as a sabre. So how do these different types of communication, the giving and the receiving, the verbal and the non-verbal work?

Two different brain systems – and two styles of communication

In *Thinking, Fast and Slow*,[2] Daniel Kahneman, the psychologist and Nobel Prize winner, discusses the two modes of human thinking, which he calls System 1 and System 2. System 1 operates automatically and quickly, with little or no effort and no sense of voluntary control. System 2 allocates attention to the effortful mental activities that demand it, including complex computations. The operations of System 2 are often associated with the subjective experience of choice and concentration.

When we think of our self, we identify with System 2, the conscious, reasoning self that has beliefs, makes choices and decides what to think about and what to do. However, as Kahneman puts it, 'Although System 2 believes itself to be where the action is, the automatic System 1 is the hero of the book. I describe System 1 as effortlessly originating impressions and feelings that are the main sources of the explicit beliefs and deliberate choices of System 2.' What, you might ask, has all this to do with language? System 2 is self-evident – it embodies the conscious thinking and language that we use all the time. System 1, however, is more of an enigma. It enables us to operate on automatic pilot, aware of what is happening but not on a conscious level. It is the part of our brain that leaps to conclusions. We are all familiar with that sensation of knowing something but not knowing how we know it. We use this ability all the time. We make judgements about people within seconds of meeting them and often we are proved right. This is all down to System 1, the part of the brain that is intuitive, that senses what is happening. It can anticipate danger and take evasive action even before our conscious brain is aware of it. Although it has no language, it is an effective communicator, for example through posture or tone of voice and, as such, it is an invaluable ally.

Developing greater awareness and paying more attention to people's speech and body language can provide us with a huge amount of useful knowledge, at conscious and non-conscious levels. It helps us to understand what is important to them, what drives them, what they want to achieve, what makes them fearful and how they relate to other people around them. Understanding people better is clearly a useful skill, especially if we are working with them, but it requires attention and interest. And in the process we learn much about ourselves as well. Building rapport with work colleagues enables us to short-circuit preliminaries; the basis of mutual trust has already been established. This is particularly important when the topic of the conversation is contentious. When working as a team is critical.

Sandy Pentland, an MIT professor, created a device worn around the neck to compare patterns of communication, recording tone of voice, body language, gesturing and other exchanges among team members. The resulting data confirmed that particular patterns of communication are vital to team success. They are as significant as all other factors – individual intelligence, skill, decision-making – combined.[3]

But who says that this is just a human activity? Some animal species are at least as intuitive as we are when it comes to body language.

Dogs do it so well

On a beach in India, I watched two dogs negotiate power relations. One of the dogs (Top Dog) belonged to the beach restaurant. He had a collar, which gave him authority and territorial rights. The other dog (Underdog), looked superficially similar to Top Dog, but his manner was very different. He was slightly smaller and very watchful. As I stood on the beach admiring the view, Underdog stood some twenty yards from me, stock still. His total attention was on me, his eyes locked onto mine. I stared back for a while – stray dogs can be dangerous – but I decided that he was friendly. I made a small movement towards him. Instantly he trotted over to me, not too fast to frighten me, but cautiously, just in case I attacked him. He was clearly used to being chased away, or worse. As he came closer, there was sudden activity behind me. I had been watching Underdog and not paying attention to Top Dog, but he had been standing at the borders of the restaurant – *his* restaurant, where he lived – and had been observing the scenario play out. With speed, and a certain elegance, he ran down the beach to where Underdog and I were getting to know each other. By the time he got there, I was stroking Underdog and he was timidly enjoying it. The situation changed in an instant. Once Underdog spotted Top Dog, his whole body changed. He just drooped and backed off, clearly wary. He did not run away, but he would not let me stroke him. Top Dog did not make eye contact with him. The most interesting response was from Top Dog. Having rushed to the scene, he was now nonchalant. He confidently came up to me to be stroked. He then walked towards Underdog but behaved as if he had not seen him; it was as if Underdog was so unimportant, so low down the pecking order that it was not worth expending the energy to see him off. Besides, it was not necessary. Underdog posed no threat. His tail was between his legs and he was shivering. Clearly Top Dog did not consider him worthy of a fight.

I walked back to the restaurant marvelling at the sophistication and symmetry of the dogs' behaviours. Both dogs were acutely aware of their environment; how they each fitted into it and how they related to one another. This enabled them to coexist, provided they each played by the rules. We can learn a lot by observing dogs. We are not so different from them. Perhaps we are a little less obvious in our posturing and jostling for status and power, but even that is arguable. Both humans and dogs have shared the same environments and threats for millennia. We are not so different from one another. Top Dog could not have said it better himself.

The interpretation of language

Language is an imprecise medium. When we talk with someone, the message that we convey, consciously or otherwise, is not necessarily the message that they receive. What we hear isn't necessarily what was said. All language is interpreted through our past individual experiences and expectations, and each of us has a lifetime of upbringing, experiences, training, cultural norms and so on that colour the ways in which we interpret communications. Added to this is the influence of context, which can have a huge impact on our behaviour and language. For example, meeting your future in-laws for the first time probably requires a code of dress, behaviour and language that may be far removed from your normal persona. It is easy to get it wrong. Equally, a football supporter may be good mates with his Asian neighbour, as they exchange pleasantries over the garden fence, but take him out of that context and put him in a football crowd and he may become a racist thug. Context always shapes our behaviour, even if we are unaware of it. It is a crucial influence on our language and behaviour and can be minefield.

Context is critical. Language and behaviour can be a minefield that we must all learn to navigate, while bearing in mind the possible meanings, interpretations, and precise verbal and non-verbal cues, conscious or otherwise, that constitute everyday working life and interaction. Given the complexity of all this, it really is extraordinary that the human mind is capable of disentangling and making sense of it all.

You might wonder why we have developed such imprecise language. Surely it would be better to have fixed meanings for everything so we all know where we are. However, this assumes a constancy that we do not possess. As Chime Paden described in Chapter 9, although we think of ourselves as constant beings, in practice we are imperceptibly changing second by second. How else can we explain the difference between 'me' at four and 'me' at forty? Our lives are like rivers, constantly flowing, ever-changing. Imprecise language allows us to play with new ideas, to adapt our thinking to the needs of the situation and the time. It enables us to create, to challenge thought, to forge new vistas. Without fluid language we would be robots.

Living in the moment – or not

A few months ago, I went to an event at the Royal Society of Arts. Daniel Goleman, who famously 'invented' emotional intelligence, was giving a talk on his new book, *Focus: The hidden driver of excellence*. It was a great talk. Goleman came across as a warm, gentle man, who was genuinely interested in the people who came up to speak with him after his talk. There were a limited number of his books for sale outside the lecture theatre and the audience jostled – in a very discreet and middle-class way – to order and secure a signed copy of the book. None of us wanted to appear pushy, but as there was no obvious queue, we shuffled and slithered silently forward in order to maintain our intellectual posturing while, at the same time, ensuring that we grasped a signed book. In my case, it was worse. I had acquired two books – one for a colleague – and I could see the sideways glances I was attracting. Two books were considered to be really greedy.

The woman in front of me was keen to talk with Goleman and he was very receptive. He chatted and she reciprocated, while the rest of us became slightly tetchy. As far as I was concerned, this was a transactional exchange. Buy copies of books. Queue up. Get books signed. Get back home on the Tube as soon as possible. My turn came. I smiled and held out my books – no time to talk. Daniel looked me in the eye; not for ages, but long enough for me to start feeling uncomfortable. He had an open, friendly expression on his face. I felt confused; torn between my impatience to leave and not wanting to appear rude. He did not seem bothered that people were waiting. He was totally focused on the person in front of him. In this case, me. However, in my mind, I was already in the future, happy to have secured my two signed books and plotting my journey home. As interesting as Goleman's talk was, that momentary exchange – which in retrospect I realized I had wasted – was the most important lesson he passed on to me. 'Being in the moment' is such a trite and overused phrase that it is easy to underestimate its importance. However, it is one of the most useful skills to practise. When we are truly in the moment, with all our senses focused and attuned to the situation or person we are communicating with, we are able to absorb huge amounts of information that they emit from myriad sources. We can hear what he or she says, make sense of its meaning by the words they use, how they use them and the hesitations between. We can understand their mood or state from their tone of voice through our instincts, take in and interpret their body language, and observe how these cues are changing. However, much of the time we miss these cues, as I did, because we are simply not paying attention. The dogs on the Goan beach were more able to live in the moment than I was.

In organizational life, we are often positioned – or more likely we position ourselves – in the past or the future. The past may shape our current behaviour and our expectations may colour the future. It is often hard to be in the present and totally focused on what is going on at that moment, although that moment is all we can hope to control. If we spent more time being in the present and less worrying about the past or future, we would be much more productive. Being fully focused on the person we are engaged in conversation with is, perhaps, the greatest compliment that we can pay them.

Changing organizations through conversation

Honest communications and a better understanding of the people we work with are crucial in any successful working environment. According to psychologists Sarah Rozenthuler and Andreas Priestland of Dialogos,[4] employees spend up to 80 per cent of their working time in conversation. This does sound an extraordinary percentage, and doubtless it varies according to the nature of the organization but, if it is only half true, it highlights the crucial *role* of conversation at work. Indeed, it makes talk our key action tool in that it is a fundamental and primary means through which change happens in organizations.

Equally, the *way* in which we converse with one another at work is pivotal to the success of the organization. Changing the nature of conversations in organizations can be the single most powerful way to bring about an innovative mindset and performance breakthrough.[5] Dialogue is increasingly acknowledged to help build trust and cohesiveness in teams, and is a key benefit in times of uncertainty, complexity and rapid change.

Indeed, people who engage in more substantive conversations have been found to have higher levels of well-being and happiness than those who don't.[6] Empirical research also shows that high-performing teams talk together in distinctive ways that lead to:

- greater productivity and profitability;
- higher levels of customer satisfaction;
- better relationships with colleagues.[7]

Changing how we talk – in small, sometimes imperceptible ways – can be a very powerful and non-threatening way to bring about change. Most importantly, this change can be subtle, non-hierarchical and contagious. Ferdig and Ludema[8] describe organizations as:

> networks of conversations. Conversation is not only a tool for communicating change, it is the very medium through which change occurs. Changing the way people talk and listen to each other changes the way people act. Creating the conditions for constructive dialogue, through promoting a climate of inquiry, inclusion, spontaneity, possibility and freedom, increases levels of interconnectivity, strengthens shared identity and promotes better utilization of resources. Together these outcomes lead to transformative change.

The nature of our conversations is therefore crucial to the kind of organization we seek to create. Healthy, productive, innovative organizations arise out of high-quality, creative, engaging conversations. While innovation per se cannot be designed, it can be encouraged by putting in place the conditions for reflective dialogue. Creating a climate where people can question and challenge current operating norms and form new understandings is at the heart of dialogic practice and strategic innovation.[9]

Within and outside organizations

Understanding cultural trends and communication patterns *within* an organization is just as important as understanding trends *outside* in the consumer environment. Arguably it is more important, because corporate culture inevitably bleeds into the consumer world through customer–staff interface. Product quality, the level of customer service, speed of answering the phone all tell the customer something about the corporate culture of the organization they are dealing with. The growth in awareness of the critical importance of the customer–staff interface has boosted organizational research: examining the customer interface, developing change management programmes and highlighting training and communication needs. However, of all these factors, the most important is the communication between staff and customers. Apocryphal as it may be, one bad customer experience with an organization is shared with twenty potential customers, whereas a good experience is shared with only two.

Convening successful meetings within organizations

There are endless variations on the organizational meeting. The common denominator, however, is that meetings are made up of people in conversation. We will talk about how people behave in meetings and how, as team leaders, we might influence this process. How can we best hone our ability to engage with others, both on a one-to-one basis and as part of a community of co-workers, without seeming authoritarian, patronizing, indifferent or some other undesirable state?

While there is a wealth of academic research on using dialogue to change conversations in organizations, it is an area that can also be addressed in a pragmatic and hands-on way, incorporating some themes that can be easily adopted and incorporated into everyday conversation in organizations – and indeed outside them as well. Some of these themes will be self-evident. Hopefully others will trigger thoughts and ideas on how to increase engagement in your meetings at work.

Establishing rapport

The leader or moderator sets the tone of the meeting within the first few minutes. This is the most important stage and rapport needs to be quickly established. How this is achieved will depend on several factors, including whether people already know one another, if the meeting is friendly, if the group is cohesive and so on. Until we can achieve a sufficient level of rapport, empathy and trust among participants, progress will be difficult. The greater the fear levels in the organization, the stronger the need for reassurance, openness and a willingness to listen to the views of others. We all have different *ways of being*. We see the world differently. As Carl Rogers, the founder of humanistic psychology, put it, we do not have to agree with people, just recognize and respect them.[10]

There are basic housekeeping rules: greeting people in a friendly and appropriate manner; mirroring their style; being clear about who other participants are or the topics to be covered; asking participants to introduce themselves; and so on. A degree of formality *might* be appropriate, depending on the group mix, as will reassurances about who will have access to the content of the meeting and such like. Emphasizing that people have been invited to give their views – *which will probably differ* – gives permission for diversity. Equally, stressing that *everyone's view counts* sows the seeds for discouraging the over-talkative. Neuro-linguistic programming (NLP), in spite of its name, offers very practical, hands-on techniques which can be used to establish rapport quickly. For example:

- Matching voice tone and speed of speaking – not in the sense of mimicry, but more like two instruments harmonizing.

- Using the same technical vocabulary, where appropriate, is a way of establishing professional credibility.

- People will often mark out words and phrases that are important to them. Using the same words or phrases in your reply show that you hear and respect their meaning.

- Body and voice matching with the participants creates rapport at the behaviour level.

- The strongest rapport comes from acknowledging a person's identity, ie using their name, acknowledging their opinions and way of life.

Self-awareness and empathy

These are umbrella skills, which are particularly useful if you are moderating the meeting. How we present ourselves to others influences their response to us. Therefore being aware of how people might see us is useful. Equally, honing our ability to monitor an ongoing conversation while at the same time being in the loop of conversations that are going on around us is a very useful skill which can be mastered with some practice. When we are aware of how we are acting and being perceived, we can make choices about how to behave, speak and interact with the individual or group in order to create the appropriate environment to explore the relevant topics of discussion. This is not being *false* – other participants immediately pick up on insincerity – it is *being in the flow*, a mental state in which the individual is totally immersed in what they are doing.[11] An essential characteristic of a good engager is someone who is genuinely interested in understanding other people and their concerns. Participants will recognize this quality and respond to it. Being aware is to do with choosing a facet of ourselves that is appropriate with *this* group, within *this* context, when talking about *this* subject. This may sound trite, but actually it lies at the core of successful communication: we are primed to respond to people who are genuinely interested in us.

The conversational dance

Conversation can be viewed as a dance between participants, which is both choreographed and improvised at the same time. Participants can explore the topics of conversation and also go beyond them, so that the conversation is both known and unknown simultaneously. This cannot be achieved by simply asking people a string of direct questions. First, this is likely to alienate participants, so they will not open up and engage. Second, the convenor may not know the nuances of the subject area. There will be aspects that emerge in conversation that some of the participations will not be familiar with. Third, participants may themselves discover aspects of their own behaviour or attitudes of which they were not previously aware.

The style of moderation and interaction obviously needs to reflect the nature of the group and its purpose, so that participants can recognize and feel reassured by the environment. One of the essential moderator skills is to recognize when to lead and when to follow – and this takes considerable experience. When I talk about leading, I am not referring to the actual questions asked, but to the process of steering the participants through the relevant agenda, without bias. This avoids leading questions that may influence the participants and skew their responses.

We can never *truly* know how participants experience the situation but if we stay sensitive to what is happening in the group interactions we can often *gauge the mood* and adjust our behaviour in order to help keep the group on track. This means being aware, moment by moment, of the interaction. We can plan what we want to achieve in a meeting, but the plan is just a guide. Anticipate deviation. To do this, we need improvisational skills. Effective communication involves observing other people's behaviour: how they express themselves, how they respond in the particular situation and how they interact with different participants.

As moderator, your responsibility is to create an atmosphere that is conducive for participants to share their views, thoughts and feelings with the rest of the group. This can be quite a challenge. There need to be ground rules, which will vary depending on the mix of people attending and the topics under discussion. Ideally a spectrum of views would be encouraged and the conversation would cover the areas that are relevant, of interest and reflect the agreed topics. Encouraging people to speak out can be a challenge, but is important, to ensure a mix of views. This needs to be done in such a way that the free-flowing conversation within the group is not inhibited. The aim is to foster an environment in which participants are relaxed, comfortable and feel as if they are having normal, everyday conversations.

There is an obvious contradiction here. As moderator you need to act like a duck: smooth and unruffled on the surface, but paddling madly under the water as you steer the conversation subtly in order to cover the objectives of the meeting. You need to recognize important areas when these emerge and encourage the group to discuss these in detail, using a variety of verbal and non-verbal moderating skills. The group dynamic needs to be handled constructively and participants encouraged to speak out and feel comfortable doing so. It is quite a challenge.

Developing moderating skills

There is a paradox in moderating meetings. A good moderator will make the process look easy and it is common for an observer to comment, 'That was a really good meeting.' In practice, it was a really good moderator, but really good moderation is invisible.

Becoming *really good* at moderating meetings takes time, practice and ideally the guidance of an experienced mentor. Experienced researcher and moderator Joanna Chrzanowska describes how moderating is a delicate balancing act, involving the integration of different factions, possibly clients and other participants with different agendas:

> You are managing the power relations between moderator and participants, choosing how to frame questions and when to make interventions and being sensitive to the group dynamics as well as the feelings and issues of the individual participants – all at the same time. It happens as a set of moment-by-moment moderator choices. Colloquially speaking, these happen in the moderator's head. Since the moderator is working simultaneously on several different levels it might be more accurate to say they happen in the body-mind (using inputs from the physical, emotional and intuitive levels).[12]

This may seem quite an esoteric explanation and difficult to grasp initially. Certainly, in the early stages it is normal for a new moderator to interview 'from their head', that is, the interview is largely a cerebral process as the moderator struggles to stay in control, get through the agreed agenda and keep the meeting on track. However, over time, and with experience, more of the senses come into play. An experienced moderator may choose to loosen their intellectual control and allow their senses to inform their understanding of what is going on. Experienced moderator Rosie Campbell described this type of awareness to me as:

> a bit like butterflies in my stomach – hard to describe. It's like I know emotionally, before I get the intellectual understanding. I'm onto something important and I have to just wait and be alert. Sometimes it's when things are confused or when, for no apparent reason, I get really interested in what is going on.

There are a number of ways in which these skills can be developed but it is worth pointing out that the most important moderator skill is establishing rapport. Everything else can be forgiven.

Non-verbal communication (NVC)

Human beings have an extraordinary ability to communicate with one another in a myriad of ways. In Western culture, we tend to overplay language because we prize *rational thought* and *speech* over other forms of communication. However, non-verbal communications such as eye movements, frowning, grimacing, the way we walk, our accent, our dress, a smile, being overfamiliar and so on can all complement – or undermine – the words we use. Equally, the words we *choose* and the *way* we use them – our intonation, silences, tone of voice – are just as important as the words themselves. Some non-verbal communication is overt and intentional, whereas much of it is outside our conscious awareness.

It is useful to develop an awareness of the huge range of NVC communication because it opens the door to a greater understanding of others and their needs, attitudes and behaviours. The range of non-verbal communications discussed here is just the tip of the iceberg. There is much to explore.

The role of non-verbal communication (body language)

Non-verbal communication or *body language* is essentially communication without words. It includes any bodily expression, such as eye or facial movements, posture and actions to which an observer attributes meaning. It also includes vocal cues or signals: crying, shouting or silences, although these cues are, strictly speaking, verbal. According to Mark Earls, 'more than 90 per cent of what is communicated by any speaker lies in the (largely unconscious) nuances of tone of voice and body language and only 10 per cent of effective communication comes from the content of what is said'.[13] It makes you wonder if it is worth talking at all. Different researchers challenge this proportion, but whatever proportion we adopt, it is clear that NVC is a very important element of communication.

Body language often acts at an unconscious level: we may transmit *signals* without being aware that we are doing so, although they might be noticed by an observer. Equally, body signals can be learnt and consciously used by the sender: for example, maintaining eye contact or smiling to encourage rapport. Body language is often described as more primitive and powerful than verbal communication and it acts in different ways. For example, communication containing strong emotional content, (comfort, love and apology) may be better communicated non-verbally, as these messages can be more ambiguous and subtle. More likely this is a reflection of our generalized belief that spoken language is the superior form of communication because it is believed (erroneously) to be more rational.

Verbal messages can be superseded or, alternatively, reinforced by body language and topics that are rarely discussed tend to have underdeveloped vocabularies. Body language can fill the gaps. For example, it might be easier to *demonstrate* how you brush your teeth, rather than explain. Most importantly, body language enables conversation to flow, by offering a common code that all of those involved in the dialogue will understand, eg taking turns to speak, adopting another's mood state, empathizing, consoling etc.

Most of us have a degree of skill in using body language. We do it all the time, often without thinking about it. However, becoming more *aware* of what we do and how we do it enables us to choose the most appropriate body language to convey our meaning in specific situations. The range of body language is almost endless. It includes: leaning forward, silence, smiling expectantly, making or avoiding eye contact, looking down or away, grimacing, laughing – in fact the whole spectrum of human emotions. Sometimes we might be looking for consonance or dissonance between verbal and spoken behaviour; for example, what someone says may contradict what they do. The more we observe, the better we become at accurately interpreting the body language.

Body language also differs from country to country and there are recognized and reliable cultural differences in non-verbal communication. Consider differences in greetings: in parts of Europe it is appropriate to bow with a slight click of the heels; in Japan, a deep respectful bow is required; the gallant hand kiss is used in France, the bear-hug in Russia.

Expressing ourselves through our senses

We all have preferences in the way in which we use our senses. Some people think in words. Others are visually oriented and think in pictures. Some trust their feelings or instincts. In NLP, these different sensory preferences are called *representational systems*, which can be expressed as:

Sense	Representational system
sight	visual
hearing	auditory
feeling	kinaesthetic
tasting	gustatory
smell	olfactory

The way in which people express themselves provides clues to their preferred representational system. Someone who repeatedly starts a sentence with 'I feel' is likely to be strongly kinesthetic, whereas a person who starts with 'Sounds like' may be more auditory. Mirroring a participant's language can encourage them to open up and expand on a subject. Those with a visual preference may be interested in drawing, visual arts, film or interior design. With an auditory preference they might be interested in language, writing or drama. Kinesthetic people are typically drawn to sport or working with their hands. These are, of course, stereotypes, and people may use all sorts of combinations of these representational systems at different times, while having one that comes more naturally to them. The important thing is to be aware that people think differently. Knowing this, we can use various approaches to understanding how individuals make sense of their world. By paying attention to *in the moment* interactions in conversation, *being present*, we can absorb and understand much more information.

Language tools to aid understanding

There is a variety of simple linguistic tools that can be used as an aid for understanding.

Reflecting can help us to view a situation as if through the eyes of another: for example, 'It sounds as if you are pretty angry at the way you were treated in the surgery.' This gives the participant the opportunity to confirm, deny or clarify what they have said. In doing so, he or she may delve deeper into their own experiences and be able to give a fuller or more emotional description of their feelings. This is not therapy. It is helping the participant to understand his/her reactions, so that they respond appropriately.

Summarizing may help a smooth transition to the next topic or be used to confirm understanding. It is also an opportunity to *clarify*. A participant's meaning when they use certain words may seem self-evident, but sometimes, just asking, 'What does it mean when you call him xxx?' reveals quite surprising answers.

Silence, when appropriately used, can be a very powerful way of communicating respect, empathy and interest in something a participant has just said. It also allows the participant to work through their own thoughts, which is especially important when exploring areas that are difficult to articulate. These strategies demonstrate to the participant that the moderator is both concentrating on, and actively processing, what he or she is saying – the hallmarks of active listening.

Open and closed questions. Questions can be either *open* or *closed*. Open (non-directive) questions, often start with 'what', 'why', where', 'who' and provide space for the participant to answer in his or her own words and to decide how to develop the conversation. For example, 'Describe a typical day at work' gives participants considerable leeway to steer the conversation in whatever way they choose and to focus on areas that they consider to be important. This type of question is appropriate when exploring broad topic areas, because it helps the moderator to highlight key areas that are important to participants, and which can be explored in more detail.

Neither open nor closed questions are *better*. Each has its place and the skill is in understanding which type of question is appropriate at a particular moment in time, in order to elicit the type of response that is needed. It is common for novice moderators to ask more closed questions, because they feel that they have greater control over the interaction. However, this makes for a staccato conversation, which may bypass the key issues.

The meaning of language, revealed through qualitative research

Language lies at the heart of organizational life. Even when we employ imaginative, innovative techniques, we develop, discuss and demonstrate them through language.

What people *say* and what is created in conversation (or written in discourse) *creates* reality, not least because we hear it as we speak it. Listen to a participant in a market research session explaining her laundry routine:

> I'm afraid I'm the one who has the obsessively tidy house. I plump up my cushions at night. I have to put clean clothes away. I don't feel comfortable with myself until I do.

This woman is not just describing what she does. She is relaying a well-rehearsed story. *Obsessively tidy* is a personal theme that is used to explain and contextualize who she is.

The ways in which people use language are hugely revealing. Listening to people's stories – how they describe events, the words they use, what they choose to focus on – tells us a great deal about who they are. Indeed, how we use words contains the code for our beliefs and motivations. In the hurly burly of everyday life it is hard to make time to reflect seriously on language. But if we do, we can unearth an Aladdin's cave of cultural, social and personal meaning. It is only through hearing the language, with its intonation, hesitation, pace etc, that we can absorb the full flavour of the communication – bearing in mind that we inevitably *fill in the gaps* to create our own unique meaning. Language can be analysed at different levels. Here are a few examples of the ways in which it can reveal meaning on cultural, social and personal levels.

Language as cultural discourse

We often use language in ways that are so rooted in our culture that we do not notice how *odd* they are until we question them. The bizarreness of the language becomes what Professor John Shotter, a communications specialist, calls 'rationally invisible'.[14] For example, 'What's he worth?' is generally understood as 'How much money has he got?' In a society where one's wealth is the definition of worth, this seems normal, but in societies in which wealth is measured by other criteria, such as status in the community or age, it seems very odd. Then there is the never-ending lure of property:

> '. . . *the security of bricks and mortar* . . .'
> '*You can't go wrong with property!*'
> '*Safe as houses.*'

These quotes reflect cultural assumptions, which were regarded as *truths* until the 2008 world recession proved otherwise.

Language as social meaning

We often adopt family or group *truths* which become *shared reality*, so that denying the *truth* is particularly upsetting:

> 'In my family, debt is always frowned upon.'

For this research participant, getting into debt would bring more than simply anxiety about money. It would bring shame and challenge her family allegiances.

Language as personal meaning

'*Money just slipped through my fingers.*'

'Slipped through' and 'my fingers' are very close up, worried descriptions, in which the teller feels things happen to him. This is a common use of language, in which the narrator distances him- or herself from the activity and denies agency. It was 'not my fault'. An area where this is particularly pronounced is in weight loss, as illustrated by comments made by overweight women in a focus group:

> '*It was the car that put the weight on me . . .*'

> '*I look and think, "What are these rolls? Why have they decided to settle on me?"*'

Language as storytelling

Language is the food of stories that both describe the past and define the future:

> '*When I had a thin summer in my mid-twenties, I wasn't actually all that happy . . . I felt like I was waiting all the time, feeling anxious that the weight would come back . . . and of course, it did . . . Sometimes I wonder why I'm obsessed by losing weight . . .*'

Making sense of participants' experience

In real life, how we *experience* something is dependent on a complex mix of intellect, bodily reactions, emotions, in a soup of personal history. A truism of NLP is 'The meaning of the communication is the response you get.' This may seem odd, initially. We tend to think that *we* are the source of the communication and therefore if it is misunderstood, then it is the fault of the recipient. However, turning this around gives a different perspective. We may get curious and ask how the misunderstanding is possible. What is the participant's world view that encourages him or her to interpret the communication in this way? By paying attention, staying curious and asking questions around a topic, we can gain an understanding of where the participant is coming from, who they are and what drives him or her. Language is arguably the most important theme in this book. It is through language that we will be enabled to change our organizations. Language is capable of changing hearts and minds, but only if we work together and only if we really care.

How talk transformed the East Coast main-line railway[15]

Karen Boswell joined the East Coast as managing director in late 2009. Her remit was to restore financial stability to the line before handing over to a new private sector operator 18 months later. Two previous franchise owners had run out of money, and the government took the company back into public control as a wholly owned not-for-profit subsidiary.

The job turned out to be bigger than Boswell anticipated and the problems too great to be quickly resolved. The job she was appointed to do, and the length of time she had to do it, changed completely. Before Boswell joined, the only research available was the mandatory employee survey, so she and her team set to work to develop a rigorous programme of research and insight. Boswell has now overseen several stages of employee insight work, including a series of focus groups. The team talked with a vast swathe of passengers and with staff from a wide range of jobs. They identified problems and good practices in all parts of the business and talked about how the problems could be resolved. Then they went back again to check that the solutions had worked.

The outcomes helped the company to develop its employer brand, based on four key promises: different every day, pride in what we do, warm and friendly people, and smarter ways of working. 'You have to be dogged and honest about your approach – and when people see you doing what you said you would do, they gradually come with you,' said Boswell.

A second piece of work, talking with still more passengers and staff, used the initial insights that emerged throughout the year to help leaders and teams to improve. The objective was to shift the company from its traditional rules and process-driven approach towards a more customer-focused orientation. Forty-five focus groups were conducted along the East Coast route to find out how the highest performers did their job, with particular attention paid to train guards and station staff, these being the roles that have most direct impact on passengers. As Stephanie Oerton, head of learning and development on the East Coast line put it, 'There's no point in having a great marketing campaign if your staff let you down.'

Boswell is a visible and accessible leader, but the culture she sets from the top is reinforced by a comprehensive communications programme, designed to reach engineers working overnight in the Craigentinny depot in Edinburgh as easily as it does frontline staff at King's Cross. Communication is two-way, though. The rigorous and continuous staff engagement and customer satisfaction programmes that Boswell instigated when she joined the company have given the East Coast an unprecedented insight into what its people and customers value, and this has allowed the company to deliver more of it. 'We changed the employee satisfaction survey to the "employee engagement survey" because engagement plays to advocacy and there is a clear link between advocacy and profitability,' says Boswell. Engagement is not soft and fluffy – it is about pure revenue and profit. Between 2010 and 2013 staff engagement scores, based on an annual survey, rose from 62 per cent to 73 per cent – higher than the comparable train companies measured – while staff participation increased from 52 per cent to 78 per cent. By the time the line is re-privatized in February 2015 it is expected to have returned £1 billion to the government.

The East Coast main line is a success story, thanks to Karen Boswell and her team. By using consumer insight gleaned from talking extensively with passengers and staff, they gradually came to understand what makes a successful main line. Then they put it into practice. The overriding theme that emerges is of a team who threw themselves into the project, who motivated others to get on board and who swept everyone along with their enthusiasm and commitment. It is this passion to succeed that sustained them. They won hearts and minds in the process. This use of language may not be as earth-shattering as that of Martin Luther King, but it is certainly effective. And perhaps the last word should go to Rudyard Kipling: 'Words are, of course, the most powerful drug used by mankind.'

Notes

1 Active Listening, in (ed) Lisa M Goven, *The Sage Encyclopedia of Qualitative Research Methods*, Vol 1 Part 7, Sage

2 Kahneman, D (2012) *Thinking, Fast and Slow*, Penguin

3 Pentland, S (2012) The new science of building great teams, *Harvard Business Review*, April

4 www.diagolos.com

5 Shaw, P (2002) *Changing Conversations in Organizations: A complexity approach to change*, Routledge

6 Isanski, B (2010) Talking your way to happiness: Well-being is related to having less small talk and more substantive conversation, *Association for Psychological Science* [online] https://www.psychologicalscience.org/media/releases/2010/mehl.cfm

7 Losada, M and Heaphy, E (2004) The role of positivity and connectivity in the performance of business teams – a non-linear model, *American Behavioural Scientist*, **47** (6) pp 740–65

8 Ferdig, M and Ludema, J (2005) Transformative interactions: Qualities of conversion that heighten the vitality of self-organizing change, *Research in Organizational Change and Development* **15**, pp 169–205

9 Jacobs, C and Heracleous, L (2005), Answers for questions to come: reflective dialogue as an enabler of strategic innovation, *Journal of Organizational Change Management*, **18** (4) pp 338–52

10 Rogers, C (1961) *On Becoming a Person*, Constable

11 Csikszentmihalyi, M (2002) *Flow: The psychology of happiness*, Rider

12 Chrzanoswka, quoted in Keegan, S (2009), *Qualitative Research: Good decision-making through understanding people, cultures and markets*, Kogan Page

13 Earls, M (2002) *Welcome to the Creative Age: Bananas, business and the death of marketing*, John Wiley

14 Shotter, J (1993), *Conversational Realities: Constructing life through language*, Sage

15 Simms, J, How talk transformed the East Coast Railway, Abridged article from *Impact Magazine*, 2014

Building a culture of innovation

Why do I stand up here? . . . I stand upon my desk to remind myself that we must constantly look at things in a different way . . . Just when you think you know something, you have to look at it in another way, even though it may seem silly or wrong . . . Now, when you read, don't just consider what the author thinks, consider what you think. DEAD POETS SOCIETY

Banishing fear of the unknown

Fear and over caution can be the death of innovation within organizations. Fearful of making mistakes, of blundering into costly ventures that end in disaster, of being seen as foolish, we hold back, or wait for the right moment. But there is no right moment. Innovation by its very nature is always a risk. However much we plan and research and try to consider all the issues, at the end of the day we cannot know whether we will succeed or fail until our baby is launched. Before we start, we have to accept that we may fail. Only through this acceptance can we liberate ourselves to 'feel the fear and do it anyway'. As Steve Jobs put it, 'Innovation distinguishes between a leader and a follower.'

Creating ideas

Among the things a company needs to consider when innovating are acceptable timescales and risk, says innovation consultant Lida Hujic.[1] Timescales can range enormously depending on the project. Breakthrough or disruptive innovation takes the longest time and carries the most risk; it involves thinking beyond the company's brands and beyond product categories. According to UK innovation charity, Nesta, which tracks emergent innovation, we have moved on from the 20th-century models of innovation that were driven by big labs and programmes funded by governments, or by the research and development capacities of huge firms. Companies are increasingly looking for external ideas. Many industries use open innovation in this way.

Crowdsourcing has thrived in recent years. For instance, LEGO has a crowdsourcing platform called Cuusoo (recently relaunched as Lego Ideas) to which people can submit new designs for LEGO products. If the LEGO community supports the idea, LEGO will produce it and give the designer a share of the revenue. NASA has also become involved in crowdsourcing by running a competition to invent a more efficient astronaut glove and it encourages individuals, student groups and private companies to participate in R&D through cash prizes. The UK department store John Lewis has announced the launch of an open innovation scheme, JLab, which encourages start-ups to find ways that customers can shop across channels and simplify their lives using in-store personalization.[2]

Thinking differently as a way of life

During the long years of the economic downturn, considerable energy was focused on keeping organizations afloat and functioning – whatever it took. Meanwhile, over-control in organizations has had the effect of discouraging risk-taking among employees; squashing initiative and dispelling creativity and novel thinking. We are creatures of habit. As the adage goes, 'If you keep doing the same thing, you will get the same result.' Even as the economic climate changes, we do not necessarily recognize the change. It is too easy to become locked into tunnel vision and continue on the same trajectory.

To recapture our enthusiasm and creativity, we need to be willing to experiment, and to risk failure. In her book *Daring Greatly*, Brene Brown describes individual creativity as the combination of one's personal experiences, knowledge of others' experiences and other factors such as education; the combined outcome gives each person a quite unique perspective. 'I think that is what sparks innovation and seeing things differently. We wouldn't be able to innovate and come up with new ideas if they could not be birthed from our unique and creative perspectives,' says Brown.[3]

Perhaps more than anything else, we need noisy, productive, good-natured and creative dissent in organizations. This is not only helpful; it is essential. There is a considerable body of research pointing to the importance of diversity as a route to developing new ideas.[4] The creativity guru Sidney Parnes, when talking about our propensity to resist change, quipped, 'All that a man wants now is a womb with a view.' He was probably right; the urge to clutch to the known is sometimes overwhelming. Parnes continues: 'The man who wants to emerge from the cocoon will need a radical change in his thinking. And as with most changes, he may have to practise it for quite a while before he appreciates its worth.'

Indeed, we may need to push ourselves into uncomfortable situations, to endure alternative perspectives, bring outsiders to the table to offer fresh ideas, get out of the office, come into the office and even interact face to face! Any novel situation will challenge stale ideas and assumptions, and help foster a culture in which employees are thinking, reassessing, reviewing and creating. Energy, skill, enthusiasm and tenacity are some of the key qualities that are most needed for innovation. To rejuvenate organizations, we need people who can think and act in these different ways. However, humans are born with the innate desire to problem-solve, which can translate into innovation, but sometimes we just forget about it.

Google famously asks its employees to spend one day a week working on projects outside their usual job description to encourage innovation. Human curiosity, when fostered correctly, is what leads people to pioneer new cures for diseases, more efficient forms of energy and new ways to see the world. You don't need to hire a team of geniuses to achieve innovation, but you do need to give your workforce the confidence and incentive to solve the problems around them, until problem-solving becomes an integral part of the culture.

Innovation doesn't need to be complex or expensive either, although it may require a shift in mindset. Recently I listened to a talk by a Procter & Gamble scientist. He told the story of how the company had developed teeth-whitening strips which you stuck onto your teeth like Sellotape. Ten minutes later you pulled off the strip and uncovered sparkling white teeth. However, as simple as it sounds, the research team had struggled for years. They had been modelling the process on an earlier design, which was a rigid plate that covered all the teeth to the back of the mouth. However, they just couldn't work out how to design the strips so that they could be easily attached to the back teeth. The scientist explained the eureka moment. 'We were really stuck. We couldn't find a way to do it. Then a newly arrived member of the team asked the killer question: "Why does it matter if your back teeth are white? No one sees them there."' Sometimes we can just get too close to a problem. P&G went back to the drawing board and designed the strips to cover the *visible* front teeth. The product was simple and cheap to produce and it was very effective. A successful product was launched.

Innovation is what we *are*

Innovation is not simply a function of what employees do. Innovation is central in terms of how employees see themselves and how they view their level of engagement within the organization itself. Ideally employees can use the hive networks within organizations to make informal connections and establish communication routes. They can short-circuit traditional communication channels and build connections that can facilitate innovation hubs, which may cut across hierarchies and functions. Social media provide opportunities to develop innovation communities that can span geography, function and interests and come up with some extraordinary innovation. Included in the Google Top 20 inventions of 2014 are: a bed that massages you to sleep, an artificial pancreas, a super-strong spade, washing gloves with a built-in soap dispenser, a portable flood defence system and 'Tappy', a bath tap protection for small children that transforms into a hand puppet.

If innovation is what we are, how do we express this? There are many ways. It may be that we set aside a 15-minute slot in a weekly sales and marketing meeting and ask everyone at the table to talk about one interesting innovation they have seen in the company's industry, or better yet, an industry in another sector. We can offer examples that are most applicable to the business, then charge one person or team to flesh out that idea or ideas. We might monitor progress monthly in the same team meetings. Success breeds success; feedback and inclusivity are its lifeblood. If innovation is truly what we are, then we will see opportunities wherever we go.

The paradox of innovation

Innovation is something of a paradox. On the one hand it is put on a pedestal as the idealized goal: 'Innovate or die!' Companies that are highly innovative are revered, often regardless of their financial successes. On the other hand, innovation is feared. It is a high-risk activity and, if it goes wrong then the employees who are involved are likely to bear the brunt. But innovation does not always need to be monolithic; it needs to reflect the needs of the organization or indeed the specific task at hand. Clearly if you are Apple, innovation is the root of the brand. If you are Sainsbury's or Andrex or Marks and Spencer, there is more of a balance needed between innovation and constancy – which bits to change, which to keep and develop. It may be more evolution than revolution. Indeed, prioritizing constancy has been a very effective strategy for many brands. Look at brands such as Wickes, Hovis and John Lewis. Clearly predictability and reliability should not be dismissed if they are core brand values.

There is often a pressure to innovate; it is taken to be a sign of a dynamic company. But exploring the obvious questions – such as 'how/when/where/why do we want to innovate?' – is not a bad start for any innovation programme. There are sound reasons to innovate and, equally, there are valid reasons why innovation – or particular routes to innovation – are not valid for a particular organization at a particular time. Fear is not a valid reason to avoid innovation, yet it is frequently the unspoken barrier. The first step is to acknowledge our fear of failure, exposure and ridicule, and how it can freeze and blinker us. Both fear and habit stop us communicating effectively with one another and they limit our perspectives at the expense of creativity and innovation. New ideas rarely spring from a culture of gloom. The second step is to assess the risks – or what may turn out to be an overblown perception of them – and work out ways of reducing the risks involved, for example by combining forces with another department, seeking expert help, staggering the process, instigating a trial run and so on. If innovation is viewed as a necessary mindset, an ongoing part of organizational life in which every employee can potentially be involved and which inevitably produces failures – as well as occasional successes – then the perception of risk is much smaller.

The concept of *jugaad*

In India, there is often less angst about failure in innovation, because trial and error and making do are culturally ingrained. A very interesting concept has developed, born out of necessity in poorer areas of India – although it has spread and been reconfigured throughout the country. *Jugaad*, sometimes referred to as *jugard*, is a colloquial Hindi word applied to creative or innovative ideas that provide a quick and cheap alternative way of solving or fixing a problem. Roughly it translates as 'overcoming harsh constraints by improvising an effective solution using limited resources'. An innovative fix or a simple workaround can also be referred to as *jugaad* and it is sometimes used to describe solutions that bend rules or a resource that can be used, such as a person who can solve a complicated issue. It is very roughly the equivalent of the British 'make do and mend' although, through ingenuity and necessity, Indians have elevated *jugaad* to an art form. I have seen derelict cars brought back to life, shoes crafted from old tyres, delicious, impromptu meals cooked over an open fire in the desert, all referred to as *jugaad*. It can also be used to describe enterprising street mechanics, who are used to mending machinery and tools with limited resources but a good deal of ingenuity and creativity. This ability to rethink the problem in such a way that it enables a possible, previously unconsidered, solution is a very precious resource and invaluable in terms of thinking innovatively.

Jugaad *in action*

Paperclips have a long history of versatility. They have opened locks and acted as toothpicks. However, Dr Pushkar Waknis, a maxillofacial surgeon from Pune, India, has found an unexpected use for them, that is, to keep the skin flap in place while operating on the face. Not only is this effective, but paperclips are more easily accessible than surgical clips, which are both expensive and hard to find in India. 'The paperclip can bring down the cost of surgery. This can be a big amount for poor patients,' says Dr Waknis.[5] *Jugaad* is increasingly being used by surgeons who are replacing costly, disposable imported surgical devices with cheaper, more common and locally sourced tools. Being frugal, the doctors insist, does not mean compromising on quality. 'We come up with *jugaads* because we have to cater to all patients, whether poor or rich,' says Dr Suresh Vasistha, joint secretary of the Association of Surgeons of India.[6] Other forms of medical *jugaad* are also commonly used. For instance, doctors have used mosquito net mesh in hernia operations because the tube costs just a few rupees.[7] 'Whenever there is an effective local option, which has been documented and proven to be safe, we try to use it,' says Dr Pillai. In 2012, surgeons at the All India Institute of Medical Sciences published a paper that showed that honey healed wounds better and faster than povidone-iodine, the standard ointment used in such cases.[8] 'As long as you follow basic principles of sterilization and operative techniques, and provide good post-op clinical care, it is safe to use low-cost substitutes,' says Dr Satish Shukla, an oncology surgeon based in Indore and president of the Association of Surgeons of India.

Jugaad: *expanding into management*

Jugaad is becoming a mainstream concept in India. It is already recognized as an acceptable form of frugal engineering, adopted as a practice to reduce research and development costs. It is also increasingly accepted in India as a management technique, where it is applied to some forms of management thinking, such as creative out-of-the-box ideation, which maximizes resources for a company and its shareholders. The principles of *jugaad* are simple but intriguing and they are increasingly being applied to a range of problem-solving situations. According to the authors of *Jugaad Innovation*,[9] companies such as 3M, GE, PepsiCo, Procter & Gamble and Siemens are already using *jugaad*.

Bring on the new

We often underestimate our power and abilities. We are not just passive observers. We are all – individually and collectively – responsible for developing an engaged, productive and energized workforce. We all know from our own experience that it is easier to achieve our goals when we are confident, optimistic and enthusiastic. Successful innovation is more likely to grow out of a positive, cooperative work climate in which there is a combination of factors such as strong, involved management support and an acceptance of a variety of different perspectives; where there are time, tenacity, trial and error and, to varying degrees, budget. But most of all it needs passion within the teams that are leading the projects and the managers who are sponsoring them. If employees regularly see innovation displayed in a positive and fun light, and they are rewarded for their more innovative personal pursuits, they will be much more likely to mimic that behaviour in the workplace.

We take small personal risks every day: crossing the road, building an Ikea cupboard, making a new LinkedIn contact. Can we not foster organizational cultures in which greater individual autonomy and small organizational risks are simply part of everyone's job? We tend to place too much faith in senior managers and too little faith in the workforce as a whole to deliver commitment, innovation and entrepreneurial spirit. Often we expect more of senior managers than they are able to deliver. They are our co-workers and subject to many of the same anxieties, doubts and fears as the rest of us although they may have more responsibility and inevitably get paid more. It is often the collective mind of the workforce or team that brings about the breakthrough thinking which fuels innovation. To achieve this requires commitment and effort on behalf of the designated team. Nonetheless, board members who are motivated to fan the flames of innovation are a great bonus, not least because they have the clout to command financial and other resources.

Organizations need to loosen old habits that have become set during the downturn, and that are now holding back new thinking and experimentation. Energy needs to be directed into growth and innovation. Where possible, governments need to support the organizations that are struggling to innovate. If we are to turn our fortunes around as societies and as individuals, we need a degree of bravery all round, in order to shrug off the despondency and uncertainty of the last five years and take a leap of faith into the future.

Why do birds fly in a V formation?

Trust is the glue that binds us. If we can share our fears and cooperate wholeheartedly with our work colleagues, then the collective power and knowledge of the group can be more than the sum of its parts. This is something that we humans find difficult to do, but strangely enough, birds manage it very easily. Perhaps we can learn something from them.

It has long been a mystery as to why birds fly in a V formation. Scientists from the Royal Veterinary College now think they have the answer.[10] They have fitted data loggers to a flock of rare birds that were being trained to migrate by following a microlight aircraft. They discovered that the birds flew in the optimal position – gaining lift from the bird in front by remaining close to its wingtip. The study, published in the journal *Nature*, also showed that the birds timed their wing beats perfectly. As a bird's wings move through the air, they are held at a slight angle, which deflects the air downward. This deflection means that the air flows faster over the wing than underneath, causing air pressure to build up beneath the wings, while the pressure above the wings is reduced. This makes the most of upward-moving air generated by the bird in front. As a result, the other bird wants to put its own wingtip in the upwash from the bird in front, to reduce its own efforts. The lead researcher Dr Steven Portugal explained: 'They're seemingly very aware of where the other birds in the flock are and they put themselves in the best position possible. This can give a bit of a free ride for the bird that's following.'

A previous experiment with pelicans was the first real clue as to the energy-saving purpose of the V formations. It revealed that the birds' heart rates went down when they were flying together.[11] The birds work collaboratively. They are constantly in tune with their fellow birds, each automatically making minor, individual adjustments to their behaviour in order to maximize the efficiency of the flock as a whole. It is a very precise process, but also a constantly adaptable one. It saves energy. It puts less effort on the bird's heart and supports both the individual bird and the flock as a whole. What a lot we could learn from birds.

'We are family'

Western culture has an obsession with the individual and our illusion that we are each autonomous beings, who can exist and can make decisions without the influence of others. The reality is that we are constantly being influenced in all sorts of ways by our environment and by the people we come across, although we may not be aware of it. At best we are interdependent individuals, working cooperatively, trusting, sharing our anxieties, our strengths and our vulnerabilities. This not only provides us with a broader canvas on which to work but it also acknowledges the essentially human activities we are engaged in. The birds understand intuitively that by cooperating, by working together, they can become stronger. We humans sometimes forget this truth. Brene Brown, in *Daring Greatly*, quotes Peter Sheahan, the CEO of ChangeLabs, a global consultancy building and delivering large-scale behavioural change projects:

> If you want a culture of creativity and innovation, where sensible risks are embraced on both a market and individual level, start by developing the ability of managers to cultivate an openness to vulnerability in their teams. And this, perhaps paradoxically, requires that first they are vulnerable themselves.

Cultural preparedness and reducing risk

We can try to manage the risks and reduce the fear factor in a number of ways. For instance, we can prepare and train employees to be more receptive to innovation. We can do this by developing a cultural preparedness in which employees throughout the organization are primed to be receptive to – and work with – the exploratory nature of innovation. This sets the scene for the development of innovation from all levels and functions within the organization.

Alternatively, and in conjunction, we may adopt a strategy of ongoing, low-risk research processes, eg parallel work teams exploring the same issues, involving clients and/or customers in qualitative research, creative workshops, ethnographic immersion or other activities that encourage them to question their preconceptions and develop parallel perspectives. We may decide to nominate a chief of innovation, whose job it is to keep everyone on track, ensuring that innovation is an ongoing part of organizational life. We might be actively on the lookout for tipping points in the organization, where small shifts can trigger significant changes. We may also be actively experimenting and learning from our mistakes, fostering a *hive* culture where ideas and initiatives can be shared, and group organizational learning activities used to increase autonomy and trust between employees.

These activities clearly need to be tailored to the particular organization, so that they make sense to employees and motivate them. However, they do not necessarily have to be linked to a specific innovation. Staff at all levels and in various functions can help to develop a culture of innovation that challenges both habitual ways of thinking and the insidious effects of inertia. These, and other initiatives, can help foster an organization that punches above its weight, so that innovation becomes part and parcel of the organizational culture, mindset and behaviour.

Finding a voice

Innovation is often thwarted because staff feel embarrassed or afraid to speak out, to draw attention to themselves or simply because they are afraid of being wrong. In organizational cultures where people are afraid to speak freely, employees often withhold opinions, suggestions or knowledge that may be very useful to other employees or to the organization as a whole. They need a climate that facilitates speaking out. They may not want to talk about big issues. Their suggestions might relate to local problems or ideas to improve their own working practices. However, small changes can sometimes make big differences.

There is so much untapped potential in most organizations. By understanding and encouraging employees, with all their diverse experiences, knowledge and creativity, to think and work together on new ideas and new ways of doing things, we can set in motion processes of rolling innovation – provided there is a management culture that encourages and supports this. This is more than the passive suggestions box. It needs to be an active and inclusive process in which staff feel involved and in which they participate freely. In this way, innovation and experimentation at a local level become normalized and part of every employee's responsibility. Equally, encouraging different perspectives, often at a micro-level – through individual initiatives or by small, informal groups working on initiatives in their specific area – fosters a climate of micro-innovation that can spread across the whole organization. This approach has the advantage of capturing and utilizing the wide range of creative skills that employees have, but historically do not bring to the workplace. By utilizing these skills, employees become more engaged, more confident and more strongly linked to both their work teams and the organization. Trial and error, experimentation, improvisation and measured risk-taking become part of organizational life.

Essentially, these initiatives are about building engagement within the workforce, which is simple to say but often hard to do. Indeed workplace engagement can be seen as a process of re-humanizing the environment in which people are working and fostering cooperation, enthusiasm and pride in their work. From this perspective, the processes of building innovation can be seen as the art of building human relationships and skills, rather than 'the science of organizational change' – a description that, to me, manages to bypass the human element altogether.

It is possible to change corporate culture over time and to encourage employees at all levels of the organization to be more innovation-receptive, although this does require consistent, well-thought-out strategies, a core of staff throughout the organization who are motivated to create change, and strong management initiation and support. There are many forms that this can take, for instance Synectics, neuro-linguistic programming (NLP), creative workshops, brainstorming and a variety of training options. Essentially, in these approaches employees are encouraged to address innovation issues that are within their domain, areas in which they may be knowledgeable, or where they have particular concerns and where they are authorized to initiate changes that will improve their working lives. At best these initiatives can foster a climate in which employees develop a heightened awareness of, and involvement with, their work environment and with their co-workers, and also with innovative thinking and practice which can improve the quality of work.

Developing strong, cooperative relationships between co-workers, including managers, reaps huge benefits in terms of collaborative innovation. In many organizations there is tension between different levels – the classic 'us and them' scenario. Much of this stems from mutual mistrust based on past experiences or simply tradition: the age-old suspicion between the managers and the workers. NLP techniques, for instance, are particularly good at challenging these stereotypes and encouraging people to view situations or problems from different perspectives.

A simple NLP technique that I have found useful for encouraging individuals to articulate their views or to understand another person's perspective, especially in conflict situations, involves changing perspectives. The 'client' involved takes on three different roles in succession. Initially he or she adopts 'first position': they stand up, face an audience and discuss the contentious issue for five minutes, focusing on their own views. Then they physically move to 'second position', to face where they had stood as first position, taking on the role of their opponent and spending five minutes discussing the issue from the opponent's perspective. Finally, they take up 'third position', that of the independent observer. In this role, they are asked to take a neutral role and spend five minutes evaluating the relative merits of the two previous positions. Simply voicing the views of 'the other', which the individual previously rejected, generally makes the client more flexible and more broad-minded in their thinking. I have observed this very simple exercise played out on many occasions and I am constantly surprised that such a simple technique can be so effective in building trust, encouraging participants to consider different perspectives, and helping them to understand how other people experience the world.

Innovation and shame

These two concepts, innovation and shame, may not seem natural bedfellows. What have they got to do with one another? Brene Brown, in *Daring Greatly*, quotes Peter Sheahan again. He very eloquently describes the role of shame in undermining innovation:

> The secret killer of innovation is shame. You can't measure it, but it is there. Every time someone holds back on a new idea, fails to give their manager much-needed feedback and is afraid to speak up in front of a client you can be sure fear plays a part. That deep fear we all have of being wrong, being belittled and of feeling less than, is what stops us taking the very risks required to move our companies forward.

Innovation as a way of seeing things differently

We have a tendency, at least in the Western world, to view reality as 'out there', something solid and immutable, which enables us to recognize the familiar, to name and use it appropriately. A chair is a chair is a chair. But of course, a chair can also be a prop, or a weapon; it can be fuel, it can be a means of blocking a door. When we set about the processes of innovation, we may want to challenge these taken-for-granted assumptions in order to open up our minds to different ways of thinking or doing. Innovation is, by its nature, a process of construction as well as discovery.

We select, consciously or otherwise, what we pay attention to and how we interpret it.

The greater the diversity of perspectives, of thinking, hypotheses, off-the-wall ideas and wacky creativity that can be fed into innovation – especially in the initial stages – the greater the potential range of ideas that can emerge. Engaging clients, customers, researchers and whoever else may contribute in some way, as co-creators, in the innovation process can only increase the scope of our knowledge and options. However, this does not necessarily mean that all contributions are equal or that the process needs to be egalitarian. There are judgements to be made about how best to manage the involvement of different parties in the process.

The improvisational nature of innovation

Over the years, a great deal has been written about creativity and innovation and how we can foster creative climates within organizations. But there is no formula that can be applied universally. If it was that easy, we would all just read the book and do it. Situations differ from one another and they evolve over time. Much of innovation is an accident – serendipity which, in retrospect, is described as planned – and there is almost always a strong element of improvisation in the processes of innovation, as we explore alternative routes.

Most of our discussion so far has focused on preparing the ground: cultivating an organizational climate which is receptive to innovation and which recognizes something new when it emerges. This is important. Few innovations are born fully formed and the more major and complex the initiative, the more likely it is that there will be a long process of trial and error, of frustration and promise, before useful innovation is glimpsed – if indeed it ever is. Acceptance of this process of trial and error is essential. In particular, if senior management is too impatient for signs of progress, then they both raise the fear levels in the innovation teams and simultaneously undermine confidence in the process itself.

A model of marginal gain

A great example of how small gains can deliver huge rewards was spelled out by the British cycling team in the 2012 Olympics. The approach, used with spectacular success by British cycling's performance director Dave

Brailsford, became part of Olympic history. Brailsford went on BBC Breakfast TV to explain the secret of the GB cycling success:

> The whole principle came from the idea that if you broke down everything you could think of that goes into riding a bike, then improved it by 1 per cent, you will get a significant increase when you put them all together.

There are two interesting themes in this explanation. First, it is a low-risk strategy; Brailsford was not making 'one giant leap for mankind', so presumably the fear of failure was reduced. Second, he was making very small but meticulous, painstaking and thorough improvements. It must have been very hard work, but he persevered. There is much to be learnt from this approach to risk reduction, attention to detail and perseverance. We need to model (sensible) risk-taking. We need to work hard and persevere, even when we fail in the early stages. Although everyone in the organization needs to be tuned in to innovation so that it becomes a state of mind, part of the hive, innovation doesn't necessarily have to be rocket science. Success may be built on a number of small steps throughout the organization. Initiatives that originate at local levels spread the message that this is an organization that fosters innovation. As much as anything, this is a way of developing stronger interdepartmental and inter-seniority links, so that the hive mode of communication becomes stronger.

Try, try and try again . . .

We can learn a lot about this process of trial and error and serendipity from major medical discoveries over the years. A great many important scientific discoveries were the result of accidents or luck: Sir Alexander Fleming discovering penicillin, Marie Curie's discovery of radium, Faraday's discovery of electricity. These radical advances for mankind were accidental discoveries. However, we have to remember the old adage that luck favours the well-prepared. These scientists had spent years studying their subject area and had a shrewd idea of what success would look like. So they recognized it when they saw it. Paul Schoemaker, a professor at Wharton Business School in Pennsylvania, encourages 'brilliant mistakes' in his students, mistakes that move things forward in a way that getting things right would not have done. He says:

> This is counter-intuitive. Some people reject the whole notion of a brilliant mistake as an oxymoron. But brilliant mistakes are an opportunity to learn.

If you think of them as a chance to challenge your thinking, they can prove to have a silver lining . . . it's about creating opportunities for serendipity and being able to recognize what can often be quite weak signals.[12]

Most organizations and individuals try to avoid making mistakes. But mistakes, provided they are managed in a controlled fashion and provided they are viewed as learning, not failure, are part of the innovation process. As Schoemaker says, 'If you avoid all mistakes, you will not get better, so you need to find opportunities to learn in a low-cost environment.' Or equally a low-risk, low-fear environment.

Inspirational market research and creative development work

I have left this area until last, not because it is less important than other areas, but because, in my opinion, it is a priority and because it generally involves bringing in specialists from outside the organization. The bedrock of any innovation process is an understanding of the market you will be selling into, whether this is an internal organizational market, a consumer market or a social context, irrespective of the nature of the innovation. Who is the target audience? Is it fragmented or cohesive? What do they want? What is missing? What are they looking for? Why do they want this? How will it fit into their lives? Will they change their behaviour to accommodate it? What role will it fulfil, emotionally, practically? How will they use it? Is usage likely to change over time? How can it be improved? And so on. These basic issues need to be covered. But so too do the more amorphous areas such as the consumer's relationship with 'it', what it says about them. And it is not enough to ask the questions. You will need to see the prototype in action; how it is actually used, its limitations, its possibilities. And how will it be three weeks later? Will it be incorporated into everyday life? Will it be discarded as boring, the excitement spent?

'Market research' is something of a misnomer. It suggests data gathering, statistical analysis, hard data. However, it is much more than this, especially if we are talking about qualitative research, in which researchers, clients, consumers, designers and others are engaged in a highly creative process of developing and shaping concepts and ultimately products. Good, professional research and creative development are critical for reducing fear and increasing knowledge in the innovation process. There is a tendency, in times of austerity, to cut back on research spending, to curb research on initial ideas, prototypes and advertising ideas. Research may also be avoided for fear that it will throw up negatives. But as we have seen, mistakes or anomalies can be an important source of learning. Research is the friend of innovation, not the enemy.

Counter-intuitive as it may seem, in straitened times it is more necessary than ever to reduce risk – and thereby fear – through investing in meticulous research and planning. It will prove to be money well spent, even if it highlights a problem with the concept at an early stage.

Developing an innovative organization

Innovation is exciting, scary and, if you get it right, exhilarating. To sum up, here are a few key themes you might like to explore and use to experiment with within your organization:

- Trust is the foundation of employee productivity and innovation. Work hard to build trust, involvement and engagement.

- Curiosity and openness are good starting points. Put your rational mind to one side and let your creative juices play with possible directions. Engage with the problem and the question. Stay curious, in the moment, throughout the project and open to whatever emerges. Being engaged with the problem or question means that you will be sensitized to possible solutions. Creating possible solutions to problems is part of being alive. If you help define the problem, there is much more interest in helping to solve it.

- Be conscious of both hierarchical structure and hive culture. Hierarchy is often less important than you imagine and hive culture is often more important. Try keeping them in your mind as parallel influences.

- Encourage healthy dissent, diversity and challenge; but make it fun and cooperative rather than challenging and undermining to others. New thinking grows out of bringing new and unfamiliar ideas together.

- Knowledge is not static. It is constantly evolving. We can get a fix on particular issues but bear in mind that they are almost inevitably work in progress.

- Question why you want to innovate and what you want to achieve. Particular innovations may not be right for your company/brand/ service at this time. Continuity is often underrated. Some of the most successful brands have traded on predictability and constancy.

- Innovation often needs full-body involvement. Be conscious of your feelings, your intuitions, guesses and hunches. Any or all of these can lead you into surprising and productive hypotheses.

- Encourage trial and error – learn from failure.

- If possible, give people some resources and time to experiment and develop ideas in small local teams. This doesn't have to be costly. It could be an hour on a Friday afternoon, but it supports the idea that all employees are responsible for the success of the organization.

- Starting from scratch is OK, provided you keep an open mind. As the famous social process consultant Edgar Schein put it: 'We need to access our areas of ignorance.'[13] In this way, we can treat questioning as part of the research process, rather than a challenge to other people's authority.

- New and creative thinking often occurs when we are outside our comfort zone, when we encourage diversity. We need to goad our team to think the unthinkable and do the undoable – within reason.

- Don't overdo the targets and performance monitoring; they usually restrict rather than prompt creativity.

- Innovation doesn't have to be 'big'. A series of small innovations may be more sustainable and less daunting. Innovation in small steps allows you to adapt and modify your original ideas as you go along.

- Identifying the influencers in the work group is essential. There are generally one or two individuals who set the tone for the group. If they can be brought on side, the task of motivating the whole group will be half done.

- Ensure that senior managers are aware of these initiatives and publicly applaud them. Too often lack of communication means that such initiatives are not appreciated and employees become disillusioned and ultimately cynical.

- Remember that, deep down, most people want to feel needed, to contribute and to grow as individuals. If this isn't obvious, it is usually because their experiences in various workplaces have taught them to be wary, cynical and withdrawn. It may take time and consistency to build trust.

- The nature of large organizations is changing. Senior managers today have the almost impossible task of managing and steering organizations that are complex, fluid, geographically dispersed, viral and virtual. Organizational structures will need to evolve to accommodate these changes. Leadership is not the preserve of leaders. In the future, improvisational leadership will increasingly be a skill that many people throughout the organization will be required to demonstrate, in order to deal with increasingly fast-moving and unpredictable situations. Welcome to a new world.

- Think about the project from a variety of angles; there is rarely just one perspective to be considered. Try out your ideas on people who come from different backgrounds or different industries. It is easy for us to become locked into a narrow way of thinking.

- Immerse yourself in the project without trying to solve the problem; allow your unconscious to mull on it. The old adage of sleeping on it is based on fact. The unconscious mind often has the ability to solve problems that we cannot resolve through our rational minds alone.

- Defining the problem is part of the solution. If we accept the problem on a platter, we do not have the opportunity to help shape it. However, if we accept that knowledge is created, then the problem is also created through the way we choose which aspects we will pay attention to, and there are often many possible options. Shaping the question is central to the task of the research process, is part of the research, in that the way the question is shaped will inevitably influence the outcome.

- Knowledge is constantly moving on, being recreated. It is never static. We can get a fix on a particular research problem or issue and create potential solutions – and this is generally good enough for our purposes – but it is always work in progress, not the final solution.

- The role of research and innovation is to facilitate the creation of knowledge and ideas, but it cannot always adopt the sole responsibility for delivering an answer to the client. It is important that the thinking, guidance and potential routes that we offer can be further worked on with our clients or managers, so that there is the greatest possible input to decision-making. Working on the potential directions together, either as part of the feedback session or at a separate session afterwards, is the most fruitful way of bringing all the knowledge together, rather than the more common sequential process, in which the researcher is dismissed while the client group decides what to do with the research findings.

- We are participants in the research process, not observers. As such our emotional responses in the research situation are just as valid as our rational responses – in fact are invaluable - in understanding and constructing possible outcomes of the research.

- As researchers, starting from a position of ignorance is OK. We may be experts in research approaches, but we are probably not experts in the subject matter we are focusing on or in creating solutions to the particular problem we are exploring. In relation to our clients we tend to adopt the role of the supplier–client or expert–patient. In both of these role relationships, the power balance is stuck and the possibilities for interaction and development of ideas is stilted, because the roles tend to define the interaction. Clients generally feel that they ought to know the research question. Researchers generally feel that they should not be too challenging to the client's defined objectives. In the ideal world, if both sides chilled out and put their roles to one side, the researcher would be able, as Schein puts it, 'to access her areas of ignorance' without fear of appearing stupid, and the client could accept the questioning as part of the research process, rather than a challenge to his or her authority. We need to work together as colleagues, co-creating the possible routes forward.

- New and creative thinking occurs when we are outside our comfort zone and when we are able to think in different ways, to think the unthinkable and do the undoable. The job of researchers, innovators, clients, managers and whoever else is part of the innovation project is to encourage diversity, new ways of thinking and new ways of connecting ideas to create novel insights.

Notes

1 www.run-riot.com/users/lida-hujic

2 Excerpts from 'Open to ideas' by Bronwen Morgan, in *Impact,* 5, April Issue 2014

3 Brown, B (2013) *Daring Greatly: How the courage to be vulnerable transforms the way we live, love, parent, and lead,* Portfolio Penguin

4 For example: Florida, R and Gates, G, Technology and Tolerance: The Importance of Diversity to High-Technology Growth, *Urban Institute Publications* [online] www.urban.org/UploadedPDF/1000492_tech_and_tolerance.pdf

5 Dr Waknis works at the Dr D Y Patil College of Dentistry and Nursing. He co-wrote a paper on this innovation which was published in the Journal of Maxillofacial and Oral Surgery in 2013: http://link.springer.com/article/10.1007%2Fs12663-011-0225-x#page-1

6 Surgeons do *jugaad* in the OT; *Sunday Times, India* [online] http://timesofindia.indiatimes.com/india/Surgeons-do-jugaad-in-the-operation-theatre/articleshow/30491175.cms

7 A Novel Use for Mosquito Nets, *BBC News* [online]www.bbc.com/news/health-23944195

8 http://timesofindia.indiatimes.com/home/science/Honey-heals-wounds-faster-than-betadine/articleshow/30496472.cms

9 Radjou, N, Prabhu, J and Ahuja, S (2012) *Jugaad Innovation: Think frugal, be flexible, generate breakthrough growth*, John Wiley & Sons

10 www.nature.com/nature/journal/v505/n7483/full/nature12939.html

11 www.bbc.co.uk/nature/life/Pelican#p00mrckh

12 Discover the wonder of brilliant blunders, *The Sunday Times* [online] www.thesundaytimes.co.uk/sto/public/Appointments/article873765.ece

13 www.cihm.leeds.ac.uk/new/wp-content/uploads/2011/06/edgar_schein-process_consultation_revisited.pdf

What about the future?

15

> *The opening up of new markets, foreign or domestic, and the organizational development from the craft shop to such concerns as US Steel illustrate the same process of industrial mutation – if I may use that biological term – that incessantly revolutionizes the economic structure from within, incessantly destroying the old one, incessantly creating a new one. This process of Creative Destruction is the essential fact about capitalism.* JOSEPH SCHUMPETER

The age of transformation

It is a truism that the pace of change in Western cultures, and elsewhere, is accelerating rapidly. Increasingly we face multiple and rapidly accelerating changes that happen simultaneously. These changes will inevitably transform our workplace structures, practices and our personal futures. As the economist John Mauldin puts it:

> It is a tendency of ours to take our recent past and project it in a linear fashion into the future. That's the way we are hard-wired. And while we all acknowledge that change is happening faster today than it did 20 or 30 years ago, we really don't expect the pace of change to quicken in the future. The next 20 years, we figure, will more or less unfold as the last 20 years has. Not a chance. That assumption is missing the second derivative of change – the acceleration of the pace of change.[1]

Mauldin's view of the future is terrifying or exhilarating, depending on your constitution. He predicts multiple technologies bursting into our lives, taking centre stage and becoming disruptive. 'It will be as if the steam engine and electricity and the automobile and telecommunications all appear at the same time, after having been developed in the background for many decades,' he says.

Artificial intelligence, automation, the internet of things, advanced robotics, cobots (robots intended to physically interact with humans in a shared workspace), nanotechnology, renewable energy, mobile and wireless internet, energy exploration, as well as a host of technologies that we cannot even imagine, will become commonplace and will radically change the way we live and work. Joseph Schumpeter described capitalism as the 'perennial gale of creative destruction' and generations of economists have adopted this term as a shorthand description of the market's messy way of delivering progress.[2] Short of unforeseen catastrophe it is hard to imagine how progress will slow down. The cycle of renewal and destruction will likely continue apace and with accelerating speed. In China they are literally 3D printing 3,000-square-feet houses in a day. One company is planning to print a car with 20 moving parts, using advanced materials much stronger than steel and aluminium. Both Facebook and Google are developing technologies to place 'high balloons' and permanent solar drones at 65,000 feet in order to blanket the globe with WiFi. We will have life-altering bio-tech breakthroughs. A technique in development at King's College, London, does away with fillings and instead encourages teeth to repair themselves. We're already starting to print human organs. If Moore's law[3] keeps working we will see more change in the next 20 years than we saw in the last 100.

Living in a brave new world

Of course we have had many changes in the past, but we have never had to face simultaneous, multiple, transformational trends playing out within such a very short period of time. Such changes demand that we adapt – and continually adapt *as a way of life* if organizations (or whatever they become) are to survive. Historically human beings have evolved slowly over time as a process of trial, error and adaptation. This need to change so rapidly is a big challenge.

Change will be thrust upon us. Like it or not, we have no option but to accept it. To some extent we can ride the crest of change if we can overcome our fear of it. As we have seen, fear, uncertainty and overcaution within the current business climate can be the death of employee engagement, productivity and innovation. Fearful of making mistakes, of blundering into costly ventures which end in disaster, we hold back; we wait for the right moment. There is no right moment. Innovation is always a risk, however much we plan and research and try to consider all the issues. At the end of the day we can never be sure of success or failure until our baby is launched and tested in the roller coaster of life. And if it fails? Well then we just have to lick our wounds, learn from our mistakes and try something different. In our new world, experimentation, risk-taking and thinking in radically different ways will not only be useful, they will be essential to our survival.

We must learn to manage the risks and reduce the fear factor as best we are able. We can prepare our organizations so they are ripe for innovation. This means developing a culture that encourages risk-taking and rewards courage – a culture that is led from the top *and* the bottom. Employees throughout the organization need to be primed for innovation, encouraged to challenge the status quo, to be excited by change and experimentation, understanding that failure is tolerated but giving up is not. This sets the scene for all employees to contribute to innovation and adaptation from all levels and functions within the organization. This will not be easy to achieve. It requires commitment from all staff – and it is a tough call.

In particular it is important to identify the 'Influencers' in the work group. As outlined in Chapter 14, these are generally one or two individuals who set the tone for the group. Often they are the mavericks and the rebels. They see things differently and that is exactly what is required. However, they may need to be brought on side; again, not an easy task. If this can be done, the task of motivating the whole group will be halfway achieved.

A human workforce

But to revert to the theme that we have circled around throughout this book: we abandon our humanity at our peril. Human beings have a primal need to achieve, to belong as part of a community, to be acknowledged, to be treated with respect. We want to feel needed, to contribute and to grow as individuals. If this isn't obvious, it is usually because our experiences in various workplaces have taught us to be wary, cynical and withdrawn. It takes time and consistency to build trust and even longer to restore trust that has been lost. But it is worth the effort, not only for the sake of employees but also because of the other theme that has permeated this book, namely that engaged, resilient, curious and experimental employees are more productive. There is a strong economic argument for developing a psychologically healthy workforce.

Turning a workforce round from disengagement to engagement can be a very tough and lengthy process, but human beings can often be delightfully unpredictable. Sometimes it is not fear or threat which re-engages a workforce. It can be the bizarre, the unexpected, the humorous or the pure farcical that grabs people's imagination and motivates them to engage.

A fruity option

A colleague told me a true story of something that had happened in her organization. It was in the thick of the recession and the management was trying to cut back on costs, wherever possible. One cost that was under review was the fruit bowl. Each Monday morning, staff would be greeted by a large bowl of fruit at reception. It was extravagant and costly, but it was part of the company tradition and employees were very attached to it; they proudly pointed it out to visitors, who were suitably impressed. The fruit bowl was more than a bowl of fruit. It was a company mascot and a symbol of the company culture of care, good taste and consideration for its staff. One Monday, a rumour went round. The fruit bowl had to go. Everyone was very upset. Much of the fear and anxiety that had dogged them in the tough years came to be focused on the loss of the fruit bowl. There was so much anger about this seemingly trivial issue that little work was done that day. By the next day, one of the managers had an idea. 'How about you taking this on?' he said to one of his staff. 'If you can make the saving somewhere else, then the fruit bowl can stay.' Once this message had spread throughout the organization, the staff set to work. By the end of the day they had found savings that were four times the value of the weekly fruit bowl. There was a huge sense of achievement. Everyone was happy and work resumed as normal. We humans like games and we like challenges. Too often these qualities are not brought to the workplace. When they are, as we see with the fruit bowl story, they can generate excitement and healthy competitiveness and bring the workforce together.

Studies repeatedly emphasize trust in the workplace as critical to ensuring a happy and productive workforce. Trust grows from familiarity, working together and taking risks as a community. It may seem counter-intuitive, but placing greater emphasis on human values of trust, participation and greater autonomy in the workplace has been shown to promote a happier, more engaged and more proactive workforce. People stay longer, put in more effort and work together more cooperatively. Equally important, productivity increases. This has been shown to hold true even in times of restructuring and redundancies.

In the flow

If we can bring engagement, cooperation, adaptability, skill and trust together into the workplace, we may have the recipe for a successful organization. It just requires one last ingredient: flow. The concept of flow grew out of positive psychology and was developed by the psychologist, Mihaly Csikszentmihalyi,[4] who was fascinated by artists who became lost in their work. Flow is the mental state in which a person performing an activity is fully immersed in a feeling of energized focus and enjoyment in the process of the activity. Essentially it is a state of complete absorption. Csikszentmihalyi describes this as 'focused motivation': positive, energized and aligned with the task at hand. There are certain conditions that promote flow; for instance, one must be involved in an activity with a clear set of goals and progress (this adds direction and structure); the task must have clear and immediate feedback; and one must have confidence in one's ability to complete the task at hand.

Flow can have a very important role in the workplace. It is linked with achievement and its development can have concrete implications in increasing workplace satisfaction and accomplishment. Flow researchers, such as Csikszentmihalyi, believe that certain interventions may be performed to enhance and increase flow in the workplace through which people would gain intrinsic rewards that encourage persistence. He argues that with increased experiences of flow, people 'move towards complexity'; they flourish as their achievements grow and with that comes the development of increasing 'emotional, cognitive and social complexity'.[5]

Flow in action

I had the great privilege of watching Mo Farah win the 5,000-metres race at the 2012 Olympics in London, seven days after taking gold in the 10,000 metres, making him the first Briton to win two gold medals at the same Olympics. Mo streaked past the stands where I and thousands of near-hysterical British fans cheered ourselves hoarse. He was totally focused; his movements appeared effortless and relaxed, as if he was expending the absolute minimum energy required. He was a joy to behold. All aspects of his body, mind, thought and intention were focused on winning the race. And win he did, amid the cacophony of cheers. In his characteristic gesture, Mo dropped to his knees, bowed his head and kissed the ground. The crowd continued to cheer until they had no voice left. This was flow in action.

The coming decades may well be the most challenging that the human race has ever faced – and not only in the workplace. The human faculties that we have discussed throughout this book will hopefully stand us in good stead as we face the accelerating unknown, but we need to continuously strengthen these abilities and resist the mechanization of our thinking and behaviours, which can undermine our ability to adapt. Our humanity lies at the core of our collective being. It is our shared responsibility to protect, nurture and develop it. The various themes that we touch upon within this chapter – the age of transformation, the accelerating pace of change – present both opportunities and challenges. At the same time, the very human drives to protect symbols of unity such as the precious fruit bowl and, in a very different context, the ecstasy of Mo Farah bringing home gold for England reflect the complex mix of what it is to be human.

In conclusion

In this book I have attempted to cover much ground and probably I have been overambitious. There are topics that deserved more attention that I have not done justice to. There are others that I included because they excite me. In spite of these limitations, I hope that the whole has become more than the sum of the parts.

Reducing excessive fear at work is a priority in many workplaces and needs to be addressed through a variety of means, such as strong and fair management, coaching, good leadership, the principles of positive psychology and approaches such as appreciative enquiry and collaborative working. However, there are two sides to this story. In addition to lowering levels of workplace fear, we need to raise levels of risk-taking. It is important to encourage and support employees to take (measured) risks, to experiment, to learn, to improvise, to experience flow, to collaborate and to think outside the box. There is much work to do in order to transform fearful workplaces into environments that people enjoy working in, where they go to work with a sense of joy and adventure.

Notes

1 Mauldin, J (2014) The Age of Transformation, *Mauldin Economics* [online] www.mauldineconomics.com/frontlinethoughts/the-age-of-transformation

2 Schumpeter, J (1942) *Capitalism, Socialism, and Democracy*

3 http://en.wikipedia.org/wiki/Moore's_law

4 Csikszentmihalyi, M (1990) *Flow: The psychology of optimal experience*, Harper Perennial

5 Visser, Coert [accessed 26 September 2012] Good Business: Leadership, Flow, and the Making of Meaning [online]http://articlescoertvisser.blogspot.com/2007/11/good-business-leadership-flow-and.html

INDEX

NB: chapter notes/references are indexed as such page numbers in *italic* indicate tables